The Lunar Garden

PLANTING BY THE MOON PHASES

E.A. CRAWFORD

Copyright © 1989, 2000 Cynthia Parzych Publishing, Inc.

All rights reserved. No reproduction of this book in whole or in part or in any form may be made without written authorization of the copyright owner.

Published by Capital Books Inc.
22841 Quicksilver Drive
Sterling, Virginia 20166

Library of Congress Cataloging-in-Publication Data
Crawford, E.A.
The lunar garden: planting by the moon phases/
by E.A. Crawford. –2nd ed. p. cm.
Bibliography: p.
ISBN 1-892123-36-3 (alk. paper)
1. Astrology and gardening. 2. Moon—Phases—Miscellanea.
I. Title.
BF1729.G35C73 2000
133.5'8635—dc20

Produced by: Cynthia Parzych Publishing, Inc., New York, N.Y.
Edited by: Jean Hoots
Horticultural consultants: Renée Shepherd and Beth Benjamin
Calendar design by: Kathleen Nosti

Manufactured in Italy by Sfera International Srl

Table of Contents

1. A History of Lunar Gardening	5
2. The Influence of the Moon	9
3. Why the Moon Phase System Works	13
4. The Waxing and Waning Moon	19
5. Flower, Leaf, Root and Seed Days	25
6. Sample Seeds and Recipes	33
7. Tips for Planting by the Moon	47
8. Using the Lunar Planting Calendar	51
The Lunar Planting Calendar	55
Bibliography	128

Chapter One

A History of Lunar Gardening

To men and women throughout time, the moon has been a tangible illustration of the cycle of birth, life and death. In its short cycle of $29^1/_2$ days, early men and women saw the patterns of their own life spans mirrored faithfully and understandably in nature. The moon's disappearance and reappearance assured them that "to every thing there is a season and a time to every purpose under the heaven."

Because of its relationship to tidal flow and the human menstrual cycle, the moon became associated with fertility and cycles of regeneration. Traditionally, the new moon was associated with menstruation. The full moon symbolized fertility, ovulation and birth. Studies have substantiated these primitive theories; it is a fact that more births occur around the full moon than at any other time of month.

Farmers and gardeners, dependent upon the whims of nature, watched the moon carefully and studied its effects on planting and crop growth. Their observations were passed down in brief notations, sage witticisms, proverbs, folk tales and "histories." The Roman historian Plutarch confidently stated that, "The moon showeth her power most evidently in those bodies which have neither sense nor lively breath; for carpenters reject the timber of trees fallen in the full moon as being soft and tender, subject also to the worm and putrefaction, and that quickly by means of excessive moisture."

The Koreans and the Japanese taught their children to see in the full moon two large hares beating rice. The Chinese believed the most fortunate of all animal signs, the hare, lived on the moon. Cora Native Americans told tales of the sky Eagle conversing the night through with Titewan, the moon goddess who ruled the underworld.

The famous magician Paracelsus, born in 1493 near Zurich, recommended a moon talisman be worn to protect travelers, expatriots, and those susceptible to violent death. A talisman of the moon was said to protect its wearer from epilepsy, dropsy, apoplexy and madness.

It is said in England there was never a north wind at the exact appearance of the moon. To this day, Gaelic speakers use the phrase "son of the moon's dark circle" in a deprecatory way to describe someone with hidden agendas, whether it be his intention or not, in reference to the late-rising, waning moon.

The Scots were convinced that at the moment of the moon's increase a bull's horns were loose and could easily be pulled off or put on again if the bull's owner so desired. It was considered that one was courting insanity to sleep under a full moon.

In the eighth century, B.C., Hesiod wrote a lunar calendar. Using his method of calculation as a model, agricultural calendars became lunar-based and more and more standardized. Two thousand years ago, Ptolemy wrote that farmers used the full moon to plant, to transplant seedlings and to breed animals. The new moon encouraged activities like pruning, castration and some types of harvesting.

Every culture and country developed its own moonlore. Much of what remains is obscure, oddly conceived or incomplete, but certain patterns have emerged intact. First, gardening by the moon's phases can be divided into two basic cycles: waxing and waning. The waxing moon is recommended for activities involving new growth and beginnings. The waning moon is recommended for ventures that require stabilization or cutting back of excessive growth. In the Middle Ages, gardeners were advised to plant during the waxing moon crops that produce above ground, and during the waning phase, crops producing below ground.

A second consideration is the position of the moon on the horizon. Is it riding close to the earth or high in the heavens? Middle Europeans believed that gardening when the moon is at its height encourages maximum growth and production. Sowing, in particular, was advised for this time. The theories on the position of the moon spread to England and, later, to America where they became standard information in many gardening almanacs.

A third factor, simplified in this century by Maria Thun, a student of Rudolph Steiner, classifies growing things according to the elements ruling the twelve signs of the zodiac. Each month, the moon passes through the belt of twelve constellations surrounding the earth, remaining in each constellation for one to two days. According to Thun, the moon's position in the zodiac has positive effects on plants depending on whether the plant is a root plant, a leaf plant, a plant grown primarily for its fruit, or a flowering or ornamental plant. Thun's simple theory will be explained and developed more fully in chapter three.

Today's scientists and agriculturalists, like Maria Thun, have established the validity of many traditional and ancient claims concerning the moon's effects on plants. Gardening in consideration of the phases of the moon produces abundant, healthy plants or crops. Dr. Bernard Dixon wrote in a December 1978 *Omni* article, "There seems little doubt that the lunar cycle influences the life processes of plants." Add to that the satisfaction of working in harmony with natural rhythms, and gardening by the phases of the moon becomes a creative response to a cosmic ecology, an encouraging activity to lift the mind and heal the spirit.

Chapter Two

The Influence of the Moon

The moon's orbit around our planet affects the rising and falling tides, air currents on the earth's surface, and the occurrence of thunderstorms. The gravitational pull of both the sun and the moon affects us, but we feel the effects of the moon more acutely. While the moon has a much smaller mass, it is 390 times closer to us than the sun.

Tides manifest the gravitational pull of the moon as it circles the earth. If you think of the water on the earth as a thin skin on the surface mass of the planet, it is easy to understand how the gravitational effects of the moon's orbit can pull the water mass gently from side to side. The tide cycle follows the same time cycle as the rising moon, occurring faithfully every twenty-four hours and fifty minutes. Tides rise in lakes and rivers as rhythmically as in oceans.

The correlation of moon and tide may not seem to have anything to do with planting or gardening, but consider the fact that the water content of the earth responds to the same tide cycle as the massive bodies of water that cover our planet. Any gardener knows the importance of the soil's water content to a germinating seed. It makes sense to consider, when planting your garden, the pull of the moon and the moon's position in order to give seeds the best chance to germinate, grow and develop. The effects of water content and of the moon's phases on seeds and their growth is recorded in *The Moon and Growth of Plants*, written by L. Kolisko and published in London in 1936. In her book, *Planetary Planting* (Simon and Schuster, New York; 1975) Louise Riotte states:

> There is a definite connection between the moon and the water in the earth. One could say in regard to root crops that those sown in the waxing phase of the moon can more strongly take up into themselves the watery element than those sown in the waning phase of the moon. The new-moon plants tend toward woodiness while among the full-moon plants hardly any woody plants could be found.

Rainfall, like the water content of the earth, is affected by the cycles of the moon as surely as the tides, which reach their highest point every 14.6 days or twice a month. Rainfall cycles mirror the two-week tide cycle in response to the position of the moon. The highest rainfall occurs just after the full and new moons.

Once a month, when the moon is at perigee (nearest the earth), tides are pulled 30% higher than at apogee, the point at which the moon is farthest from the earth. Both perigee and apogee are reported in A. L. Lieber's book *The Lunar Effect*, published in 1979, as being biologically stressful times for human beings.

Even more interesting, in 1981 D. R. Currie, an American mathematician, claimed from his study that droughts in the U.S.

were strongly effected by the 18-cycle Saros cycle. The Saros cycle is one complete rotation of the lunar nodes around the earth. The weathermen of antiquity used the Saros cycle to predict eclipses. They watched and charted the movements of the earth, sun and moon. When all three were aligned it signaled the beginning of one set of cycles.

Dr. Currie suggested the Saros cycle affects rainfall and atmospheric tides, resulting in rain patterns and drought. He put forth the theory that the 1930s Dust Bowl was a result of the Saros cycle and predicted the next major drought to occur in 1991 or 1992.

Not only does the gravitational pull of the moon affect the tides and rainfall, but it affects the air currents on the surface of the earth as well. Plants are extremely sensitive to any tiny energy fluctuation. This was first proven in the seminal studies conducted by the Indian scientist Sir Jagadis Chandra Bose at the turn of the century. Later scientific research has substantiated his findings. By designing his own apparatus and taking systematic measurements, Bose proved that plants have a great ability to respond to simple stimuli. This is an important fact to remember when considering air currents on the earth's surface.

Lunar winds on the earth's surface, moving at $1/20$ of a mile per hour, are too minute to be felt on the human skin, but they come, as do tides, twice daily. In the morning they flow east, in the evening to the west, influencing the growth of plants as surely as sunshine and rainfall.

The moon also affects the surface of the earth itself. A Columbia

University study, conducted in 1970 across the continental United States, measured earth tides and found that land surface changes an average of twelve inches each day.

Tides, lunar winds, earth tides and rainfall, together with the subtle effects of the moon on the shifting of the earth's crust and the moon's effects on the patterns of thunderstorms and their corresponding effect on ionization in the air, convince us that the effects of the moon on our planet are constantly coming into play, influencing the growing things of the earth. These factors considered, gardening in accordance with the phases of the moon seems not so odd after all.

Chapter Three

Why the Moon Phase System Works

The time at which a seed is sown is the beginning of its life cycle. Final plant yield, as every gardener knows, is crucially affected by the conditions encountered by the seed. It is certainly not surprising that so much folklore and tradition has surrounded the sowing of seeds. But what actual evidence is there to prove that the position of the moon at the time of sowing has any effect on seed germination?

Many biogardeners and agriculturalists have undertaken to answer this question. Thanks to their experiments, we have come to understand the influence of the position of the moon on the potential development of the seed.

The person most responsible for formal experimentation in this area is Maria Thun, whose research on her farm in Darmstadt, Germany, has been financially supported by a group of biodynamic farmers.

In 1952, Thun developed a method of sowing a fixed number of crop rows over a sidereal month. The term sidereal refers to the position of the moon in relationship to the stars or constellations in the sky behind it. In other words, Maria Thun sowed according to varying phases of the lunar cycle. Once the crop came to maturity, it was weighed and studied, and the results were recorded. Thun's findings were accumulated over a ten-year period from 1952 to 1962. The crop Thun chose to study initially was potatoes; subsequently she studied not only other root crops but also leaf crops, fruit-bearers and flowers.

Thun's results were surprising. She discovered that if potatoes were planted when the moon was in the constellations of Taurus, Capricorn or Virgo (traditionally termed "root days"), the crop was more prolific than if she planted when the moon was positioned in other constellations of the zodiac belt. After some thought, she concluded that potatoes did better if planted while the moon was clearly positioned in earth signs than at any other time. Potato crops planted when the moon was positioned in the constellations Cancer, Scorpio or Pisces—the water signs of the zodiac—did poorly.

The results of Thun's studies fascinated another experimenter in Germany. Graf repeated her method from 1973 to 1975, this time using many different types of soils, and planting radishes as well as potatoes. Graf discovered that sowing on root days affected positively the growth and production of crops, and got best results when using chemically untreated, organic soils.

In 1976, Kollerstrom and Muntz, Sussex market gardeners, repeated the experiments of Graf and Thun and gained a 45% increase in yield for crops sown on root days. Conducted over a period of two months, their study did not show that the phase of the moon, waxing or waning, made as much difference as the moon's placement in the sky at the time of sowing.

The effect of the phases of the moon on seed germination and growth was first studied by L. Kolisko in 1930. Using wheat, Kolisko found that seeds germinated faster and more prolifically when sown at the full moon. The new moon gave him the most unsuccessful results. Later experiments on cress confirmed Kolisko's findings. Recent studies at Northwestern University, conducted by Professor F. Brown, have shown that, even under equal temperatures, seedlings absorb more water at the full moon than at the new moon. The findings lend credibility to adages that recommend harvesting at the full moon. It seems plants have less water content at the new moon phase. Professor Brown went so far as to test plants in the darkened laboratory where they would have no direct access to effects of sun or moon. The plants still responded to the moon phases.

Other experiments have been conducted at Wichita State University and at Tulane University. All have achieved the same results. Experimentation indicates that seeds sown just before or around the full moon have a higher rate and speed of germination than those sown at the new moon because seeds are able to absorb more water at the full moon.

Human beings and animals respond to the phases of the moon as well. Dr. Harry Rounds has reported a decrease in stress hormones in mice and humans during the full and new moon and an increase during the waxing moon. Although no one knows exactly why, the rhythm of our world and our bodies respond to the cycles of the moon. We routinely cut our hair during the waxing moon to enhance growth. Doctors schedule much of their surgery during the new or waning moon, having found that operations during the full and waxing moon often cause more bleeding in surgical patients. Through experiments conducted by Evanston, Illinois scientist J. R. Brown, it was found that, although oyster shells open and shut according to regular intervals in the ebb and flow of tides, when the oysters were moved 1,000 miles inland in sealed tanks, they reset their programming to match the phases of the moon in Chicago—proving that their cycles were controlled not by the tides but by the moon.

The moon moves on a tilted elliptical orbit around the earth, waxing and waning as it reflects the light of the sun from various angles. It is backdropped, as are the other planets of our solar system by the belt of constellations. (See Diagram One on page 17.)

Once every twenty-seven days the moon is at the farthest point from the earth that its orbit reaches. Its orbit around the earth is tilted, and so two times each month the moon sinks five degrees above or below the angle at which the earth is orbiting the sun. These bimonthly points are called the nodes of the moon. The two node points north and south, occur when the moon's orbit intersects the path of the Sun (the ecliptic). Historically, the north node was called the *Carpat Draconts* or Dragon's Head. The south, or descending node was the Dragon's Tail or *Cauda Dragonis* and both nodes spanning the sky conjured the image of a huge sky dragon devouring the moon during its eclipses. (See Diagram Two on page 18.)

Eclipses occur when a new or full moon passes through one of the nodes, at which time it is possible for the earth to come between the moon and the sun. The moon is not visible to the naked eye because there is no sunlight to illuminate it.

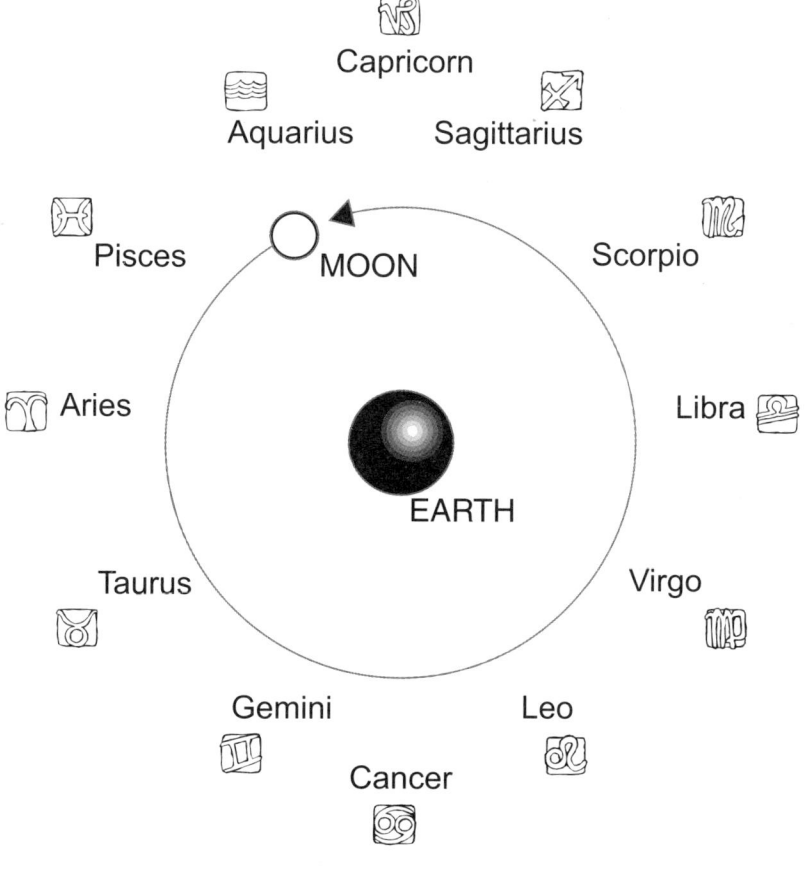

Diagram One

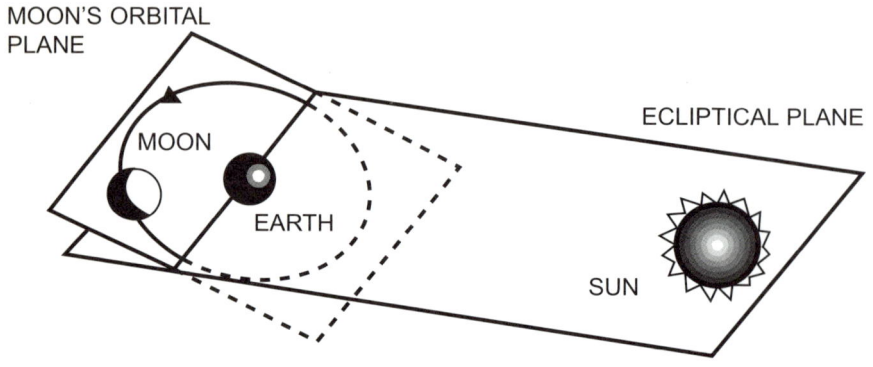

Diagram Two

Chapter Four

The Waxing and Waning Moon

The lunar month is divided into two basic moon activities: waxing and waning. The beginning of each process is designated by the new and full moon. A full moon occurs when the moon is 180 degrees opposite the sun, in position to receive sunlight over the maximum volume of its surface. A new moon occurs when the sun and moon are so closely aligned that it is impossible for the moon to give off any reflected sunlight. Waxing occurs in the period between the new and the full moon. Waning describes lunar activity between the full and the new moon. When the moon is waxing, it is said to be in its first and second quarters. The waning of the moon brings the phases through the third and fourth quarters of the cycle.

The waxing moon phase is a good time to encourage plant growth and proliferation. The waning moon phase is a useful time to control plant growth and keep down garden pests. Historically, cutting timber at the new moon was such an accepted practice that South American loggers stamped the moon phase on their timber, and the French, from 1669 until the French Revolution, could sell only timber cut at the new moon. Timber cut at the new moon or in the waning phase resists parasites and cures more effectively.

Should you want to try your hand at cutting wood by the phases of the moon, August is the best month in which to engage in this activity.

We have already seen evidence asserting growth and liquid absorption peaks at the full moon, and drastically declines during the new moon. Even the cells of the human circulatory system seem to respond to moon phases. Many surgeons in the United States postpone until the new moon operations which can be complicated by excessive bleeding, and refuse to perform such procedures during the full moon, when bleeding increases.

We know from fluctuations in the electrical field of plants, made visible through Kirlian photography, as well as through experience, that plants grow and absorb water at an irregular rate. Rapid growth rate is often followed by a period of rest. Fruit bearing is followed by a period of dormancy. Although we do not know the full effects of the waxing and waning moon on plant growth, we do know that synchronizing phases of plant growth with the phases of the moon produces healthier plants and more abundant yield.

Traditionally, gardeners have been advised to sow seeds at the full moon, perhaps because our ancestors discovered that seeds germinated more rapidly then. Many people today sow at the new moon in order to ensure germination before the growth spurt given the plant by the full moon.

The moon phase is associated with harvesting. Over centuries, farmers found that apples, cabbages, potatoes and onions store better if harvested at the waning moon, when water content is decreased. Fruits or vegetables meant to be eaten immediately are at their best when gathered at the waxing moon. And tomatoes have been found to ripen most satisfactorily when harvested at the full moon, when water content is highest.

Although general principles hold, it is best to be specific when organizing gardening activities according to waxing and waning moon phases.

THE WAXING MOON
1. Sow large areas during the waxing moon. Use this time to sow lawns, to put down sod and plant wheat and grains.
2. Sow crops like leafy vegetables and flowers, which produce yield above ground and do not rely on extensive root development.
3. Plant flowers grown for beauty or fragrance in the first quarter of the waxing moon.
4. Plant cane, such as raspberries, blackberries and gooseberries, in the second quarter of the waxing moon.
5. Always plant roses in the first or second quarter of the waxing moon.
6. During a period of drought, sow seeds when the moon is waxing as close to the full moon as possible.
7. Perform any grafting chores. Cut grafts in late January, before the sap flows, in the first or second quarter of the waxing moon.
8. Transplant and repot houseplants during the waxing moon so

the plant can capitalize on the full moon growth.

9. In the first or second quarter of the waxing moon, take cuttings from plants you wish to propagate. Once the cuttings are rooted, pot in the first or second quarter of the waxing moon.

10. Water plants during the waxing moon. If plants need a food boost, it is a good idea to water down the fertilizer and add it to the soil as close to the full moon as possible, particularly if the plants require phosphorus.

11. Pick fruits and vegetables intended for immediate consumption. Salads are best when made with ingredients picked during a waxing moon. Because the water content of the ingredients is higher, salads are crunchier, juicier and free from woody, unpleasant textures.

12. Harvest grapes to be used in winemaking as close to the full moon as possible. The grapes will retain more juice and bouquet.

13. Gather herbs that are to be used for their essential oils. Oil content is more concentrated at this time.

14. Water your compost heap.

THE WANING MOON

1. Sow crops that produce their yield below ground. This includes root vegetables such as beets, carrots, parsnips, potatoes, onions and turnips.

2. Always plant trees and saplings in the third quarter, waning moon, as well as plants that remain in the soil for more than one growing season. Successful fruit trees are generally those planted during the waning phase of the moon. This position of the moon

encourages development of root growth and tree bark instead of forcing the plant to proliferate above ground before it has a strong grounding. Saplings with firmly established roots are less in danger of damage and deterioration due to loss of branches or top growth during the winter.

3. Plant strawberries or their runners in the third quarter of the moon. Most strawberries thin out and die because ground heaving during winter breaks their roots. Planting during the waning moon ensures that root growth is strong and well-developed, even before the plant begins to fruit.

4. Divide your perennials in the third or fourth quarter of the waning moon.

5. If your crops require potassium, fertilize at the waning moon. Potassium absorption is at its peak at the new moon.

6. Start your compost heap during the waning moon. This phase aids in decomposition of plant matter.

7. Spread and turn compost and organic fertilizer.

8. Mulch in the third quarter. When mulching fruit trees or roses, leave a small space around the trunk or base of the plant.

9. Always spray fruit trees in the fourth quarter of the waning moon.

10. Kill weeds and thin out plants.

11. In the late summer, mow your lawn in the waning moon to retard growth, if you live in an area with heavy summer rainfall.

12. Prune and cut back plants.

13. Harvest crops requiring long-term storage like apples, cabbage and potatoes.

14. Harvest flowers and seeds that will be stored until the next year.

15. Use the waning moon to help cut spring grass. This phase discourages growth and keeps your lawn under control.

16. The waning moon is a good time to dig herb roots or harvest leaves and bark intended to be used in medicinal teas. Herbs will retain maximum potency at this time and dry more easily.

17. Perform all drying activities. Dry herbs, flowers and fruit. Herbs and fruit dry well on old window screens in shady, well-ventilated spots. Hang baby's-breath, cockscomb, gaillardia, globe amaranth, larkspur, strawflowers and zinnias in a shady, dry place, upside-down, for beautiful dried flowers.

Remember, the waxing moon is the time to encourage rapid new growth. If you want to retard or control growth, or encourage hardy rooting, perform the necessary activities during the waning moon.

Chapter Five

Flower, Leaf, Root and Seed Days

esterners have traditionally seen living things as composed of four elements: earth, air, fire and water. These elements ruled parts of the human body, types of human personality, plants, and the constellations of the zodiac.

In the zodiac, each of the four elements rules three signs. Aries, Leo and Sagittarius are said to be fire signs; Taurus, Virgo and Capricorn are ruled by earth; Gemini, Libra and Aquarius by air; and Cancer, Scorpio and Pisces by water.

The water signs of the zodiac are said to be fertile, fruitful and fecund. The moon's passing through any of these signs is a propitious time for sowing seed. The fire signs are considered the most unfertile time, as they are dry and barren.

Maria Thun examined ancient and medieval theories of planting by the zodiac and began to work with them in experimental conditions. As we have seen, she had positive results from planting potatoes when the moon was passing through the constellations ruled by earth signs. Thun continued her work for thirty-five years. She concluded that each plant is composed of four essential parts: leaf, root, flower and fruit or seed. Each plant is cultivated to yield one of the four qualities. Tomatoes, for instance, are a fruit or seed crop; nasturtiums are a flower crop.

Each of the four essential plant parts is ruled by an essential element. According to Maria Thun's model, leaves are ruled by water, roots by earth, flowers by air and fruit or seed by fire. Plants are sown according to the corresponding element of the zodiac through which the moon is passing, as illustrated in the chart.

PLANT	ELEMENT	ZODIAC SIGN
Root: potatoes, radishes, turnips, parsnips, onions, etc.	Earth	Taurus, Virgo, Capricorn
Seed: apple, grapes, pears, fruits, nuts, sunflowers, etc.	Fire	Aries, Leo, Sagittarius
Flowers	Air	Gemini, Libra, Aquarius
Leaf: lettuce, cress, endive, alfalfa, Chinese celery, comfrey, etc.	Water	Cancer, Scorpio, Pisces

It is difficult to go wrong following Thun's simple principles. However, as in any theory, there are exceptions, which are listed in the following charts. Some plants fall under different categories than the obvious ones. For example, broccoli, Brussels sprouts, cabbage and cauliflower are all flowers but seem to give best results planted on leaf days.

FLOWER DAYS

PLANT	MOON PHASE	MOON POSITION
Artichokes	Plant in waxing moon, first quarter	Cancer, Pisces, Virgo
Daffodils	Plant bulbs in first or second quarter, waxing moon	Libra
Dahlias	Plant in first or second quarter, waxing moon	Libra
Flowering annuals	Sow in first or second quarter, waxing moon	Libra. For hardiness: Scorpio, Taurus
Gladioluses	Plant bulbs in first or second quarter, waxing moon	Libra
Globe artichokes	Plant in waxing moon, first quarter	For abundance: Cancer, Pisces, Virgo. Sturdiness: Scorpio. Hardiness: Taurus. For flowers: Libra
Hyacinths	Plant bulbs in third quarter, waning moon	Cancer, Scorpio or Pisces, in the month of October
Roses	Plant in second quarter, waxing moon	Cancer
Sunflowers	Sow in third or fourth quarter, waning moon	Libra

ROOT DAYS

PLANT	MOON PHASE	MOON POSITION
Beets	Sow in third quarter, waning moon	Cancer, Scorpio, Pisces, Capricorn
Carrots	Sow in third quarter, waning moon	Taurus, particularly in summer
Onions	Sow seeds during second quarter of the waxing moon.	Cancer, Scorpio
	Plant sets in third or fourth quarter, waning moon, for good rooting.	Taurus, Libra, Pisces
Parsnips	Sow in third quarter, waning moon	Taurus
Potatoes	Plant tubers in third quarter, waning moon	Taurus, Capricorn, Cancer, Scorpio; for seed potatoes, Sagittarius
Radishes	Sow in third quarter, waning moon	Taurus, Capricorn
Shallots	Plant bulbs in second quarter, waxing moon	Scorpio

SEED DAYS

PLANT	MOON PHASE	MOON POSITION
Apples	Plant trees or graft when moon is waning, third or fourth quarter	Sagittarius
Beans: navy, pea, white, kidney	Sow in third and fourth quarters, waning moon.	Leo
	Dry after full moon.	Aries, Leo, Sagittarius
	Can in waning moon.	Cancer, Scorpio, Pisces
Leeks	Plant in first or second quarter, waxing moon.	Sagittarius
Peppers	Plant in second quarter, waxing moon	Sagittarius

LEAF DAYS

PLANT	MOON PHASE	MOON POSITION
Beans: bush and pole	Plant in waxing moon, second quarter	Cancer, Scorpio, Pisces
Broccoli	Plant in waxing moon, first quarter	Cancer, Scorpio, Pisces
Brussels sprouts	Plant in waxing moon, first quarter	Cancer, Scorpio, Pisces. Transplant under these moon positions in September.
Cabbage	Seed or transplant in waxing moon, first quarter	Cancer, Scorpio, Pisces. Sturdiness: Taurus. Flowering: Libra
	Make sauerkraut in waning moon immediately after full moon.	Cancer, Scorpio, Pisces
Cantaloupes	Plant in waxing moon, first quarter. Melons are fruits but high water content is desirable, so plant in water signs.	Scorpio, Pisces
Cauliflower	Sow in first quarter, waxing moon	Cancer, Scorpio, Pisces
Celeriac	Sow in third quarter, waning moon	Cancer, Scorpio, Pisces

LEAF DAYS continued

PLANT	MOON PHASE	MOON POSITION
Celery	Sow in first or second quarter, waxing moon	Cancer, Scorpio, Pisces
Chard	Sow in first or second quarter, waxing moon	Cancer, Scorpio, Pisces, Libra
Chayote	Sow in first or second quarter, waxing moon	Cancer, Scorpio, Pisces
Chicory	Sow in the waning moon, third quarter	Cancer, Scorpio, Pisces, Sagittarius
Chinese celery	Sow in first quarter, waxing moon	Cancer, Scorpio, Pisces
Corn	Sow in first quarter, waxing moon	Scorpio, Pisces. Hill in Gemini to keep weeds and pests away.
Cucumbers	Sow in the second quarter, waxing moon. Cucumbers increase in size at the full moon.	Cancer, Scorpio, Pisces
Eggplant	Seed in second quarter, waxing moon	Cancer, Scorpio, Pisces
Endive	Seed in first quarter, waxing moon	Cancer, Scorpio, Pisces, Libra, Virgo, Gemini, Sagittarius

LEAF DAYS continued

PLANT	MOON PHASE	MOON POSITION
Garlic	Plant in third or fourth quarter, waning moon	Scorpio, Sagittarius
Kohlrabi	Sow in the second quarter, waxing moon	Scorpio, Pisces, Cancer
Lettuce	Sow in the first quarter, waxing moon	Cancer, Scorpio, Pisces, Libra, Taurus
Parsley	Sow in first quarter, waxing moon	Cancer, Scorpio, Pisces, Libra
Peas	Sow in third quarter, waning moon	Cancer, Scorpio, Pisces, Libra
Salsify	Sow early in spring in the third or fourth quarter, waning moon	Cancer, Scorpio, Pisces. Taurus for later plantings
Spinach	Sow in first quarter, waxing moon	Cancer, Scorpio, Pisces
Tomato	Plant seeds in the waxing moon, second quarter. Transplant in the waning moon so that roots will establish themselves before the foliage grows too abundant and unbalances the plant.	Pisces. For sturdiness: Cancer. During hot dry summers: Capricorn

Chapter Six

Sample Seeds and Recipes

he sample seeds included in this book were chosen because they are easy to grow, prolific, and can grow anywhere, all over the country, from backyards and solariums to rooftop gardens in urban areas.

JEWEL NASTURTIUMS

Nasturtiums may be the most popular and easiest to grow of all annuals. An old garden adage advises, "Be nasty to nasturtiums." These little plants are independent and willful and good for gardeners who tend to be preoccupied and absent-minded.

The word "nasturtium" comes from the Latin, *nasitortium*, meaning "distortion of the nose." Gerard, in his herbal, named them Indian cresses. In the first American medical book, *The Angel of Bethesda*, written by Cotton Mather more than 250 years ago, we are told that nasturtium was used to cure scurvy: "Paris Physicians have ordered a great Quantity to grow near their General Hospital."

Mather's advice was: "Take the dried Leaves . . . and Juniper-Berries; equal parts, each. After they are well-powdered, incorporate them with a sufficient quantity of despumated Honey.

Take the Quantity of the Bigness of a Walnut in a little wine. D'Ube cries up this as a pretty Opiate." Scurvy is caused by lack of vitamin C and, as most fresh growing things contain vitamin C, perhaps Mather's advice worked.

Nasturtiums produce an antibiotic similar to that found in the British herb, karse. Suffolk women steeped the boiled leaves of karse in ale for hastening childbirth. Fresh nasturtium leaf tea is recommended by herbalists to cure conditions relating to bronchitis and emphysema. It is to be taken two or three times a day.

Nasturtiums are related to the cress family. The seeds can be pickled like capers. The flowers are a lovely addition to summer salads, and the leaves, when chopped, make a tangy, cressy addition to omelets. In the garden, nasturtium plants act as good little pesticides. Because they contain an oil which attracts insects, their presence protects cabbage, cauliflower, radishes, kohlrabi, Brussels sprouts, broccoli and turnips.

Plant nasturtiums when the moon is waxing, in the first or second quarter. For flowers and scent make sure the moon is in Libra; for abundance, Scorpio and Pisces; and Taurus for hardiness.

RED RADISH

The radish is a simple, satisfying root vegetable to grow, particularly for the impatient. It matures in just four weeks. Originally, red radish was brought to Europe from China, but it has long since become indigenous to most of the world and it grows wild throughout Europe and South and North America. Culpepper recommends its use for "stone and gravel," suggesting a decoction of radish juice to be drunk with wine. People in the Middle Ages used radish as a blood purifier and it was generally administered for liver conditions. Cotton Mather enthusiastically recommends "Black Rhadishes" as a cure for colic. "Black Rhadishes, pared and dried and powdered as much as may lie on half-a-crown, drunk with a little warm Ale. This has been a great secret for Cholic. Tis now divulged."

Whatever their medicinal attributes, radishes are cheerful additions to any salad. Sow radish seed during the waning moon to establish root growth when the moon is in Libra, Taurus, Pisces or Capricorn. Radishes sprout quickly and are not sensitive to soil although they like lots of moisture. Remember that radishes are at peak eating for only a week or so. For this reason, some gardeners advise sowing small amounts every ten days. For best eating, gather radishes when moon is waxing in Pisces, Cancer or Scorpio. Radishes keep very well when picked as soon as they mature. If you cut off the tops (this is important) and store them in the fridge, they'll keep two to three weeks and taste fine. Pick radishes you want to store in your root cellar when the moon is on the wane under a dry sign: Aries, Gemini or Sagittarius.

SPINACH

Spinach was used almost exclusively as a medicinal plant until the last few centuries, when it became a popular vegetable. Culpepper recommended it for promoting the flow of urine and suggested its use for convalescents and growing children. His recommendation dragged into the present century, unfortunately for children who hate spinach and are forced to eat it anyway. Culpepper writes, "The leaves are rich in minerals and are recommended for anaemic persons."

Fresh garden spinach is vastly superior to spinach bought at the supermarket. Garden leaves can be picked as soon as they are ready to be eaten, without languishing on the market shelves for days. Spinach doesn't have to be swallowed whole. It is delicious creamed, steamed, baked and fresh.

Spinach seeds should be sown in the first quarter of the waxing moon when the moon is passing through the water signs of Cancer, Scorpio or Pisces.

SCALLOP SQUASH

Squash is a New World vegetable cultivated by the Woodland Indians of the Eastern United States, as well as by the Hopi. It is hardy, prolific, abundant and requires lots of space in which to spread out.

When squash was first imported to England from America, the British called it marrow because of the resemblance of its flesh to the marrow of bones. The vegetable got its American name from the Algonquin word *akutasquah*, which means "eaten raw."

There are two basic types of squash: summer squashes and winter squashes. Winter squashes include pumpkins and gourds from which loofahs are made. Summer squashes are meant to be eaten young, directly from the plant. Pick summer squashes when they are small; more will grow back.

Once the threat of frost is over and the soil is warm, squash can be planted in the second quarter of the waxing moon, when the moon is in Cancer, Scorpio, Pisces or Libra.

Recipes

There are almost endless ways to cook spinach, nasturtiums, squashes and radishes, once they have come to maturity. We have included several sample recipes to get you started.

NASTURTIUM SALAD
Serves four

$1/2$ cup chopped nasturtium leaves
2 ounces alfalfa sprouts
2 grated medium-sized carrots
twelve yellow cherry tomatoes
$1/4$ head romaine
chopped parsley
smattering of dill
4 tablespoons sunflower seeds

Assemble in a salad bowl and toss. Serve with Lemon Tahini Dressing and garnish with nasturtium flowers. Dressing recipe follows on next page.

LEMON TAHINI DRESSING

1/3 cup tahini
juice of 1/2 lemon
scant 2/3 cup spring water
soy sauce to taste
sea salt to taste
1/2 crushed garlic clove

Mix ingredients in a blender until desired consistency is achieved. If a thinner dressing is required, add more soy sauce. For thicker dressing, add more tahini.

NASTURTIUM CAPERS

Nasturtium seeds are located in the flower spurs.

Collect nasturtium seeds when they are still small and green and soak them in brine to cover, made from one quart water mixed with $1/2$ cup salt. Renew the brine every three days until enough seeds have been collected.

Drain the seeds and pack them in small jars. Pour over enough boiling white wine vinegar to cover, seal and store for about a week before using. Use as a piquant substitute for capers in any recipe.

PRESSED SPINACH SALAD
Serves four

3 cups spinach leaves, packed
$1/2$ chopped green pepper
$1/2$ chopped onion, medium-sized

1. Place ingredients in a shallow bowl. Put a plate on top of the bowl and a heavy object on the plate, pressing down on the ingredients in the bowl. Leave in refrigerator overnight.
2. Remove the plate and drain off liquid. Toss with Hot Bacon Dressing and serve. Dressing recipe follows on next page.

HOT BACON DRESSING

6 slices bacon
2 tablespoons sugar
1/4 cup balsamic wine vinegar
black pepper to taste

1. Saute bacon until crisp, remove from pan, drain.
2. Pour off bacon grease, retaining 3 tablespoons in pan. Add sugar and vinegar. Heat over low flame until sugar dissolves. Add pepper.
3. Crumble bacon over greens, pour dressing over greens, toss and serve.

SQUASH AND CHEESE CASSEROLE
Serves six

3 1/2 cups scallop squash, cut in bite-sized wedges
1 cup chopped onion.
1 or 2 sprigs chopped parsley
1/2 teaspoon thyme
salt and pepper to taste
2 tablespoons butter
2 tablespoons flour
1 cup milk
3/4 cup grated Jarlsberg
1/4 teaspoon nutmeg
2 lightly beaten egg yolks
dash Tabasco
1/4 cup seasoned Italian bread crumbs

1. Combine onions, chopped parsley, thyme, salt, pepper, and squash, and steam until crisp and tender.
2. Heat butter in a pan and add flour, stirring with a wire whisk until blended. Cook 2 minutes over low heat while stirring. Add milk slowly and continue to stir until the sauce is thickened.

Recipe is continued on following page.

3. Add the cheese, reserving $1/4$ cup to top the casserole, and stir until melted into the sauce.
4. Add nutmeg and egg yolks gradually, stirring until sauce is smooth and well-blended. Cook for 2 minutes. Do not allow to boil. Add Tabasco.
5. Place squash mixture into a well-buttered casserole and pour cheese sauce over the top. Sprinkle with bread crumbs and remaining $1/4$ cup cheese.
6. Bake at 325 degrees for 25-30 minutes.

SPINACH AND RICOTTA STUFFED TOMATOES
Serves four

4 tomatoes
1 1/2 tablespoons olive oil
1/2 cup finely chopped yellow onion
2 1/2 cups fresh steamed spinach
nutmeg to taste
1/2 cup ricotta cheese
1 egg yolk, beaten
1/4 cup grated Parmesan

1. Cut off the tops of the tomatoes and carefully scrape out seeds and partitions without puncturing the shell. Turn upside down and allow to drain for 20 minutes.
2. Heat olive oil in a skillet. Add onion and saute until transparent.
3. Add steamed spinach and nutmeg to taste.
4. In a bowl, mix egg yolk, ricotta and Parmesan cheese. Add spinach mixture.
5. Stuff the tomatoes with the mixture.
6. Arrange in a buttered casserole dish and bake for 20 minutes at 350 degrees.

RADISH AND ORANGE SALAD

fifteen red radishes, sliced
two medium-sized oranges, peeled and sliced
3 tablespoons sesame oil
juice of $1/2$ lemon
chopped fresh chives
salt and pepper to taste

Assemble ingredients in a salad bowl and toss. Best to serve chilled. Chopped fresh mint may be substituted for fresh chives.

Chapter Seven

Tips for Planting by the Moon

Planting with the phases and positions of the moon is a good way to enhance the gardening process. But use common sense. If the lunar calendar says to plant kohlrabi on a day when flash floods are expected, it is probably better to wait until the next elemental cycle. Plant as close to the middle of the recommended cycle as is feasible. Even with difficult intervening weather or soil conditions, you will be able to plant according to the calendar about 80% of the time.

Remember that planting by the phase and position of the moon is most effective when organic gardening procedures are used. Plants can respond best to the natural rhythms that surround them when they are sown in nonchemically treated soil. Use compost and organic fertilizers. For pesky insect problems, we include a bug spray recipe that will help to make your plants happy and insect-free. It is easy to make and easy to use, and it improves with age because it gets more potent the longer it stands.

INSECT SPRAY
1 pint spring water
1 teaspoon Tabasco
2 large crushed garlic cloves

Combine ingredients in a container with a spray nozzle. For a serious bug problem add $1/2$ teaspoon cayenne pepper. Spray your plants with this mixture during the waning moon in Gemini, Leo or Virgo.

If you wish to cultivate a plant not specifically listed in this book, use the Thun model explained in Chapter Five. It is easy and simple. The following chart summarizes the main principles of lunar gardening.

ABOVE GROUND CROPS
The best time for sowing, transplanting, planting seedlings or repotting is when the moon is in Cancer. Scorpio is good and Pisces is advantageous.

BELOW GROUND CROPS
Crops that yield below ground are sown in Capricorn for good results and Taurus for best results.

FLOWERING PLANTS
Sow seeds during the waxing moon in Libra.

WATERING
Water when the moon is waxing in Cancer, Pisces or Scorpio.

WORKING SOIL
For best results, work soil in Leo. Gemini will give good results, particularly for weeding. Virgo is effective.

HARVESTING
Harvest in Aquarius. For long-term storage, harvest in Sagittarius or Aries, at the new moon. If the harvest is to be next year's seed, try for the same moon sign as the one under which the seeds were sown.

PRUNING
Follow Pliny's advice and remember that water intake is decreased at the new moon. Pliny writes, "All cutting, gathering and trimming is done with less injury to the trees and plants when the moon is waning than when it is waxing."

DROUGHT
During growing seasons plagued by drought, sow your seeds as close to the full moon as possible, in order to ensure optimum germination.

ANNUAL CROPS
Follow the four-element sowing pattern, planting as close to the center of the relevant sign as you can. If you miss your day, don't

worry. The moon will pass through another sign with the same element in another nine days.

ECLIPSES
Never sow during an eclipse.

Chapter Eight

Using the Lunar Planting Calendar

he lunar calendar provided here gives you all the information you need to plant and work your garden. The phase of the moon, its astrological placement, and the recommended crop to be sown are listed.

There are four moon phases:

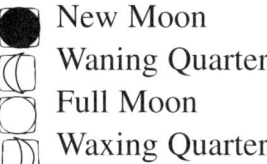
- New Moon
- Waning Quarter
- Full Moon
- Waxing Quarter

The astrological symbols are indicated as follows:

- Aries
- Taurus
- Gemini
- Libra
- Scorpio
- Sagittarius

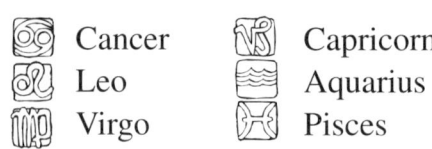

Remember, these constellations correspond to elements:

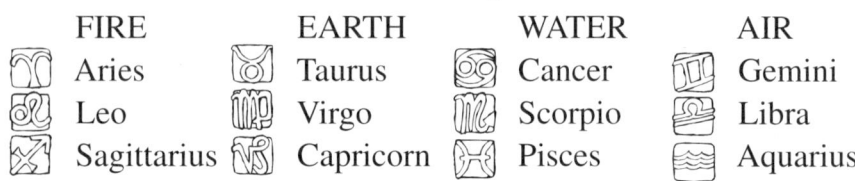

The calendar uses a twenty-four-hour clock, or "military" time, whereby the P.M. hours continue past 12. Hence, 1 P.M. is 13.00. To convert to the twelve-hour clock, simply subtract 12 from the hours. For example, to figure 21:08, subtract 12 from 21, for 9:08 P.M.

Reading the calendar is simple. Take, for example, the entry for January 1, 2001. At 22:32, the ☽ indicates a waning moon in Taurus. Taurus is an earth sign, conducive to root vegetables. On January 3, 2000, the moon moves from Taurus to Gemini. Gemini is an earth sign, conducive to flowers. Gemini is also a good sign in which to destroy weeds and pests. Therefore, on January 1, plant root vegetables, like parsnips and carrots that will get a full start under the waning moon. On January 3, plant sunflowers, which like a Gemini moon. Since this is January, northerners who choose this day for planting will want to do so indoors.

The times given in the calendar are for Greenwich Mean Time. If you live in another time zone, you will want to reconfigure your time as follows:

Time Zones:
   GMT (Greenwich Mean Time)
   Atlantic Time -4 hours
   Eastern Time -5 hours
   Central Time -6 hours
   Mountain Time -7 hours
   Pacific Time -8 hours
   Alaska -9 hours
   Hawaii -10 hours

Reading the Lunar Planting Calendar

Date

Moon waning
Moon rises at 20:52

2   20:52
     14 degrees 05

Moves from Virgo to Libra
Libra constellation rises
14 degrees 05 in heavens

Changes from Root Day
to Flower Day

The Lunar Planting Calendar
January 2001 through December 2003

MONDAY	1 ♓ 18 degrees 42	8 ♊	15 ♎ 5 degrees 46
TUESDAY	2 ☾ 22:32 ♈ 0 degrees 54	9 ○ 20:24 ♉ 6 degrees 46 lunar eclipse / no planting	16 ☽ 12:35 ♎
WEDNESDAY	3 ♈	10 ♉	17 ♏ 2 degrees 42
THURSDAY	4 ♈	11 ♌ 7 degrees 08	18 ♏
FRIDAY	5 ♉ 9 degrees 27	12 ♌	19 ♏
SATURDAY	6 ♉	13 ♍ 7 degrees 08	20 ♐ 10 degrees 26
SUNDAY	7 ♊ 7 degrees 17	14 ♍	21 ♐

22 ♑ 4 degrees 29 🍅 🥔	29 ♓ 3 degrees 40 🥬
23 ♑ 🥔	30 ♊ 3 degrees 55 🥬 🍅 🐛
24 ● ♑ 🥔	31 ♊ 🍅 🐛
25 ♒ 9 degrees 57 🥔 🌼	
26 ♒ 🌼	
27 ♓ 3 degrees 38 🌼 🥬	
28 ♓ 🥬	

Time Zones:
GMT (Greenwich Mean Time)
Atlantic Time -4 hours
Eastern Time -5 hours
Central Time -6 hours
Mountain Time -7 hours
Pacific Time -8 hours
Alaska -9 hours
Hawaii -10 hours

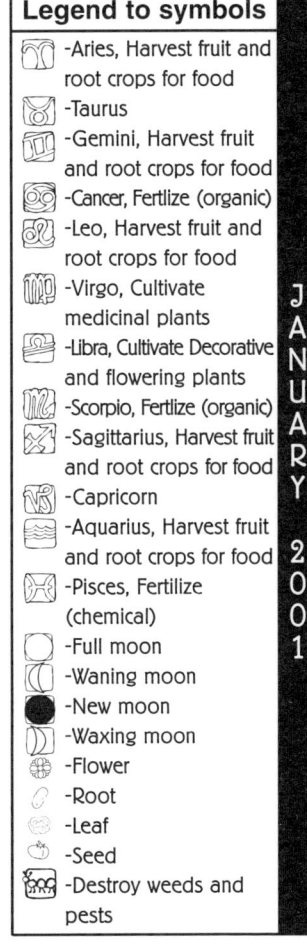

Legend to symbols

- ♈ -Aries, Harvest fruit and root crops for food
- ♉ -Taurus
- ♊ -Gemini, Harvest fruit and root crops for food
- ♋ -Cancer, Fertlize (organic)
- ♌ -Leo, Harvest fruit and root crops for food
- ♍ -Virgo, Cultivate medicinal plants
- ♎ -Libra, Cultivate Decorative and flowering plants
- ♏ -Scorpio, Fertlize (organic)
- ♐ -Sagittarius, Harvest fruit and root crops for food
- ♑ -Capricorn
- ♒ -Aquarius, Harvest fruit and root crops for food
- ♓ -Pisces, Fertilize (chemical)
- ○ -Full moon
- ☽ -Waning moon
- ● -New moon
- ☾ -Waxing moon
- ✿ -Flower
- ⌒ -Root
- ≈ -Leaf
- ◌ -Seed
- 🐛 -Destroy weeds and pests

JANUARY 2001

THURSDAY	1 ☾ 14:03 ♉ 5 degrees 09	8 ○ 7:12 ♌ 15 degrees 00	15 ☾ 3:24 ♏
FRIDAY	2 ♉	9 ♍ 0 degrees 15	16 ♐ 7 degrees 15
SATURDAY	3 ♊ 1 degree 44	10 ♍	17 ♐
SUNDAY	4 ♊	11 ♎ 0 degrees 08	18 ♑ 1 degree 30
MONDAY	5 ♊	12 ♎	19 ♑
TUESDAY	6 ♋ 14 degrees 43	13 ♎	20 ♑
WEDNESDAY	7 ♋	14 ♏ 11 degrees 46	21 ♒ 6 degrees 55

2 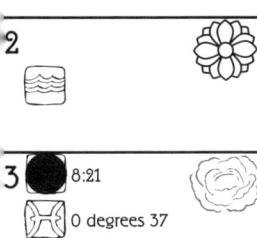	
3 ● 8:21 ♓ 0 degrees 37	
4 ♓	
5 ♓	
6 ♈ 6 degrees 60 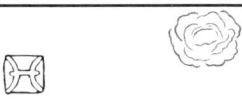	
7 ♈ 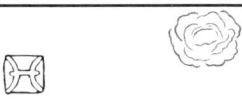	
8 ♉ 2 degrees 04	

Time Zones:
GMT (Greenwich Mean Time)
Atlantic Time -4 hours
Eastern Time -5 hours
Central Time -6 hours
Mountain Time -7 hours
Pacific Time -8 hours
Alaska -9 hours
Hawaii -10 hours

Legend to symbols

- ♈ -Aries, Harvest fruit and root crops for food
- ♉ -Taurus
- ♊ -Gemini, Harvest fruit and root crops for food
- ♋ -Cancer, Fertlize (organic)
- ♌ -Leo, Harvest fruit and root crops for food
- ♍ -Virgo, Cultivate medicinal plants
- ♎ -Libra, Cultivate Decorative and flowering plants
- ♏ -Scorpio, Fertilize (organic)
- ♐ -Sagittarius, Harvest fruit and root crops for food
- ♑ -Capricorn
- ♒ -Aquarius, Harvest fruit and root crops for food
- ♓ -Pisces, Fertilize (chemical)
- ○ -Full moon
- ◐ -Waning moon
- ● -New moon
- ◑ -Waxing moon
- ❀ -Flower
- ⌒ -Root
- ❦ -Leaf
- ⚬ -Seed
- -Destroy weeds and pests

FEBRUARY 2001

THURSDAY	1 ♉	8 ♌ ♍︎	15 ♐ 3 degrees 04 ♍︎
FRIDAY	2 ♉	9 ☽ 17:23 ♍ 8 degrees 19 ♍︎	16 ☽ 20:25 ♐ ♍︎
SATURDAY	3 ☽ 2:03 ♊ 11 degrees 23 ♍︎	10 ♍ ♍︎	17 ♐ ♍︎
SUNDAY	4 ♊ ♍︎	11 ♎ 8 degrees 04	18 ♑ 9 degrees 59
MONDAY	5 ♋ 9 degrees 10	12 ♎	19 ♑
TUESDAY	6 ♋	13 ♏ 6 degrees 31	20 ♒ 3 degrees 37
WEDNESDAY	7 ♌ 8 degrees 18 ♍︎	14 ♏	21 ♒

2 ≋	🌸	29 ⧖	🥔
3 ♓ 9 degrees 16	🌸 🥬	30 ♊ 9 degrees 21 🐛	🥔 🌸
4 ♓	🥬	31 ♊ 🐛	🌸
5 ● 1:21 ♈ 3 degrees 45 🐛	🥬 🍅		
6 ♈ 🐛	🍅		
7 ♈ 🐛	🍅		
8 ♉ 11 degrees 55	🍅 🥔		

Time Zones:
GMT (Greenwich Mean Time)
Atlantic Time -4 hours
Eastern Time -5 hours
Central Time -6 hours
Mountain Time -7 hours
Pacific Time -8 hours
Alaska -9 hours
Hawaii -10 hours

Legend to symbols

- ♈ -Aries, Harvest fruit and root crops for food
- ♉ -Taurus
- ♊ -Gemini, Harvest fruit and root crops for food
- ♋ -Cancer, Fertilize (organic)
- ♌ -Leo, Harvest fruit and root crops for food
- ♍ -Virgo, Cultivate medicinal plants
- ♎ -Libra, Cultivate Decorative and flowering plants
- ♏ -Scorpio, Fertilize (organic)
- ♐ -Sagittarius, Harvest fruit and root crops for food
- ♑ -Capricorn
- ♒ -Aquarius, Harvest fruit and root crops for food
- ♓ -Pisces, Fertilize (chemical)
- ○ -Full moon
- ☾ -Waning moon
- ● -New moon
- ☽ -Waxing moon
- ✿ -Flower
- ◯ -Root
- 🍃 -Leaf
- • -Seed
- 🐛 -Destroy weeds and pests

MARCH 2001

SUNDAY	1 🌙 10:49 ♋ 5 degrees 31	8 ☐ 3:22 ♎	15 🌗 15:31 ♑
MONDAY	2 ♋	9 ♏ 0 degrees 34	16 ♑
TUESDAY	3 ♌ 3 degrees 37	10 ♏	17 ♒ 11 degrees 43
WEDNESDAY	4 ♌	11 ♏	18 ♒
THURSDAY	5 ♍ 2 degrees 34	12 ♐ 10 degrees 51	19 ♓ 5 degrees 28
FRIDAY	6 ♍	13 ♐	20 ♓
SATURDAY	7 ♎ 1 degree 51	14 ♑ 5 degrees 56	21 ♓

2 ♊ 12 degrees 22 🐛	29 ♋
3 ● 15:26 ♊ 🐛	30 ☽ 17:08 ♌ 0 degrees 20 🐛
4 ♉ 8 degrees 12	
5 ♉	
6 ♊ 4 degrees 58 🐛	
7 ♊ 🐛	
8 ♋ 2 degrees 24	

Time Zones:
GMT (Greenwich Mean Time)
Atlantic Time -4 hours
Eastern Time -5 hours
Central Time -6 hours
Mountain Time -7 hours
Pacific Time -8 hours
Alaska -9 hours
Hawaii -10 hours

Legend to symbols

- ♈ -Aries, Harvest fruit and root crops for food
- ♉ -Taurus
- ♊ -Gemini, Harvest fruit and root crops for food
- ♋ -Cancer, Fertilize (organic)
- ♌ -Leo, Harvest fruit and root crops for food
- ♍ -Virgo, Cultivate medicinal plants
- ♎ -Libra, Cultivate Decorative and flowering plants
- ♏ -Scorpio, Fertilize (organic)
- ♐ -Sagittarius, Harvest fruit and root crops for food
- ♑ -Capricorn
- ♒ -Aquarius, Harvest fruit and root crops for food
- ♓ -Pisces, Fertilize (chemical)
- ○ -Full moon
- ☾ -Waning moon
- ● -New moon
- ☽ -Waxing moon
- ✿ -Flower
- ⌒ -Root
- ◌ -Leaf
- ◯ -Seed
- 🐛 -Destroy weeds and pests

APRIL 2001

TUESDAY	1 ♌ 🌽 🍅	8 ♏ 🥬	15 🌓 10:11 ♒ 🌼
WEDNESDAY	2 ♌ 🍅 🌽	9 ♐ 5 degrees 58 🌽 🍅	16 ♓ 1 degree 28 🥬
THURSDAY	3 ♍ 12 degrees 53 🌽 🍅	10 ♐ 🌽 🍅 🥔	17 ♓ 🥬
FRIDAY	4 ♍ 🌽 🥔	11 ♑ 1 degrees 28 🥔	18 ♓ 🥬
SATURDAY	5 ♎ 11 degrees 18 🥔 🌼	12 ♑ 🥔	19 ♈ 7 degrees 55 🌽 🍅 🥬
SUNDAY	6 ♎ 🌼	13 ♑ 🥔	20 ♈ 🌽 🍅
MONDAY	7 🌕 13:53 ♏ 9 degrees 11 🌼 🥬	14 ♒ 7 degrees 46 🥔 🌼	21 ♉ 3 degrees 33 🥔

Date		Date	
2 ♉	🫘	29 🌘 22:09 ♌ 🧹	🍅
3 ● 2:46 ♊ 0 degrees 27 🧹	🌸	30 ♍ 9 degrees 40 🧹	🫘
4 ♊ 🧹	🌸	31 ♍	🫘
5 ♊ 🧹	🌸		
6 ♋ 12 degrees 36	🥬		
7 ♋	🥬		
8 ♌ 11 degrees 12 🧹	🥬 🍅		

Time Zones:
GMT (Greenwich Mean Time)
Atlantic Time -4 hours
Eastern Time -5 hours
Central Time -6 hours
Mountain Time -7 hours
Pacific Time -8 hours
Alaska -9 hours
Hawaii -10 hours

Legend to symbols

- ♈ -Aries, Harvest fruit and root crops for food
- ♉ -Taurus
- ♊ -Gemini, Harvest fruit and root crops for food
- ♋ -Cancer, Fertlize (organic)
- ♌ -Leo, Harvest fruit and root crops for food
- ♍ -Virgo, Cultivate medicinal plants
- ♎ -Libra, Cultivate Decorative and flowering plants
- ♏ -Scorpio, Fertlize (organic)
- ♐ -Sagittarius, Harvest fruit and root crops for food
- ♑ -Capricorn
- ♒ -Aquarius, Harvest fruit and root crops for food
- ♓ -Pisces, Fertilize (chemical)
- ○ -Full moon
- ☽ -Waning moon
- ● -New moon
- ☾ -Waxing moon
- ❀ -Flower
- 🥕 -Root
- 🥬 -Leaf
- 🌱 -Seed
- 🧹 -Destroy weeds and pests

MAY 2001

FRIDAY	1 ♎ 7 degrees 43	8 ♑ 9 degrees 36	15 ♊ 3 degrees 31
SATURDAY	2 ♎	9 ♑	16 ♊
SUNDAY	3 ♏ 5 degrees 06	10 ♒ 3 degrees 49	17 ♊
MONDAY	4 ♏	11 ♒	18 ♉ 11 degrees 36
TUESDAY	5 ♐ 1 degree 38	12 ♒	19 ♉
WEDNESDAY	6 ○ 1:39 ♐	13 ♓ 9 degrees 27	20 ♊ 8 degrees 50
THURSDAY	7 ♐	14 ☽ 3:28 ♓	21 ☾ 11:58 ♊

Date			
2	♋ 7 degrees 26	29	♎
3	♋	30	♏ 1 degree 58
4	♌ 6 degrees 48		
5	♌		
6	♍ 6 degrees 04		
7	♍		
8	☽ 3:20 ♌ 4 degrees 34		

Time Zones:
GMT (Greenwich Mean Time)
Atlantic Time -4 hours
Eastern Time -5 hours
Central Time -6 hours
Mountain Time -7 hours
Pacific Time -8 hours
Alaska -9 hours
Hawaii -10 hours

Legend to symbols

- ♈ -Aries, Harvest fruit and root crops for food
- ♉ -Taurus
- ♊ -Gemini, Harvest fruit and root crops for food
- ♋ -Cancer, Fertilize (organic)
- ♌ -Leo, Harvest fruit and root crops for food
- ♍ -Virgo, Cultivate medicinal plants
- ♎ -Libra, Cultivate Decorative and flowering plants
- ♏ -Scorpio, Fertilize (organic)
- ♐ -Sagittarius, Harvest fruit and root crops for food
- ♑ -Capricorn
- ♒ -Aquarius, Harvest fruit and root crops for food
- ♓ -Pisces, Fertilize (chemical)
- ○ -Full moon
- ☾ -Waning moon
- ● -New moon
- ☽ -Waxing moon
- ✿ -Flower
- ⌒ -Root
- ≋ -Leaf
- ○ -Seed
- -Destroy weeds and pests

JUNE 2001

	SUNDAY	MONDAY	TUESDAY	WEDNESDAY	THURSDAY	FRIDAY	SATURDAY
	1 ♏	2 ♏	3 ⚼ 11 degrees 02	4 ⚼	5 ◯ 15:04 ♑ 5 degrees 58	6 ♑	7 ♒ 0 degrees 13
	8 ♒	9 ♒	10 ♓ 5 degrees 52	11 ♓	12 ♓	13 ☽ 18:45 ♈ 11 degrees 48	14 ♈
	15 ♉ 6 degrees 45	16 ♉	17 ♊ 3 degrees 08	18 ♊	19 ♋ 1 degree 14	20 ● 19:44 ♋	21 ♌ 0 degrees 48

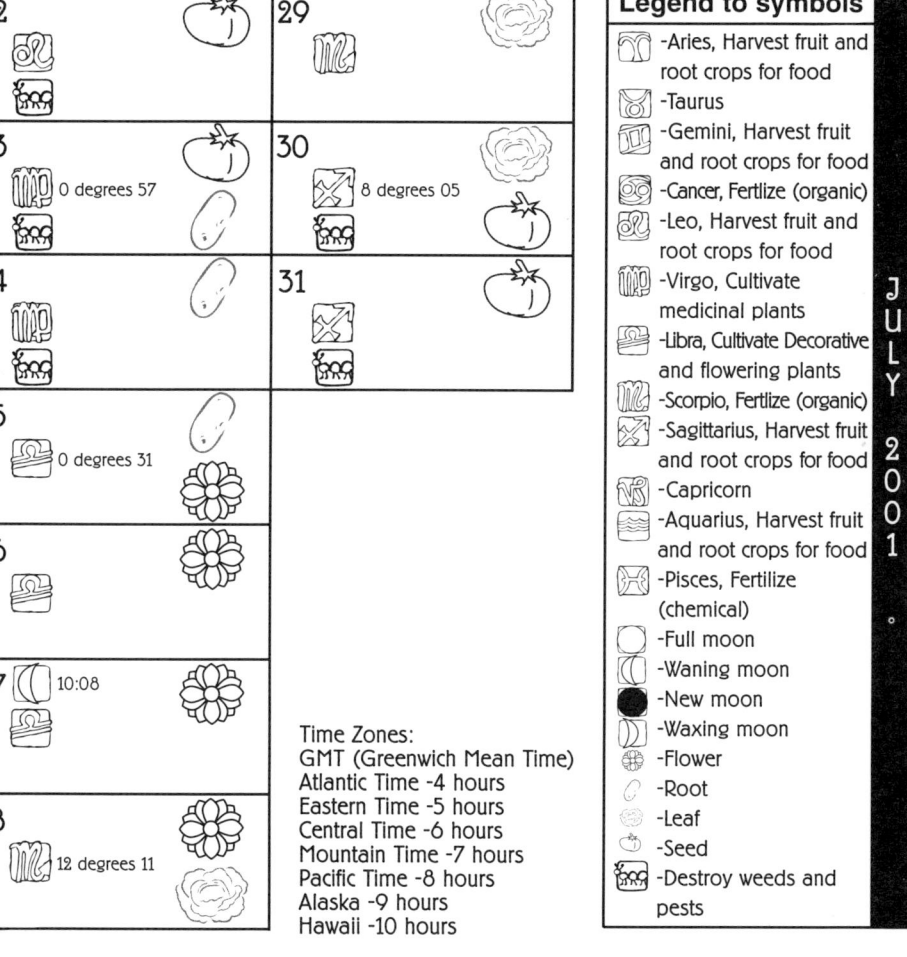

WEDNESDAY	1 ♑ 2 degrees 55	8 ♓	15 ♊
THURSDAY	2 ♑	9 ♈ 8 degrees 27	16 ♋ 9 degrees 32
FRIDAY	3 ♑	10 ♈	17 ♋
SATURDAY	4 ○ 8:56 ♒ 8 degrees 59	11 ♉ 2 degrees 54	18 ♌ 9 degrees 07
SUNDAY	5 ♒	12 ☽ 7:53 ♉	19 ● 2:55 ♌
MONDAY	6 ♓ 2 degrees 42	13 ♉	20 ♍ 9 degrees 37
TUESDAY	7 ♓	14 ♊ 11 degrees 39	21 ♍

2 ♎ 9 degrees 41	🌸 🥔	29 ♑ 12 degrees 08	🍅 🥔
3 ♎	🌸	30 ♑	🥔
4 ♏ 8 degrees 13	🌸 🥬	31 ♒ 6 degrees 02	🌸
5 🌗 19:55 ♏	🥬		
6 ♐ 4 degrees 52 🐛	🥬 🍅		
7 ♐ 🐛	🍅		
8 ♐ 🐛	🍅		

Legend to symbols

- ♈ – Aries, Harvest fruit and root crops for food
- ♉ – Taurus
- ♊ – Gemini, Harvest fruit and root crops for food
- ♋ – Cancer, Fertilize (organic)
- ♌ – Leo, Harvest fruit and root crops for food
- ♍ – Virgo, Cultivate medicinal plants
- ♎ – Libra, Cultivate Decorative and flowering plants
- ♏ – Scorpio, Fertilize (organic)
- ♐ – Sagittarius, Harvest fruit and root crops for food
- ♑ – Capricorn
- ♒ – Aquarius, Harvest fruit and root crops for food
- ♓ – Pisces, Fertilize (chemical)
- ○ – Full moon
- ☾ – Waning moon
- ● – New moon
- ☽ – Waxing moon
- ✿ – Flower
- ⌒ – Root
- 🥬 – Leaf
- 🌰 – Seed
- 🐛 – Destroy weeds and pests

AUGUST 2001

Time Zones:
GMT (Greenwich Mean Time)
Atlantic Time -4 hours
Eastern Time -5 hours
Central Time -6 hours
Mountain Time -7 hours
Pacific Time -8 hours
Alaska -9 hours
Hawaii -10 hours

SATURDAY	1 ♒	8 ⛎ 12 degrees 14	15 ♌
SUNDAY	2 ○ 21:43 ♒	9 ⛎	16 ♍ 2 degrees 44
MONDAY	3 ♓ 11 degrees 36	10 ☽ 19:00 ♊ 7 degrees 42	17 ● 10:27 ♍
TUESDAY	4 ♓	11 ♊	18 ♎ 3 degrees 9
WEDNESDAY	5 ♈ 5 degrees 31	12 ♋ 4 degrees 28	19 ♎
THURSDAY	6 ♈	13 ♋	20 ♏ 2 degrees 44
FRIDAY	7 ♈	14 ♌ 4 degrees 52	21 ♏

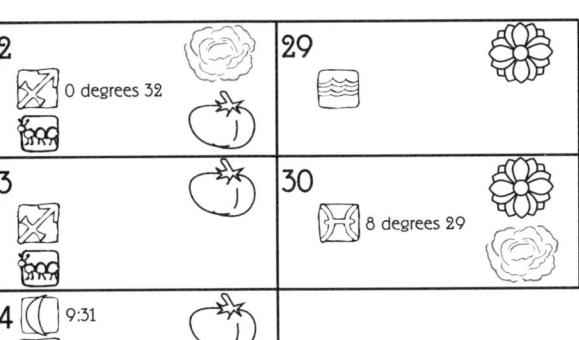

Date	Details
2	Sagittarius 0 degrees 32, Destroy weeds and pests — Leaf, Fruit
3	Sagittarius, Destroy weeds and pests — Fruit
4	Waning moon 9:31, Sagittarius, Destroy weeds and pests — Fruit
5	Capricorn 8 degrees 50 — Fruit, Root
6	Capricorn — Root
7	Aquarius 2 degrees 56 — Root, Flower
8	Aquarius — Flower
29	Aquarius — Flower
30	Pisces 8 degrees 29 — Flower, Leaf

Time Zones:
GMT (Greenwich Mean Time)
Atlantic Time -4 hours
Eastern Time -5 hours
Central Time -6 hours
Mountain Time -7 hours
Pacific Time -8 hours
Alaska -9 hours
Hawaii -10 hours

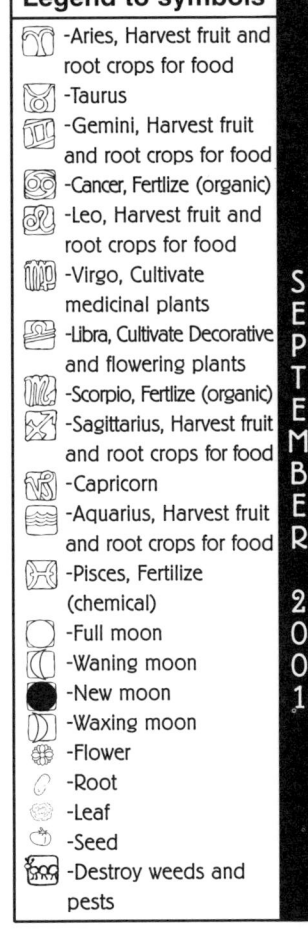

Legend to symbols
- Aries, Harvest fruit and root crops for food
- Taurus
- Gemini, Harvest fruit and root crops for food
- Cancer, Fertilize (organic)
- Leo, Harvest fruit and root crops for food
- Virgo, Cultivate medicinal plants
- Libra, Cultivate Decorative and flowering plants
- Scorpio, Fertilize (organic)
- Sagittarius, Harvest fruit and root crops for food
- Capricorn
- Aquarius, Harvest fruit and root crops for food
- Pisces, Fertilize (chemical)
- Full moon
- Waning moon
- New moon
- Waxing moon
- Flower
- Root
- Leaf
- Seed
- Destroy weeds and pests

SEPTEMBER 2001

MONDAY	1 ♓	8 ♊	15 ♍
TUESDAY	2 13:49 ♉ 2 degrees 27	9 ♋ 0 degrees 56	16 ● 19:23 ♎ 11 degrees 31
WEDNESDAY	3 ♉	10 4:20 ♋	17 ♎
THURSDAY	4 ♉	11 ♋	18 ♏ 10 degrees 49
FRIDAY	5 ♉ 9 degrees 19	12 ♌ 12 degrees 28	19 ♏
SATURDAY	6 ♉	13 ♌	20 ♐ 8 degrees 37
SUNDAY	7 ♊ 4 degrees 42	14 ♍ 11 degrees 42	21 ♐

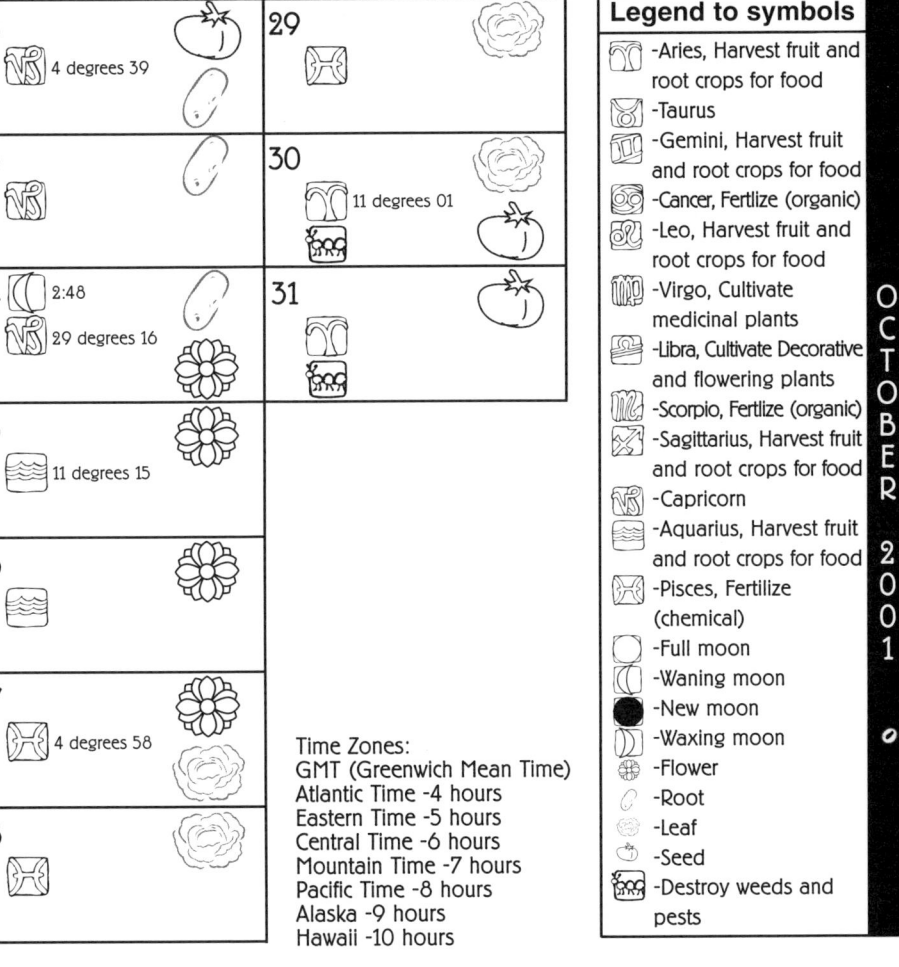

THURSDAY	1 ○ 5:41 ♉ 5 degrees 52	8 ☽ 12:21 ♌ ♒ 8 degrees 56	15 ● 6:40 ♏
FRIDAY	2 ♉	9 ♌ ♒	16 ♐ 2 degrees 56 ♒
SATURDAY	3 ♊ 1 degree 30 ♒	10 ♍ 7 degrees 15 ♒	17 ♐ ♒
SUNDAY	4 ♊ ♒	11 ♍ ♒	18 ♐ ♒
MONDAY	5 ♊ ♒	12 ♎ 6 degrees 06	19 ♑ 12 degrees 26
TUESDAY	6 ♋ 11 degrees 23	13 ♎	20 ♑
WEDNESDAY	7 ♋	14 ♏ 4 degrees 55	21 ♒ 7 degrees 08

2 🌘 23:21 ♒ 🌺	29 ♉ 🥔
3 ♓ 1 degree 03 🌺🥬	30 ♉ 🥔
4 ♓ 🥬	
5 ♓ 🥬	
6 ♈ 6 degrees 51 🐛 🍅	
7 ♈ 🐛 🍅	
8 ♉ 1 degree 31 🍅 🥔	

Time Zones:
GMT (Greenwich Mean Time)
Atlantic Time -4 hours
Eastern Time -5 hours
Central Time -6 hours
Mountain Time -7 hours
Pacific Time -8 hours
Alaska -9 hours
Hawaii -10 hours

Legend to symbols

- ♈ -Aries, Harvest fruit and root crops for food
- ♉ -Taurus
- ♊ -Gemini, Harvest fruit and root crops for food
- ♋ -Cancer, Fertilize (organic)
- ♌ -Leo, Harvest fruit and root crops for food
- ♍ -Virgo, Cultivate medicinal plants
- ♎ -Libra, Cultivate Decorative and flowering plants
- ♏ -Scorpio, Fertilize (organic)
- ♐ -Sagittarius, Harvest fruit and root crops for food
- ♑ -Capricorn
- ♒ -Aquarius, Harvest fruit and root crops for food
- ♓ -Pisces, Fertilize (chemical)
- 🌕 -Full moon
- 🌖 -Waning moon
- 🌑 -New moon
- 🌒 -Waxing moon
- 🌸 -Flower
- 🥔 -Root
- 🥬 -Leaf
- 🍅 -Seed
- 🐛 -Destroy weeds and pests

NOVEMBER 2001

SATURDAY	1 ♊ 10 degrees 29	8 ♍	15 ♐
SUNDAY	2 ♊	9 ♎ 2 degrees 23	16 ♑ 7 degrees 37
MONDAY	3 ♋ 7 degrees 49	10 ♎	17 ♑
TUESDAY	4 ♋	11 ♏ 0 degrees 29	18 ♒ 2 degrees 42
WEDNESDAY	5 ♌ 5 degrees 42	12 ♏	19 ♒
THURSDAY	6 ♌	13 ♏	20 ♒
FRIDAY	7 ☽ 19:51 ♍ 4 degrees 01	14 ● 20:24 ♐ 11 degrees 28	21 ♊ 8 degrees 50

20:56 ♓	29 ♊ 🐛
2 degrees 36 ♈ 🐛	30 10:41 ♋ 0 degrees 31
♈ 🐛	31 ♋
♈ 🐛	
♉ 9 degrees 15	
♉	
♊ 5 degrees 09 🐛	

Time Zones:
GMT (Greenwich Mean Time)
Atlantic Time -4 hours
Eastern Time -5 hours
Central Time -6 hours
Mountain Time -7 hours
Pacific Time -8 hours
Alaska -9 hours
Hawaii -10 hours

Legend to symbols

- ♈ -Aries, Harvest fruit and root crops for food
- ♉ -Taurus
- ♊ -Gemini, Harvest fruit and root crops for food
- ♋ -Cancer, Fertlize (organic)
- ♌ -Leo, Harvest fruit and root crops for food
- ♍ -Virgo, Cultivate medicinal plants
- ♎ -Libra, Cultivate Decorative and flowering plants
- ♏ -Scorpio, Fertlize (organic)
- ♐ -Sagittarius, Harvest fruit and root crops for food
- ♑ -Capricorn
- ♒ -Aquarius, Harvest fruit and root crops for food
- ♓ -Pisces, Fertlize (chemical)
- -Full moon
- -Waning moon
- -New moon
- -Waxing moon
- -Flower
- -Root
- -Leaf
- -Seed
- -Destroy weeds and pests

DECEMBER 2001

TUESDAY	1 ♌ 1 degree 06	8 ♏ 24 degrees 28	15 ♒ 10 degrees 52
WEDNESDAY	2 ♌	9 ♏	16 ♒
THURSDAY	3 ♍ 0 degrees 15	10 ♐ 7 degrees 43	17 ♓ 4 degrees 58
FRIDAY	4 ♍	11 ♐	18 ♓
SATURDAY	5 ♍	12 ♑ 3 degrees 33	19 ♓
SUNDAY	6 ☽ 6:49 ♎ 13 degrees 21	13 ● 13:29 ♑	20 ♈ 10 degrees 35
MONDAY	7 ♎	14 ♑	21 ☽ 17:46 ♈

Date		
2	♉ 4 degrees 40	🍅 / (root)
3	♉	/ (root)
4	♉	/ (root)
5	♊ 12 degrees 50 / 🐛	✿ (flower)
6	♊ / 🐛	✿
7	♋ 10 degrees 22	✿ / 🥬
8	○ 22:50 / ♋	🥬
29	♌ 9 degrees 33 / 🐛	🥬 / 🍅 / (root)
30	♌ / 🐛	🍅
31	♍ 9 degrees 37 / 🐛	🍅 / (root)

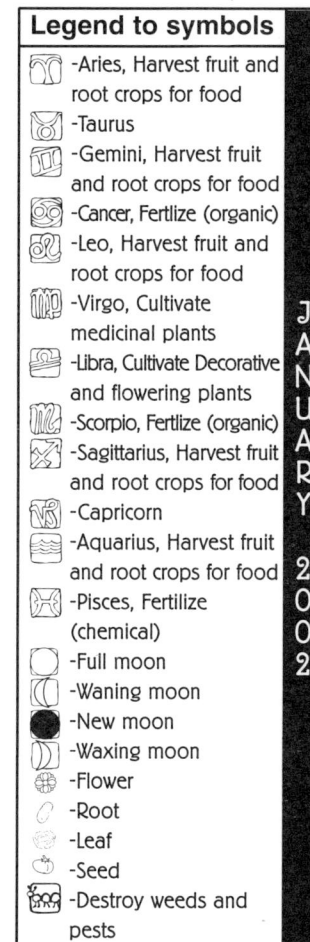

Legend to symbols

- ♈ -Aries, Harvest fruit and root crops for food
- ♉ -Taurus
- ♊ -Gemini, Harvest fruit and root crops for food
- ♋ -Cancer, Fertilize (organic)
- ♌ -Leo, Harvest fruit and root crops for food
- ♍ -Virgo, Cultivate medicinal plants
- ♎ -Libra, Cultivate Decorative and flowering plants
- ♏ -Scorpio, Fertlize (organic)
- ♐ -Sagittarius, Harvest fruit and root crops for food
- ♑ -Capricorn
- ♒ -Aquarius, Harvest fruit and root crops for food
- ♓ -Pisces, Fertilize (chemical)
- ○ -Full moon
- ◐ -Waning moon
- ● -New moon
- ◑ -Waxing moon
- ✿ -Flower
- / -Root
- 🍃 -Leaf
- 🌱 -Seed
- 🐛 -Destroy weeds and pests

JANUARY 2002

Time Zones:
GMT (Greenwich Mean Time)
Atlantic Time -4 hours
Eastern Time -5 hours
Central Time -6 hours
Mountain Time -7 hours
Pacific Time -8 hours
Alaska -9 hours
Hawaii -10 hours

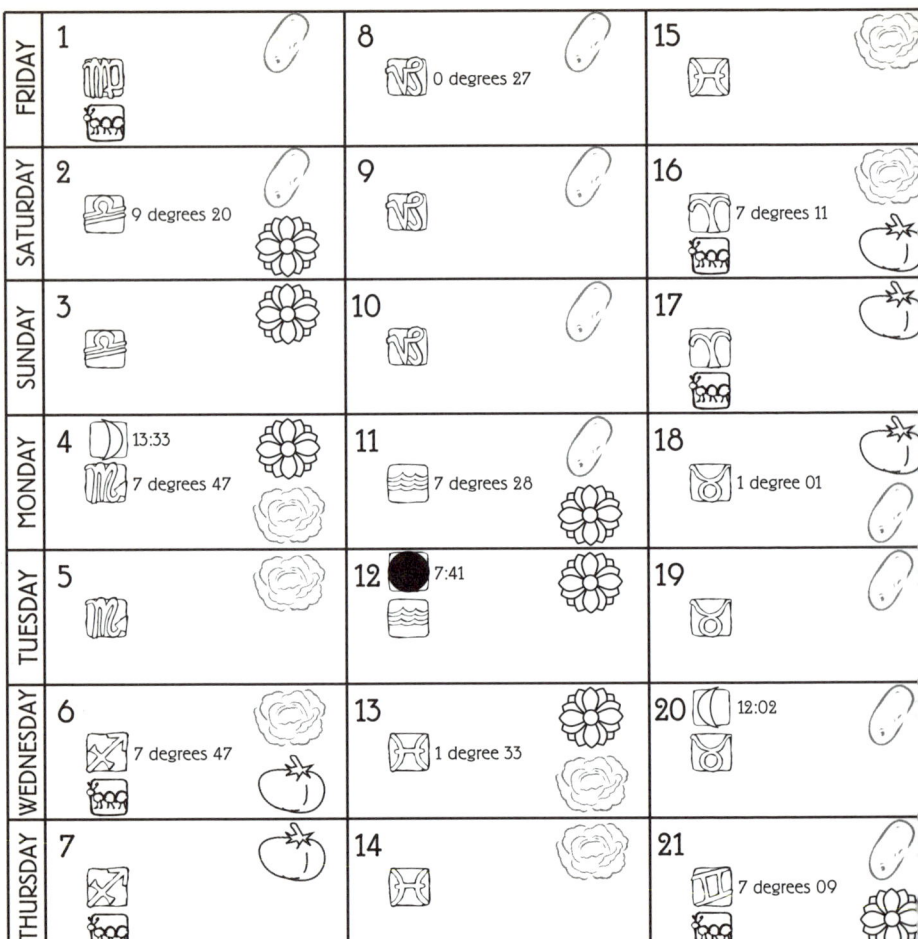

FRIDAY	1 ♍ ♒	8 ♑ 0 degrees 27	15 ♓
SATURDAY	2 ♎ 9 degrees 20	9 ♑	16 ♈ 7 degrees 11 ♒
SUNDAY	3 ♎	10 ♑	17 ♈ ♒
MONDAY	4 ☽ 13:33 ♏ 7 degrees 47	11 ♒ 7 degrees 28	18 ♉ 1 degree 01
TUESDAY	5 ♏	12 ● 7:41 ♒	19 ♉
WEDNESDAY	6 ♐ 7 degrees 47 ♒	13 ♓ 1 degree 33	20 ☽ 12:02 ♉
THURSDAY	7 ♐ ♒	14 ♓	21 ♊ 7 degrees 09 ♒

Legend to symbols

- ♈ -Aries, Harvest fruit and root crops for food
- ♉ -Taurus
- ♊ -Gemini, Harvest fruit and root crops for food
- ♋ -Cancer, Fertlize (organic)
- ♌ -Leo, Harvest fruit and root crops for food
- ♍ -Virgo, Cultivate medicinal plants
- ♎ -Libra, Cultivate Decorative and flowering plants
- ♏ -Scorpio, Fertlize (organic)
- ♐ -Sagittarius, Harvest fruit and root crops for food
- ♑ -Capricorn
- ♒ -Aquarius, Harvest fruit and root crops for food
- ♓ -Pisces, Fertilize (chemical)
- ○ -Full moon
- ☾ -Waning moon
- ● -New moon
- ☽ -Waxing moon
- ✿ -Flower
- ⌒ -Root
- 🍃 -Leaf
- 🍅 -Seed
- 🐛 -Destroy weeds and pests

FEBRUARY 2002

Time Zones:
GMT (Greenwich Mean Time)
Atlantic Time -4 hours
Eastern Time -5 hours
Central Time -6 hours
Mountain Time -7 hours
Pacific Time -8 hours
Alaska -9 hours
Hawaii -10 hours

FRIDAY	1 ♎ 3 degrees 18	8 ♑ 10 degrees 03	15 ♊ 4 degrees 10
SATURDAY	2 ♎	9 ♑	16 ♊
SUNDAY	3 ♏ 3 degrees 07	10 ♑	17 ♊
MONDAY	4 ♏	11 ♑ 4 degrees 34	18 ♉ 10 degrees
TUESDAY	5 ♐ 1 degree 10	12 ♑	19 ♉
WEDNESDAY	6 ☽ 1:24 ♐	13 ♒ 10 degrees 26	20 ♊ 4 degrees 28
THURSDAY	7 ♐	14 ● 2:02 ♒	21 ♊

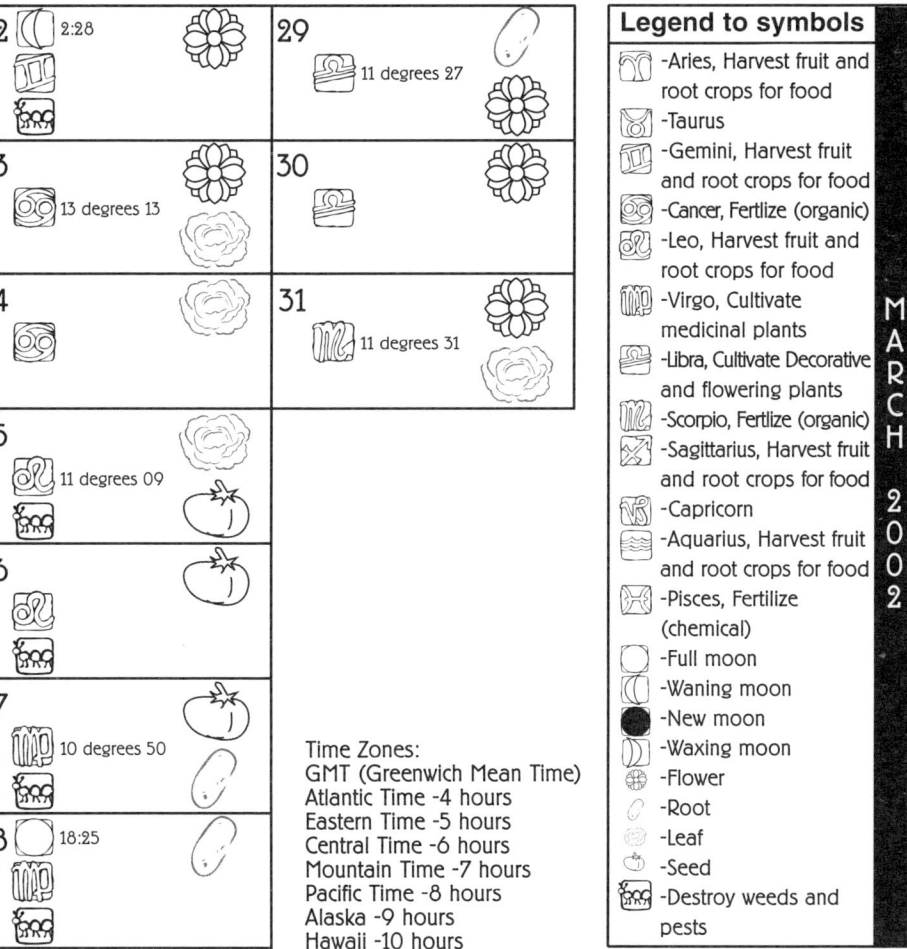

	MONDAY	TUESDAY	WEDNESDAY	THURSDAY	FRIDAY	SATURDAY	SUNDAY
	1 ♏	2 ♐ 9 degrees 57	3 ♐	4 ☽ 15:29 ♑ 6 degrees 28	5 ♑	6 ♒ 1 degree 09	7 ♒
	8 ♒	9 ♓ 7 degrees 26	10 ♓	11 ♈ 1 degree 09	12 ● 19:21 ♈	13 ♈	14 ♉ 7 degrees 05
	15 ♉	16 ♊ 1 degree 34	17 ♊	18 ♊	19 ♋ 9 degrees 44	20 ☽ 12:48 ♋	21 ♌ 6 degrees 40

2 ♌ 🐛 🍅	29 ♐ 4 degrees 02 🐛 🌹
3 ♍ 5 degrees 05 🐛 🍅 🥔	30 ♐ 🐛 🍅
4 ♍ 🐛 🥔	
5 ♎ 4 degrees 46 🥔 🌸	
6 ♎ 🌸	
7 ○ 3:00 ♏ 4 degrees 49 🌸 🥬	
8 ♏ 🥬	

Time Zones:
GMT (Greenwich Mean Time)
Atlantic Time -4 hours
Eastern Time -5 hours
Central Time -6 hours
Mountain Time -7 hours
Pacific Time -8 hours
Alaska -9 hours
Hawaii -10 hours

Legend to symbols

- ♈ -Aries, Harvest fruit and root crops for food
- ♉ -Taurus
- ♊ -Gemini, Harvest fruit and root crops for food
- ♋ -Cancer, Fertilize (organic)
- ♌ -Leo, Harvest fruit and root crops for food
- ♍ -Virgo, Cultivate medicinal plants
- ♎ -Libra, Cultivate Decorative and flowering plants
- ♏ -Scorpio, Fertilize (organic)
- ♐ -Sagittarius, Harvest fruit and root crops for food
- ♑ -Capricorn
- ♒ -Aquarius, Harvest fruit and root crops for food
- ♓ -Pisces, Fertilize (chemical)
- ○ -Full moon
- ☽ -Waning moon
- ● -New moon
- ☾ -Waxing moon
- ✿ -Flower
- ⌒ -Root
- 🍃 -Leaf
- ○ -Seed
- 🐛 -Destroy weeds and pests

APRIL 2002

WEDNESDAY	1 ♑ 1 degree 38	8 ♓	15 ♊
THURSDAY	2 ♑	9 ♈ 9 degrees 43	16 10:49 ♋ 6 degrees 45 — lunar eclipse / no planting
FRIDAY	3 ♑	10 ♈	17 ♋
SATURDAY	4 ☽ 7:16 ♒ 9 degrees 56	11 ♉ 3 degrees 46	18 ♌ 3 degrees 27
SUNDAY	5 ♒	12 ● 10:45 ♉	19 ☾ 19:42 ♌
MONDAY	6 ♓ 4 degrees 05	13 ♉	20 ♍ 1 degree 09
TUESDAY	7 ♓	14 ♊ 10 degrees 59	21 ♍

2 ♍ 🌿	🥔	29 ♑ 9 degrees 35	🍅 🥔
3 ♎ 14 degrees 22	🥔 🌸	30 ♑	🥔
4 ♎	🌸	31 ♒ 5 degrees 30 solar eclipse / no planting	
5 ♏ 13 degrees 34	🌸 🌹		
6 ○ 11:51 ♏	🌹		
7 ♐ 12 degrees 12 🌿	🌹 🍅		
8 ♐ 🌿	🍅		

Time Zones:
GMT (Greenwich Mean Time)
Atlantic Time -4 hours
Eastern Time -5 hours
Central Time -6 hours
Mountain Time -7 hours
Pacific Time -8 hours
Alaska -9 hours
Hawaii -10 hours

Legend to symbols

- ♈ -Aries, Harvest fruit and root crops for food
- ♉ -Taurus
- ♊ -Gemini, Harvest fruit and root crops for food
- ♋ -Cancer, Fertilize (organic)
- ♌ -Leo, Harvest fruit and root crops for food
- ♍ -Virgo, Cultivate medicinal plants
- ♎ -Libra, Cultivate Decorative and flowering plants
- ♏ -Scorpio, Fertilize (organic)
- ♐ -Sagittarius, Harvest fruit and root crops for food
- ♑ -Capricorn
- ♒ -Aquarius, Harvest fruit and root crops for food
- ♓ -Pisces, Fertilize (chemical)
- ○ -Full moon
- ☽ -Waning moon
- ● -New moon
- ☾ -Waxing moon
- ❀ -Flower
- 〇 -Root
- 🍃 -Leaf
- 🌱 -Seed
- 🌿 -Destroy weeds and pests

MAY 2002

SATURDAY	1 ≈ ✿	8 ☉ 12 degrees 07 🍅 🥔	15 ♌ 💀 🍅
SUNDAY	2 ♓ 0 degree 11 🥬	9 ♉ 🥔	16 ♌ 💀 🍅
MONDAY	3 ☽ 0:05 ♓ 🥬	10 ● 23:46 ♊ 7 degrees 08 solar eclipse / no planting	17 ♍ 12 degrees 07 💀 🥔
TUESDAY	4 ♓ 🥬 🍅	11 ♊ 💀 ✿	18 ☽ 0:29 ♍ 💀 🥔
WEDNESDAY	5 ♈ 6 degrees 💀 🍅	12 ♊☉ 3 degrees 10 ✿ 🥬	19 ♎ 10 degrees 34 🥔 ✿
THURSDAY	6 ♈ 💀 🍅	13 ♊ 🥬 🍅	20 ♎ ✿
FRIDAY	7 ♈ 💀 🍅	14 ♌ 0 degrees 11 💀 🍅	21 ♍ 9 degrees 02 ✿ 🥬

2 ♏		29 ♒	
3 ⚔ 7 degrees 08		30 ♓ 8 degrees 06	
4 ○ 21:42 ⚔			
5 ♑ 4 degrees 28			
6 ♑			
7 ♒ 0 degrees 44			
8 ♒			

Time Zones:
GMT (Greenwich Mean Time)
Atlantic Time -4 hours
Eastern Time -5 hours
Central Time -6 hours
Mountain Time -7 hours
Pacific Time -8 hours
Alaska -9 hours
Hawaii -10 hours

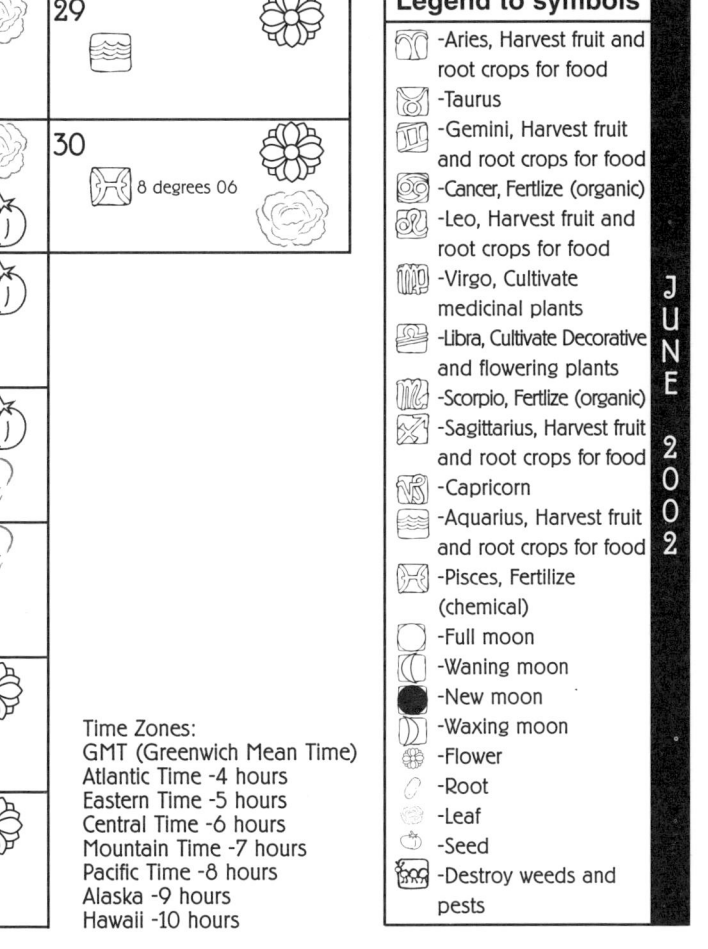

Legend to symbols

- ♈ -Aries, Harvest fruit and root crops for food
- ♉ -Taurus
- ♊ -Gemini, Harvest fruit and root crops for food
- ♋ -Cancer, Fertilize (organic)
- ♌ -Leo, Harvest fruit and root crops for food
- ♍ -Virgo, Cultivate medicinal plants
- ♎ -Libra, Cultivate Decorative and flowering plants
- ♏ -Scorpio, Fertilize (organic)
- ♐ -Sagittarius, Harvest fruit and root crops for food
- ♑ -Capricorn
- ♒ -Aquarius, Harvest fruit and root crops for food
- ♓ -Pisces, Fertilize (chemical)
- ○ -Full moon
- ☾ -Waning moon
- ● -New moon
- ☽ -Waxing moon
- ✿ -Flower
- ⌒ -Root
- ☘ -Leaf
- ⚬ -Seed
- 🐛 -Destroy weeds and pests

JUNE 2002

MONDAY	1 ♓	8 ♊	15 ♍
TUESDAY	2 ☽ 17:19 ♉ 2 degrees 04	9 ♊	16 ♎ 7 degrees 22
WEDNESDAY	3 ♉	10 ● 10:26 ♋ 12 degrees 02	17 ☽ 4:47 ♎
THURSDAY	4 ♉	11 ♋	18 ♏ 5 degrees 43
FRIDAY	5 ♉ 7 degrees 54	12 ♌ 9 degrees 55	19 ♏
SATURDAY	6 ♉	13 ♌	20 ♐ 3 degrees 23
SUNDAY	7 ♊ 2 degrees 57	14 ♍ 8 degrees 35	21 ♐

2 ♑ 0 degrees 18	29 ♓
3 ♑	30 ♊ 10 degrees 05
4 ○ 9:07 ♑	31 ♊
5 ♒ 9 degrees 11	
6 ♒	
7 ♓ 4 degrees 02	
8 ♓	

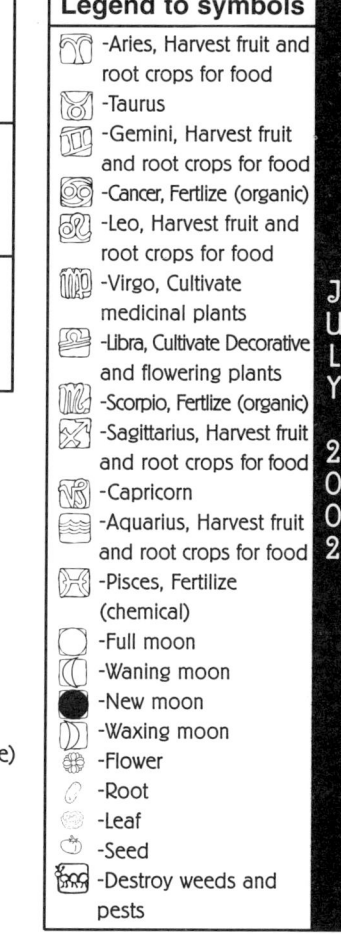

Legend to symbols

- ♈ -Aries, Harvest fruit and root crops for food
- ♉ -Taurus
- ♊ -Gemini, Harvest fruit and root crops for food
- ♋ -Cancer, Fertilize (organic)
- ♌ -Leo, Harvest fruit and root crops for food
- ♍ -Virgo, Cultivate medicinal plants
- ♎ -Libra, Cultivate Decorative and flowering plants
- ♏ -Scorpio, Fertilize (organic)
- ♐ -Sagittarius, Harvest fruit and root crops for food
- ♑ -Capricorn
- ♒ -Aquarius, Harvest fruit and root crops for food
- ♓ -Pisces, Fertilize (chemical)
- ○ -Full moon
- ☾ -Waning moon
- ● -New moon
- ☽ -Waxing moon
- ❀ -Flower
- / -Root
- ◐ -Leaf
- ˘ -Seed
- 💀 -Destroy weeds and pests

JULY 2002

Time Zones:
GMT (Greenwich Mean Time)
Atlantic Time -4 hours
Eastern Time -5 hours
Central Time -6 hours
Mountain Time -7 hours
Pacific Time -8 hours
Alaska -9 hours
Hawaii -10 hours

THURSDAY	1 ☽ 10:22 ♉ 3 degrees 50	8 ● 19:15 ♌ 4 degrees 28	15 ☽ 10:12 ♍
FRIDAY	2 ♉	9 ♌	16 ♐ 0 degrees 19
SATURDAY	3 ♉	10 ♍ 3 degrees 39	17 ♐
SUNDAY	4 ♊ 10 degrees 33	11 ♍	18 ♐
MONDAY	5 ♊	12 ♎ 3 degrees 18	19 ♑ 10 degrees 09
TUESDAY	6 ☉ 6 degrees 40	13 ♎	20 ♑
WEDNESDAY	7 ☉	14 ♏ 2 degrees 22	21 ♒ 5 degrees 37

Date			
2 ◯ 22:29 ♒	🌼	29 ♉	🥔
3 ♓ 0 degrees 25	🥬	30 ♉	🥔
4 ♓	🥬	31 ☽ 2:31 ♊ 6 degrees 14 🐛	🌼
5 ♓	🥬		
6 ♈ 6 degrees 33 🐛	🍅		
7 ♈ 🐛	🍅		
8 ♉ 0 degrees 14	🥔		

Time Zones:
GMT (Greenwich Mean Time)
Atlantic Time -4 hours
Eastern Time -5 hours
Central Time -6 hours
Mountain Time -7 hours
Pacific Time -8 hours
Alaska -9 hours
Hawaii -10 hours

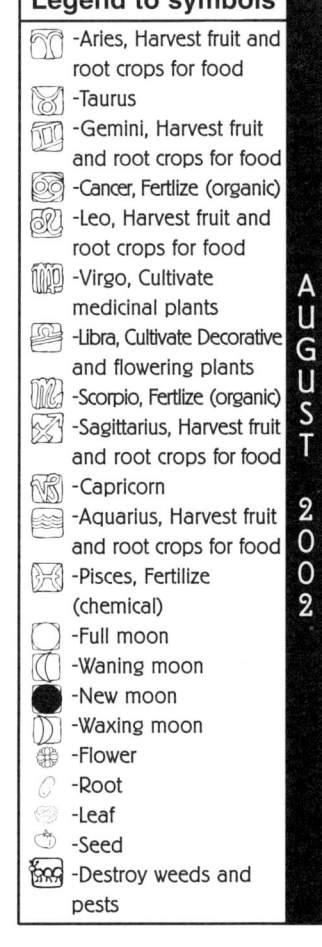

Legend to symbols

- ♈ -Aries, Harvest fruit and root crops for food
- ♉ -Taurus
- ♊ -Gemini, Harvest fruit and root crops for food
- ♋ -Cancer, Fertilize (organic)
- ♌ -Leo, Harvest fruit and root crops for food
- ♍ -Virgo, Cultivate medicinal plants
- ♎ -Libra, Cultivate Decorative and flowering plants
- ♏ -Scorpio, Fertilize (organic)
- ♐ -Sagittarius, Harvest fruit and root crops for food
- ♑ -Capricorn
- ♒ -Aquarius, Harvest fruit and root crops for food
- ♓ -Pisces, Fertilize (chemical)
- ◯ -Full moon
- ☾ -Waning moon
- ● -New moon
- ☽ -Waxing moon
- ✿ -Flower
- ⌒ -Root
- 🥬 -Leaf
- 🌱 -Seed
- 🐛 -Destroy weeds and pests

AUGUST 2002

SUNDAY	1 ♊	8 ♍	15 ♑ 7 degrees 11
MONDAY	2 ☉ 1 degree 29	9 ♎ 12 degrees 39	16 ♑
TUESDAY	3 ☉	10 ♎	17 ♒ 2 degrees 39
WEDNESDAY	4 ☉	11 ♏ 12 degrees 19	18 ♒
THURSDAY	5 ♌ 12 degrees 41	12 ♏	19 ♒
FRIDAY	6 ♌	13 ☾ 18:08 ♐ 10 degrees 32	20 ♓ 9 degrees 26
SATURDAY	7 ● 3:10 ♍ 12 degrees 20	14 ♐	21 ○ 13:29 ♓

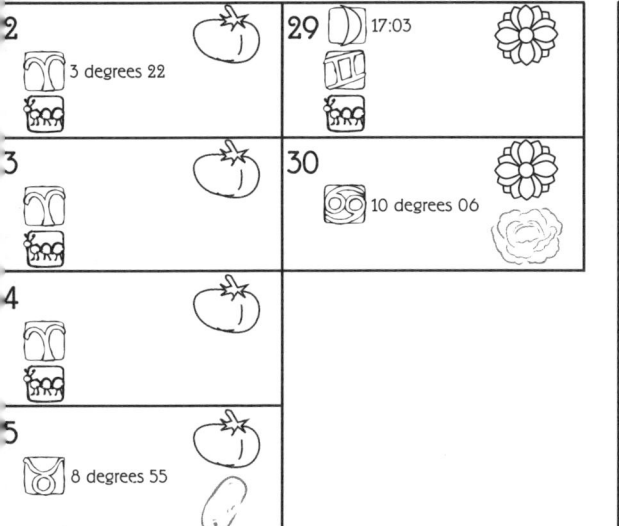

Date	Sign	Activity
2	♊ 3 degrees 22, Destroy weeds and pests	🍅
3	♊, Destroy weeds and pests	🍅
4	♊, Destroy weeds and pests	🍅
5	♉ 8 degrees 55	🥔
6	♉	🥔
7	♊ 2 degrees 47, Destroy weeds and pests	🌸
8	♊, Destroy weeds and pests	🌸
29	Waning moon 17:03, ♊, Destroy weeds and pests	🌸
30	New moon 10 degrees 06	🌸 🥬

Time Zones:
GMT (Greenwich Mean Time)
Atlantic Time -4 hours
Eastern Time -5 hours
Central Time -6 hours
Mountain Time -7 hours
Pacific Time -8 hours
Alaska -9 hours
Hawaii -10 hours

Legend to symbols

- ♈ -Aries, Harvest fruit and root crops for food
- ♉ -Taurus
- ♊ -Gemini, Harvest fruit and root crops for food
- ♋ -Cancer, Fertilize (organic)
- ♌ -Leo, Harvest fruit and root crops for food
- ♍ -Virgo, Cultivate medicinal plants
- ♎ -Libra, Cultivate Decorative and flowering plants
- ♏ -Scorpio, Fertilize (organic)
- ♐ -Sagittarius, Harvest fruit and root crops for food
- ♑ -Capricorn
- ♒ -Aquarius, Harvest fruit and root crops for food
- ♓ -Pisces, Fertilize (chemical)
- -Full moon
- -Waning moon
- -New moon
- -Waxing moon
- -Flower
- -Root
- -Leaf
- -Seed
- -Destroy weeds and pests

SEPTEMBER 2002

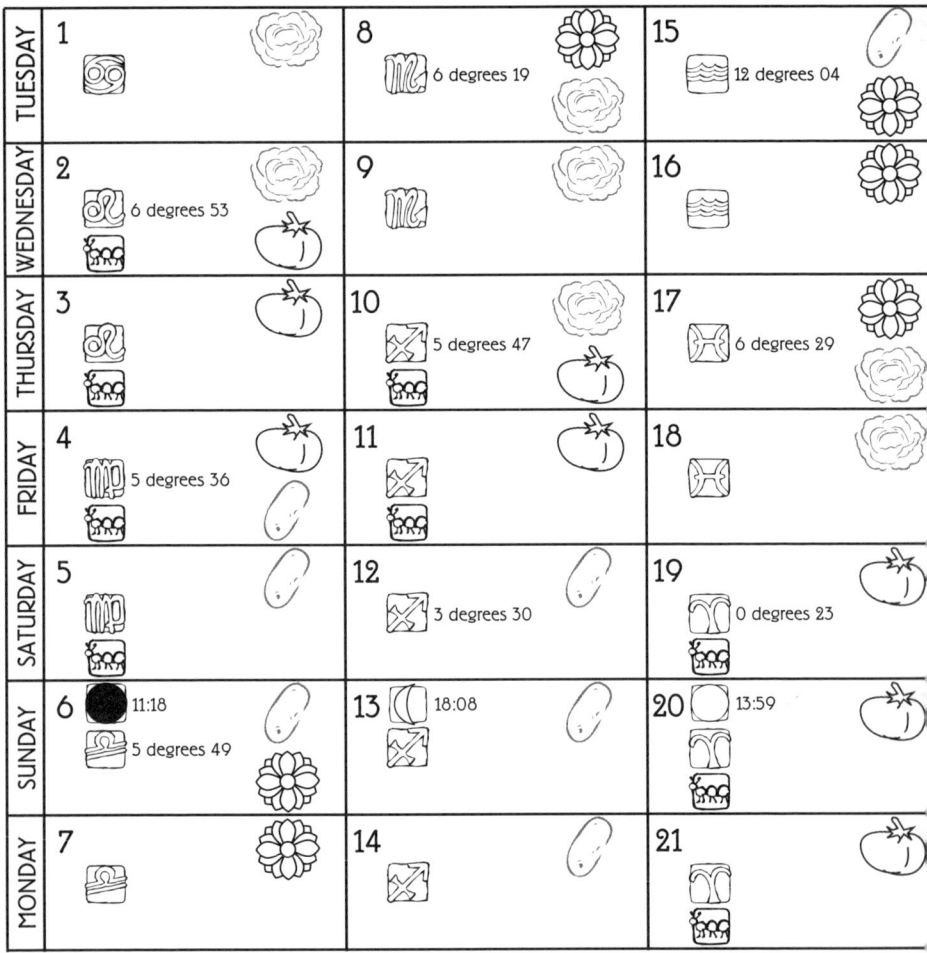

2 ⊙ 5 degrees 57	29) 17:03 ♌ 2 degrees 34
3 ♉	30 ♌ 🐛
4 ♉	31 ♌ 🐛
5 ♊ 11 degrees 57 🐛	
6 ♊ 🐛	
7 ♋ 6 degrees 42	
8 ♋	

Time Zones:
GMT (Greenwich Mean Time)
Atlantic Time -4 hours
Eastern Time -5 hours
Central Time -6 hours
Mountain Time -7 hours
Pacific Time -8 hours
Alaska -9 hours
Hawaii -10 hours

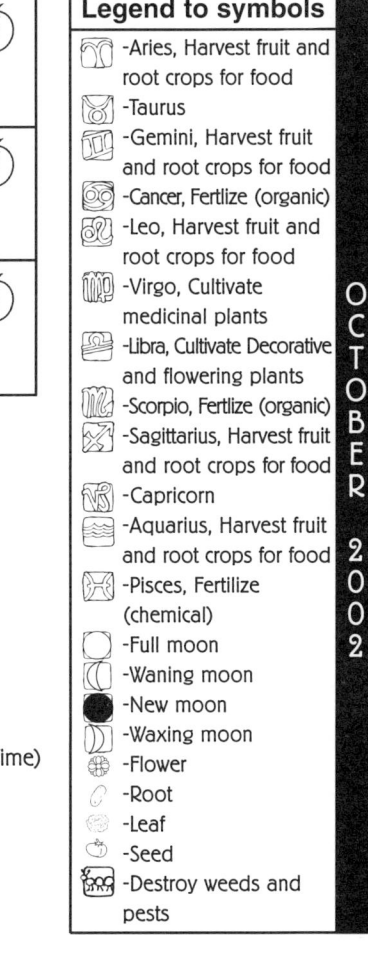

Legend to symbols

- ♈ -Aries, Harvest fruit and root crops for food
- ♉ -Taurus
- ♊ -Gemini, Harvest fruit and root crops for food
- ♋ -Cancer, Fertilize (organic)
- ♌ -Leo, Harvest fruit and root crops for food
- ♍ -Virgo, Cultivate medicinal plants
- ♎ -Libra, Cultivate Decorative and flowering plants
- ♏ -Scorpio, Fertilize (organic)
- ♐ -Sagittarius, Harvest fruit and root crops for food
- ♑ -Capricorn
- ♒ -Aquarius, Harvest fruit and root crops for food
- ♓ -Pisces, Fertilize (chemical)
- ○ -Full moon
- ☾ -Waning moon
- ● -New moon
- ☽ -Waxing moon
- ✾ -Flower
- ⌒ -Root
- 🍃 -Leaf
- ⚬ -Seed
- 🐛 -Destroy weeds and pests

OCTOBER 2002

FRIDAY	1 ♍ 14 degrees 21	8 ♐	15 ♓
SATURDAY	2 ♍	9 ♑ 12 degrees 03 — lunar eclipse / no planting	16 ♈ 9 degrees 04
SUNDAY	3 ♎ 14 degrees 05	10 ♑	17 ♈
MONDAY	4 ● 20:34 ♎	11 ☽ 20:52 ♒ 8 degrees 20	18 ♉ 2 degrees 46
TUESDAY	5 ♏ 14 degrees 24	12 ♒	19 ♉
WEDNESDAY	6 ♏	13 ♓ 3 degrees 12	20 ☽ 1:34 ♉
THURSDAY	7 ♐ 14 degrees	14 ♓	21 ♊ 8 degrees 55

2	🌸	29	🥔
♊ 🐛		♍ 🐛	
3	🥬	30	🥔
☾ 3 degrees 46		♎ 8 degrees 28	🌸
4	🥬		
☾			
5	🥬		
☾			
6 ☽ 15:46	🥬		
♌ 12 degrees 40	🍅		
🐛			
7	🍅		
♌			
🐛			
8	🍅		
♍ 9 degrees 59	🥔		
🐛			

Time Zones:
GMT (Greenwich Mean Time)
Atlantic Time -4 hours
Eastern Time -5 hours
Central Time -6 hours
Mountain Time -7 hours
Pacific Time -8 hours
Alaska -9 hours
Hawaii -10 hours

Legend to symbols

- ♈ -Aries, Harvest fruit and root crops for food
- ♉ -Taurus
- ♊ -Gemini, Harvest fruit and root crops for food
- ♋ -Cancer, Fertilize (organic)
- ♌ -Leo, Harvest fruit and root crops for food
- ♍ -Virgo, Cultivate medicinal plants
- ♎ -Libra, Cultivate Decorative and flowering plants
- ♏ -Scorpio, Fertilize (organic)
- ♐ -Sagittarius, Harvest fruit and root crops for food
- ♑ -Capricorn
- ♒ -Aquarius, Harvest fruit and root crops for food
- ♓ -Pisces, Fertilize (chemical)
- ○ -Full moon
- ☾ -Waning moon
- ● -New moon
- ☽ -Waxing moon
- ✿ -Flower
- ◯ -Root
- 🍃 -Leaf
- 🌱 -Seed
- 🐛 -Destroy weeds and pests

NOVEMBER 2002

SUNDAY	1 ♎	8 ≈ 3 degrees 22	15 ♊
MONDAY	2 ♏ 7 degrees 38	9 ≈	16 ♉ 11 degrees 01
TUESDAY	3 ♏	10 ≈	17 ♉
WEDNESDAY	4 ● 7:34 ♐ 7 degrees 21	11 ☾ 15:49 ♓ 11 degrees 25	18 ♊ 5 degrees 14
THURSDAY	5 ♐	12 ♓	19 ○ 19:10 ♊
FRIDAY	6 ♑ 6 degrees 05	13 ♈ 5 degrees 28	20 ♉ 0 degrees 15
SATURDAY	7 ♑	14 ♈	21 ♉

2 ♊ 🥬	29 ♏ 3 degrees 09 🥬
3 ♎ 9 degrees 34 🐛	30 ♏ 🥬
4 ♌ 🐛 🍅	31 ♐ 1 degree 46 🐛 🍅
5 ♍ 6 degrees 50 🍅 🥔	
6 ♍ 🥔	
7 ☽ 0:31 ♎ 4 degrees 45 🌸	
8 ♎ 🌸	

Time Zones:
GMT (Greenwich Mean Time)
Atlantic Time -4 hours
Eastern Time -5 hours
Central Time -6 hours
Mountain Time -7 hours
Pacific Time -8 hours
Alaska -9 hours
Hawaii -10 hours

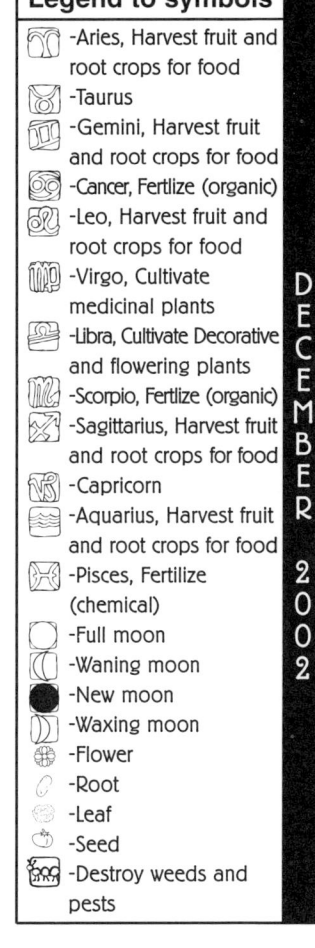

Legend to symbols

- ♈ -Aries, Harvest fruit and root crops for food
- ♉ -Taurus
- ♊ -Gemini, Harvest fruit and root crops for food
- ♋ -Cancer, Fertlize (organic)
- ♌ -Leo, Harvest fruit and root crops for food
- ♍ -Virgo, Cultivate medicinal plants
- ♎ -Libra, Cultivate Decorative and flowering plants
- ♏ -Scorpio, Fertlize (organic)
- ♐ -Sagittarius, Harvest fruit and root crops for food
- ♑ -Capricorn
- ♒ -Aquarius, Harvest fruit and root crops for food
- ♓ -Pisces, Fertilize (chemical)
- ○ -Full moon
- ☾ -Waning moon
- ● -New moon
- ☽ -Waxing moon
- 🌸 -Flower
- 🥕 -Root
- 🥬 -Leaf
- 🌱 -Seed
- 🐛 -Destroy weeds and pests

DECEMBER 2002

WEDNESDAY	1 ♐ 🍅	8 ♓ 🥬	15 ♊ 🌸
THURSDAY	2 ● 20:23 ♑ 0 degrees 10 🥔	9 ♈ 🍅	16 ♊ 🌸
FRIDAY	3 ♑ 🥔	10 ☽ 10:49 ♈ 🍅	17 ○ 10:49 ♋ 8 degrees 39 🌸 🥬
SATURDAY	4 ♑ 🥔	11 ♈ 🍅	18 ♋ 🥬
SUNDAY	5 ♒ 11 degrees 08 🌸	12 ♋ 6 degrees 60 🍅 🥔	19 ♌ 5 degrees 23 🥬 🍅
MONDAY	6 ♒ 🌸	13 ♋ 🥔	20 ♌ 🍅 🥔
TUESDAY	7 ♓ 6 degrees 51 🌸 🥬	14 ♊ 0 degrees 56 🌸	21 ♍ 3 degrees 12 🥔

22 ♍ 🐛	🥔	29 ♐ 🐛	🍅
23 ♎ 1 degree 33	✽	30 ♑ 9 degrees 23	🍅 🥔
24 ♎	✽	31 ♑	🥔
25 🌗 10:49 ♎	✽		
26 ♏ 13 degrees 60	✽ 🥬		
27 ♏	🥬		
28 ♐ 11 degrees 54 🐛	🥬 🍅		

Time Zones:
GMT (Greenwich Mean Time)
Atlantic Time -4 hours
Eastern Time -5 hours
Central Time -6 hours
Mountain Time -7 hours
Pacific Time -8 hours
Alaska -9 hours
Hawaii -10 hours

Legend to symbols

- ♈ -Aries, Harvest fruit and root crops for food
- ♉ -Taurus
- ♊ -Gemini, Harvest fruit and root crops for food
- ♋ -Cancer, Fertilize (organic)
- ♌ -Leo, Harvest fruit and root crops for food
- ♍ -Virgo, Cultivate medicinal plants
- ♎ -Libra, Cultivate Decorative and flowering plantes
- ♏ -Scorpio, Fertlize (organic)
- ♐ -Sagitarius, Harvest fruit and root crops for food
- ♑ -Capricorn
- ♒ -Aquarius, Harvest fruit and root crops for food
- ♓ -Pisces, Fertilize (chemical)
- 🌕 -Full moon
- 🌗 -Waning moon
- 🌑 -New moon
- 🌓 -Waxing moon
- ✽ -Flower
- 🥔 -Root
- 🥬 -Leaf
- 🌰 -Seed
- 🐛 -Destroye weeds and pests

JANUARY 2003

SATURDAY	1 ● 10:49 〜 6 degrees 13	8 ▭ 2 degrees 57	15 ◉
SUNDAY	2 〜	9 ◐ 10:49 ▭	16 ▢ 10:49 ૭ 13 degrees 47
MONDAY	3 ⋈ 2 degrees 10	10 ▭	17 ૭
TUESDAY	4 ⋈	11 ⬒ 8 degrees 39	18 ⬜ 12 degrees 26
WEDNESDAY	5 ⋈	12 ⬒	19 ⬜
THURSDAY	6 ⋒ 9 degrees 11	13 ◉ 3 degrees 32	20 ▱ 11 degrees 43
FRIDAY	7 ⋒	14 ◉	21 ▱

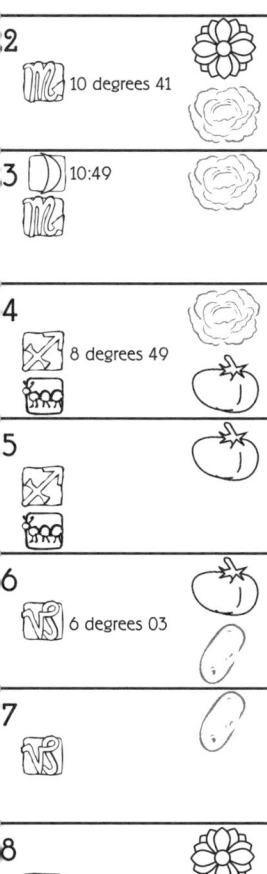

Legend to symbols

- Aries, Harvest fruit and root crops for food
- Taurus
- Gemini, Harvest fruit and root crops for food
- Cancer, Fertlize (organic)
- Leo, Harvest fruit and root crops for food
- Virgo, Cultivate medicinal plants
- Libra, Cultivate Decorative and flowering plantes
- Scorpio, Fertlize (organic)
- Sagitarius, Harvest fruit and root crops for food
- Capricorn
- Aquarius, Harvest fruit and root crops for food
- Pisces, Fertilize (chemical)
- Full moon
- Waning moon
- New moon
- Waxing moon
- Flower
- Root
- Leaf
- Seed
- Destroye weeds and pests

FEBRUARY 2003

Time Zones:
GMT (Greenwich Mean Time)
Atlantic Time -4 hours
Eastern Time -5 hours
Central Time -6 hours
Mountain Time -7 hours
Pacific Time -8 hours
Alaska -9 hours
Hawaii -10 hours

SATURDAY	1	8 11 degrees	15 7 degrees 49
SUNDAY	2	9	16
MONDAY	3 2:35 10 degrees 45	10 7:15 4 degrees 38	17 6 degrees 06
TUESDAY	4	11	18 10:49
WEDNESDAY	5 5 degrees 18	12 11 degrees 25	19 5 degrees 48
THURSDAY	6	13	20
FRIDAY	7	14	21 5 degrees 49

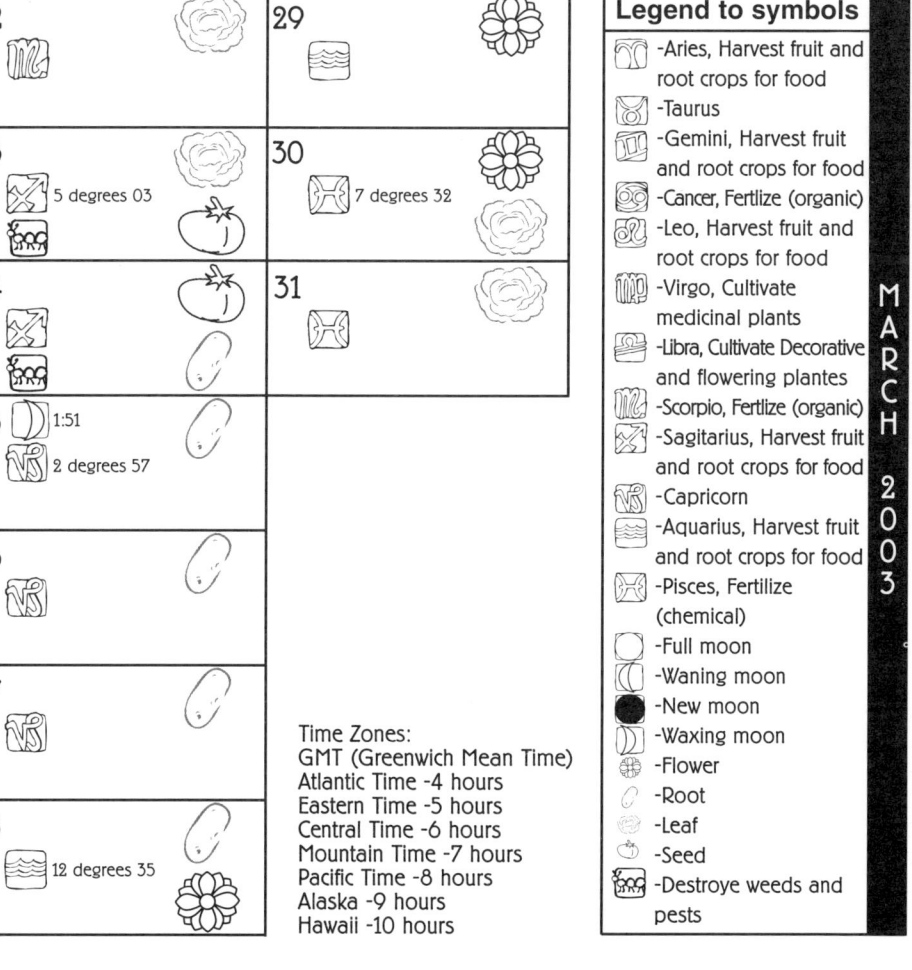

TUESDAY	1 ● 10:49 ♉ 1 degree 58 ♒ 🍅	8 ♊ ♒ 🌼	15 ♍ ♒ 🥔
WEDNESDAY	2 ♉ ♒ 🍅	9 ☽ 10:49 ♊ 7 degrees 21 🌼 🌹	16 ♎ 13 degrees 58 🌼
THURSDAY	3 ♉ ♒ 🍅	10 ♊ 🌹	17 ♎ 🌼
FRIDAY	4 ♉ 7 degrees 42 🍅 🥔	11 ♌ 2 degrees 46 🍅 ♒	18 ○ 10:49 ♏ 14 degrees 24 🌼 🌹
SATURDAY	5 ♉ 🥔	12 ♌ ♒ 🍅	19 ♏ 🌹
SUNDAY	6 ♊ 1 degree 16 ♒ 🌼	13 ♌ ♒ 🍅	20 ♐ 1 degree 13 ♒ 🍅
MONDAY	7 ♊ ♒ 🌼	14 ♍ 14 degrees 13 ♒ 🍅 🥔	21 ♐ ♒ 🍅

2 ♑ 12 degrees 35	29 ♊ 11 degrees 🕷
3 ☽ 10:49 ♑	30 ♊ 🕷
4 ♒ 9 degrees 18	
5 ♒	
6 ♓ 4 degrees 38	
7 ♓	
8 ♓	

Time Zones:
GMT (Greenwich Mean Time)
Atlantic Time -4 hours
Eastern Time -5 hours
Central Time -6 hours
Mountain Time -7 hours
Pacific Time -8 hours
Alaska -9 hours
Hawaii -10 hours

Legend to symbols

- ♈ -Aries, Harvest fruit and root crops for food
- ♉ -Taurus
- ♊ -Gemini, Harvest fruit and root crops for food
- ♋ -Cancer, Fertilize (organic)
- ♌ -Leo, Harvest fruit and root crops for food
- ♍ -Virgo, Cultivate medicinal plants
- ♎ -Libra, Cultivate Decorative and flowering plantes
- ♏ -Scorpio, Fertlize (organic)
- ♐ -Sagitarius, Harvest fruit and root crops for food
- ♑ -Capricorn
- ♒ -Aquarius, Harvest fruit and root crops for food
- ♓ -Pisces, Fertilize (chemical)
- ○ -Full moon
- ☾ -Waning moon
- ● -New moon
- ☽ -Waxing moon
- ✿ -Flower
- ⌒ -Root
- 🍃 -Leaf
- ○ -Seed
- 🕷 -Destroye weeds and pests

APRIL 2003

THURSDAY	1 ● 10:49 ♉ 4 degrees 34	8	15 ♏ 7 degrees 25
FRIDAY	2 ♉	9 ☽ 10:49 ♌ 11 degrees 56	16 ○ 10:49 ♏ lunar eclipse / no planting
SATURDAY	3 ♉	10 ♌	17 ♐ 7 degrees 43
SUNDAY	4 ♊ 10 degrees 09	11 ♍ 8 degrees 52	18 ♐
MONDAY	5 ♊	12 ♍	19 ♑ 7 degrees 12
TUESDAY	6 ♋ 4 degrees 12	13 ♎ 7 degrees 28	20 ♑
WEDNESDAY	7 ♋	14 ♎	21 ☽ 14:45 ♒ 5 degrees 04

2 ≋	🌸	29 ● 18:39 ♉	🥔
3 ♓ 1 degree 13	🥬	30 ♉	🥔
4 ♓	🥬	31 ♊ 7 degrees 10 solar eclipse / no planting	
5 ♓	🥬		
6 ♈ 8 degrees 🐛	🥬 🍅		
7 ♈ 🐛	🍅		
8 ♉ 1 degree 41	🥔		

Time Zones:
GMT (Greenwich Mean Time)
Atlantic Time -4 hours
Eastern Time -5 hours
Central Time -6 hours
Mountain Time -7 hours
Pacific Time -8 hours
Alaska -9 hours
Hawaii -10 hours

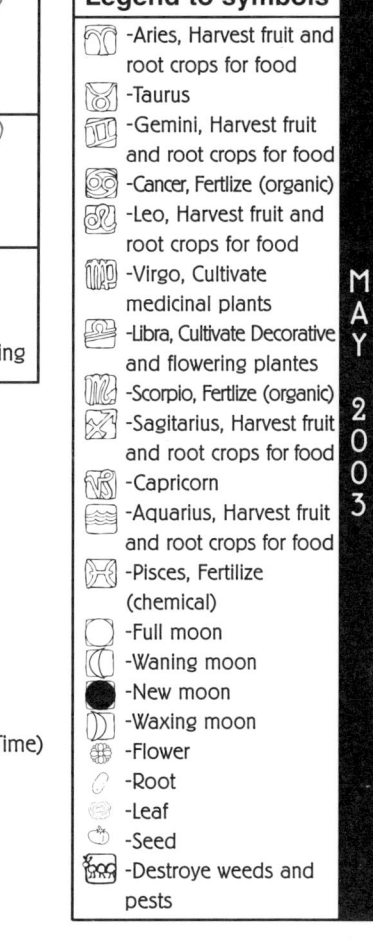

Legend to symbols

- ♈ -Aries, Harvest fruit and root crops for food
- ♉ -Taurus
- ♊ -Gemini, Harvest fruit and root crops for food
- ♋ -Cancer, Fertilize (organic)
- ♌ -Leo, Harvest fruit and root crops for food
- ♍ -Virgo, Cultivate medicinal plants
- ♎ -Libra, Cultivate Decorative and flowering plantes
- ♏ -Scorpio, Fertlize (organic)
- ♐ -Sagitarius, Harvest fruit and root crops for food
- ♑ -Capricorn
- ♒ -Aquarius, Harvest fruit and root crops for food
- ♓ -Pisces, Fertilize (chemical)
- ○ -Full moon
- ☾ -Waning moon
- ● -New moon
- ☽ -Waxing moon
- ✿ -Flower
- ⌒ -Root
- 🍃 -Leaf
- ◌ -Seed
- 🐛 -Destroye weeds and pests

MAY 2003

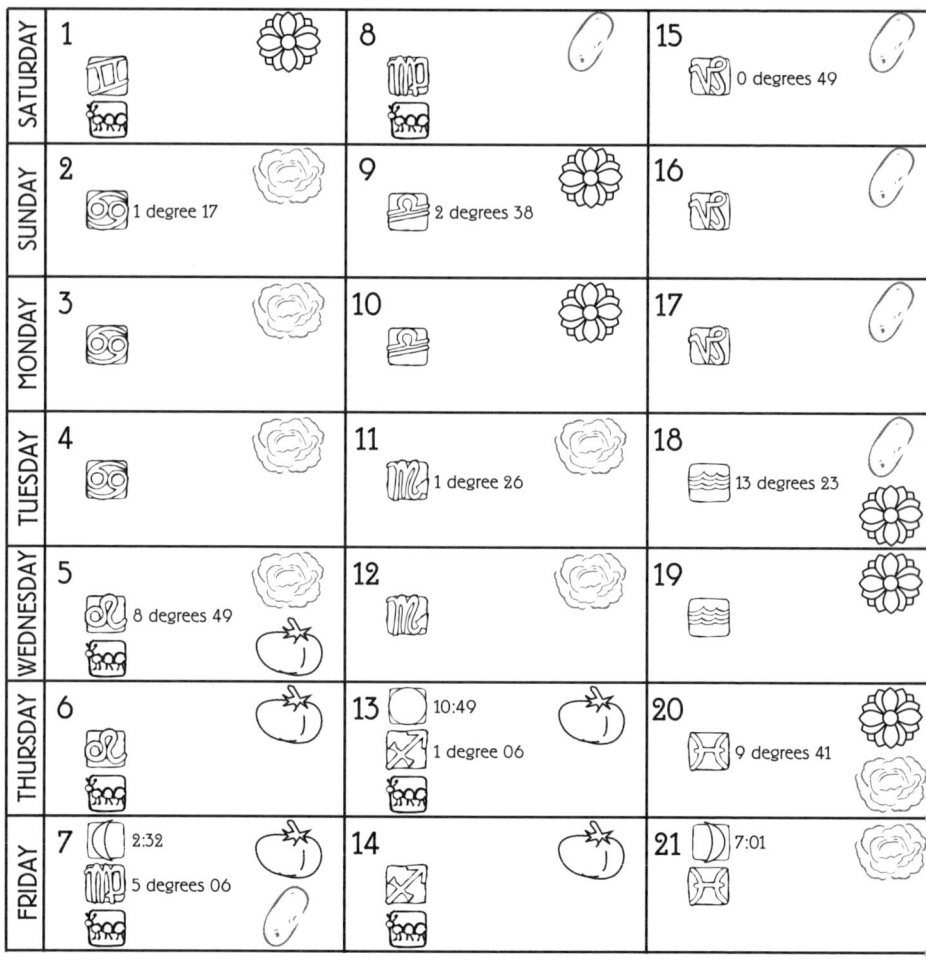

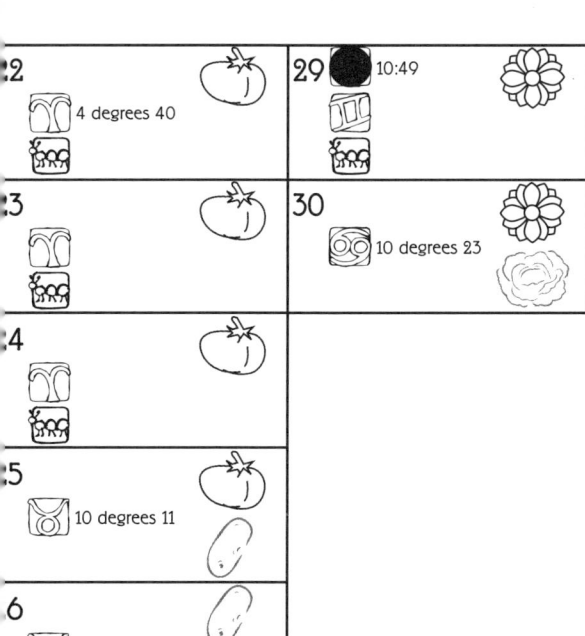

2 4 degrees 40	29 10:49
3	30 10 degrees 23
4	
5 10 degrees 11	
6	
7 3 degrees 51	
8	

Time Zones:
GMT (Greenwich Mean Time)
Atlantic Time -4 hours
Eastern Time -5 hours
Central Time -6 hours
Mountain Time -7 hours
Pacific Time -8 hours
Alaska -9 hours
Hawaii -10 hours

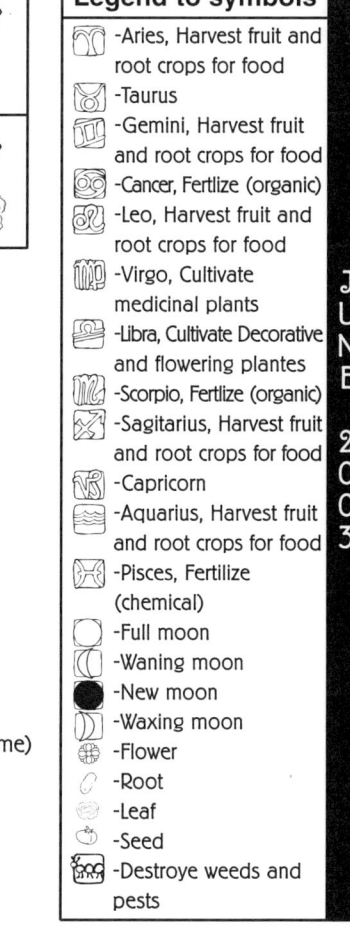

Legend to symbols

- Aries, Harvest fruit and root crops for food
- Taurus
- Gemini, Harvest fruit and root crops for food
- Cancer, Fertilize (organic)
- Leo, Harvest fruit and root crops for food
- Virgo, Cultivate medicinal plants
- Libra, Cultivate Decorative and flowering plantes
- Scorpio, Fertlize (organic)
- Sagitarius, Harvest fruit and root crops for food
- Capricorn
- Aquarius, Harvest fruit and root crops for food
- Pisces, Fertilize (chemical)
- Full moon
- Waning moon
- New moon
- Waxing moon
- Flower
- Root
- Leaf
- Seed
- Destroye weeds and pests

JUNE 2003

TUESDAY	1	8	15 ≈ 7 degrees 47
WEDNESDAY	2 ♌ 5 degrees 46	9 ♍ 11 degrees 29	16 ≈
THURSDAY	3 ♌	10 ♍	17 ♓ 4 degrees 49
FRIDAY	4 ♍ 2 degrees 04	11 ♐ 10 degrees 24	18 ♓
SATURDAY	5 ☽ 7:28 ♍	12 ☽ 4:48 ♐	19 ♈ 0 degrees 20
SUNDAY	6 ♍	13 ♑ 9 degrees 25	20 ☽ 0:48 ♈
MONDAY	7 ♎ 13 degrees 07	14 ♑	21 ♈

22 ♉ 6 degrees 30	🥔	29 ♌ 2 degrees 01 🐛	🍅
23 ♉	🥔	30 ♌ 🐛	🍅
24 ♊ 0 degrees 08 🐛	🌸	31 ♌ 🐛	🍅
25 ♊ 🐛	🌸		
26 ♊ 🐛	🌸		
27 ● 17:26 ♋ 6 degrees 31	🌸 🥬		
28 ♋	🥬		

Time Zones:
GMT (Greenwich Mean Time)
Atlantic Time -4 hours
Eastern Time -5 hours
Central Time -6 hours
Mountain Time -7 hours
Pacific Time -8 hours
Alaska -9 hours
Hawaii -10 hours

Legend to symbols

- ♈ -Aries, Harvest fruit and root crops for food
- ♉ -Taurus
- ♊ -Gemini, Harvest fruit and root crops for food
- ♋ -Cancer, Fertilize (organic)
- ♌ -Leo, Harvest fruit and root crops for food
- ♍ -Virgo, Cultivate medicinal plants
- ♎ -Libra, Cultivate Decorative and flowering plantes
- ♏ -Scorpio, Fertlize (organic)
- ♐ -Sagitarius, Harvest fruit and root crops for food
- ♑ -Capricorn
- ♒ -Aquarius, Harvest fruit and root crops for food
- ♓ -Pisces, Fertilize (chemical)
- ○ -Full moon
- ☽ -Waning moon
- ● -New moon
- ☾ -Waxing moon
- ❀ -Flower
- 🥔 -Root
- 🥬 -Leaf
- 🍅 -Seed
- 🐛 -Destroye weeds and pests

JULY 2003

FRIDAY	1 ♍ 12 degrees 15 ♌	8 ♐ ♌	15 ♊
SATURDAY	2 ♍ ♌	9 ♑ 4 degrees 40	16 ♊ 8 degrees 18 ♌
SUNDAY	3 ♎ 9 degrees 59	10 ♑	17 ♊ ♌
MONDAY	4 ♎	11 ♒ 2 degrees 39	18 ♋ 2 degrees 33
TUESDAY	5 ☽ 7:28 ♏ 8 degrees 05	12 ☽ 4:48 ♒	19 ♉
WEDNESDAY	6 ♏	13 ♒	20 ☽ 0:48 ♉
THURSDAY	7 ♐ 6 degrees 22 ♌	14 ♓ 12 degrees 58	21 ♊ 8 degrees 03 ♌

22 ♊ ♋ 🌸	29 ♍ ♌ 🥔
23 ♋ 2 degrees 10 🥬	30 ♎ 6 degrees 07 🥔 🌸
24 ♋ 🥬	31 ♎ 🌸
25 ♋ 🥬	
26 ♌ 10 degrees 31 ♌ 🥬 🍅	
27 ● 16:26 ♌ ♌ 🍅 🥔	
28 ♍ 7 degrees 50 ♌ 🥬 🥔	

Time Zones:
GMT (Greenwich Mean Time)
Atlantic Time -4 hours
Eastern Time -5 hours
Central Time -6 hours
Mountain Time -7 hours
Pacific Time -8 hours
Alaska -9 hours
Hawaii -10 hours

Legend to symbols

- ♈ -Aries, Harvest fruit and root crops for food
- ♉ -Taurus
- ♊ -Gemini, Harvest fruit and root crops for food
- ♋ -Cancer, Fertlize (organic)
- ♌ -Leo, Harvest fruit and root crops for food
- ♍ -Virgo, Cultivate medicinal plants
- ♎ -Libra, Cultivate Decorative and flowering plantes
- ♏ -Scorpio, Fertlize (organic)
- ♐ -Sagitarius, Harvest fruit and root crops for food
- ♑ -Capricorn
- ♒ -Aquarius, Harvest fruit and root crops for food
- ♓ -Pisces, Fertilize (chemical)
- ○ -Full moon
- ☽ -Waning moon
- ● -New moon
- ☾ -Waxing moon
- ✿ -Flower
- ○ -Root
- 🍃 -Leaf
- 🍅 -Seed
- 🐛 -Destroye weeds and pests

AUGUST 2003

MONDAY	1 ♏ 4 degrees 46	8 ≈ 12 degrees 14	15 ♉ 10 degrees 32
TUESDAY	2 ♏	9 ≈	16 ♉
WEDNESDAY	3 ☾ 12:34 ♐ 3 degrees 12	10 ○ 16:36 ♓ 8 degrees 38	17 ♊ 4 degrees 09
THURSDAY	4 ♐	11 ♓	18 ☽ 19:03 ♊
FRIDAY	5 ♑ 1 degree 14	12 ♈ 4 degrees 04	19 ♊
SATURDAY	6 ♑	13 ♈	20 ♋ 10 degrees 05
SUNDAY	7 ♑	14 ♈	21 ♋

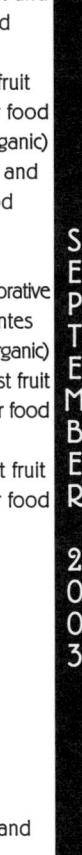

Day		
2	♌ 5 degrees 21 / destroy weeds	🥬 🍅
3	♌ / destroy weeds	🍅
4	♍ 2 degrees 15 / destroy weeds	🥔
5	destroy weeds	🥔
6	● 3:09 / ♎ 0 degrees 26	🌸
7	♎	🌸
8	♏ 0 degrees 04	🥬
29	♏	🥬
30	♏	🥬

Legend to symbols

- ♈ -Aries, Harvest fruit and root crops for food
- ♉ -Taurus
- ♊ -Gemini, Harvest fruit and root crops for food
- ♋ -Cancer, Fertilize (organic)
- ♌ -Leo, Harvest fruit and root crops for food
- ♍ -Virgo, Cultivate medicinal plants
- ♎ -Libra, Cultivate Decorative and flowering plantes
- ♏ -Scorpio, Fertlize (organic)
- ♐ -Sagitarius, Harvest fruit and root crops for food
- ♑ -Capricorn
- ♒ -Aquarius, Harvest fruit and root crops for food
- ♓ -Pisces, Fertilize (chemical)
- ○ -Full moon
- ☽ -Waning moon
- ● -New moon
- ☾ -Waxing moon
- ✿ -Flower
- ⌒ -Root
- 🍃 -Leaf
- ● -Seed
- 🗑 -Destroye weeds and pests

Time Zones:
GMT (Greenwich Mean Time)
Atlantic Time -4 hours
Eastern Time -5 hours
Central Time -6 hours
Mountain Time -7 hours
Pacific Time -8 hours
Alaska -9 hours
Hawaii -10 hours

WEDNESDAY	1 ☾ 4:25 ♐ 13 degrees 50	8 ♓	15 ♊
THURSDAY	2 ♐	9 ♈ 0 degrees 27	16 ♊
FRIDAY	3 ♑ 11 degrees 57	10 ○ 7:27 ♈	17 ♉ 6 degrees 08
SATURDAY	4 ♑	11 ♈	18 ☽ 12:31 ♉
SUNDAY	5 ♒ 9 degrees 03	12 ♉ 6 degrees 56	19 ♌ 0 degrees 41
MONDAY	6 ♒	13 ♉	20 ♌
TUESDAY	7 ♓ 5 degrees 11	14 ♊ 0 degrees 36	21 ♌

2 ♍ 10 degrees 15' 🐛	🍅 🥔
3 ♍ 🐛	🥔
4 ♎ 8 degrees 50	🥔 ❀
5 ● 12:50 ♎	❀
6 ♏ 8 degrees 41	❀ 🥬
7 ♏	🥬
8 ♐ 8 degrees 46 🐛	🥬 🍅

29 ♐ 🐛	🍅 🥔
30 ♑ 8 degrees 01	🍅 🥔
31 ♑	🥔

Legend to symbols

- ♈ -Aries, Harvest fruit and root crops for food
- ♉ -Taurus
- ♊ -Gemini, Harvest fruit and root crops for food
- ♋ -Cancer, Fertilize (organic)
- ♌ -Leo, Harvest fruit and root crops for food
- ♍ -Virgo, Cultivate medicinal plants
- ♎ -Libra, Cultivate Decorative and flowering plantes
- ♏ -Scorpio, Fertilize (organic)
- ♐ -Sagitarius, Harvest fruit and root crops for food
- ♑ -Capricorn
- ♒ -Aquarius, Harvest fruit and root crops for food
- ♓ -Pisces, Fertilize (chemical)
- ○ -Full moon
- ☾ -Waning moon
- ● -New moon
- ☽ -Waxing moon
- ❀ -Flower
- ⌒ -Root
- 🥬 -Leaf
- 🌰 -Seed
- 🐛 -Destroye weeds and pests

OCTOBER 2003

Time Zones:
GMT (Greenwich Mean Time)
Atlantic Time -4 hours
Eastern Time -5 hours
Central Time -6 hours
Mountain Time -7 hours
Pacific Time -8 hours
Alaska -9 hours
Hawaii -10 hours

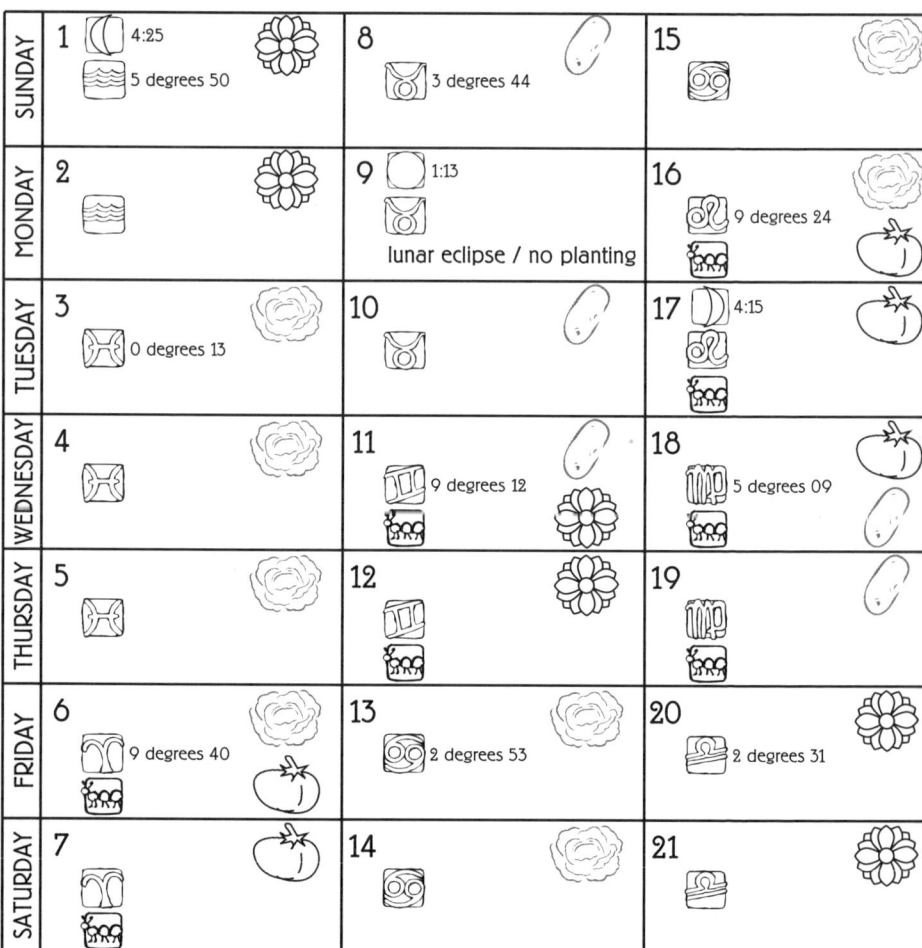

2 ♏ 1 degree 36	🥬	29 ♒	🌸	**Legend to symbols** ♈ -Aries, Harvest fruit and root crops for food ♉ -Taurus ♊ -Gemini, Harvest fruit and root crops for food ♋ -Cancer, Fertilize (organic) ♌ -Leo, Harvest fruit and root crops for food ♍ -Virgo, Cultivate medicinal plants ♎ -Libra, Cultivate Decorative and flowering plantes ♏ -Scorpio, Fertilize (organic) ♐ -Sagitarius, Harvest fruit and root crops for food ♑ -Capricorn ♒ -Aquarius, Harvest fruit and root crops for food ♓ -Pisces, Fertilize (chemical) ○ -Full moon ☾ -Waning moon ● -New moon ☽ -Waxing moon ✿ -Flower ⌒ -Root 🍃 -Leaf ⚫ -Seed 🐛 -Destroye weeds and pests
3 ● 22:59 ♏	🥬	30 ☾ 17:16 ♒	🌸	
4 ♐ 1 degree 52 🐛	🍅			
5 ♐ 🐛	🍅			
6 ♑ 2 degrees 09	⌒			
7 ♑	⌒			
8 ♒ 1 degree 17	🌸			

Time Zones:
GMT (Greenwich Mean Time)
Atlantic Time -4 hours
Eastern Time -5 hours
Central Time -6 hours
Mountain Time -7 hours
Pacific Time -8 hours
Alaska -9 hours
Hawaii -10 hours

NOVEMBER 2003

	Monday	Tuesday	Wednesday	Thursday	Friday	Saturday	Sunday
	1 ♓ 11 degrees 41	**2** ♓	**3** ♈ 6 degrees 41	**4** ♈	**5** ♉ 0 degrees 44	**6** ♉	**7** ♉
	8 ○ 20:37 ♊ 6 degrees 10	**9** ♊	**10** ♊	**11** ♋ 11 degrees 54	**12** ♋	**13** ♌ 6 degrees 20	**14** ♌
	15 ♍ 6 degrees 32	**16** ☽ 17:42 ♍	**17** ♍	**18** ♎ 11 degrees 53	**19** ♎	**20** ♏ 10 degrees 04	**21** ♏

2 ♐ 9 degrees 52 🌿 🍅 🥬	**29** ♓ 🥬 🍅
3 ● 9:43 ♐ 🌿 🍅	**30** ☾ 10:03 ♊ 3 degrees 03 🍅
4 ♑ 10 degrees 05 🥔 🍅	**31** ♊ 🌿
5 ♑ 🥔	
6 ♓ 9 degrees 30 🥔 🌸	
7 ♓ 🌸	
8 ♓ 7 degrees 13 🌸 🥬	

Time Zones:
GMT (Greenwich Mean Time)
Atlantic Time -4 hours
Eastern Time -5 hours
Central Time -6 hours
Mountain Time -7 hours
Pacific Time -8 hours
Alaska -9 hours
Hawaii -10 hours

Legend to symbols

- ♈ -Aries, Harvest fruit and root crops for food
- ♉ -Taurus
- ♊ -Gemini, Harvest fruit and root crops for food
- ♋ -Cancer, Fertilize (organic)
- ♌ -Leo, Harvest fruit and root crops for food
- ♍ -Virgo, Cultivate medicinal plants
- ♎ -Libra, Cultivate Decorative and flowering plantes
- ♏ -Scorpio, Fertilize (organic)
- ♐ -Sagitarius, Harvest fruit and root crops for food
- ♑ -Capricorn
- ♒ -Aquarius, Harvest fruit and root crops for food
- ♓ -Pisces, Fertilize (chemical)
- ○ -Full moon
- ☽ -Waning moon
- ● -New moon
- ☾ -Waxing moon
- ✾ -Flower
- ⌒ -Root
- 🍃 -Leaf
- ○ -Seed
- 🕸 -Destroye weeds and pests

DECEMBER 2003

Bibliography

We found these books to be most helpful in exploring and understanding lunar gardening.

Best, Simon, and Nick Kollerstrom. *Planting by the Moon*. 1983/1984. San Diego: ACS Publications, Inc., 1982.
Riotte, Louise. *Planetary Planting*. New York: Simon and Schuster, 1975.
Wright, Machaelle Small. *Perelandria Garden Workbook*. Jeffersonton, VA: Perelandra Ltd., 1987.

For herblore, these books are entertaining additions to anyone's reading list.

Gerard, John. Edited by Marcus Woodward. *Gerard's Herbal*. London: Spring Books, 1924. Reprinted 1964
Mather, Cotton. *The Angel of Bethesda*. Barre, MA: Barre Publishers and American Antiquarian Society, 1972.
Potterson, David, ed. *Culpepper's Color Herbal*. New York: Sterling Publishing Company, 1983.

Acknowledgements

The Author wishes to thank Thomas Bliss, Kevin Brown, Marc Glick, Sue, Don and Meghan Herner, Harry Kahn, Pat LoBrutto, Peter Nevraumont, Cindy Parzych, Ann Perrini, David Taub, John Turner, and Marc Weidenbaum for their help and inspiration in preparing this book.

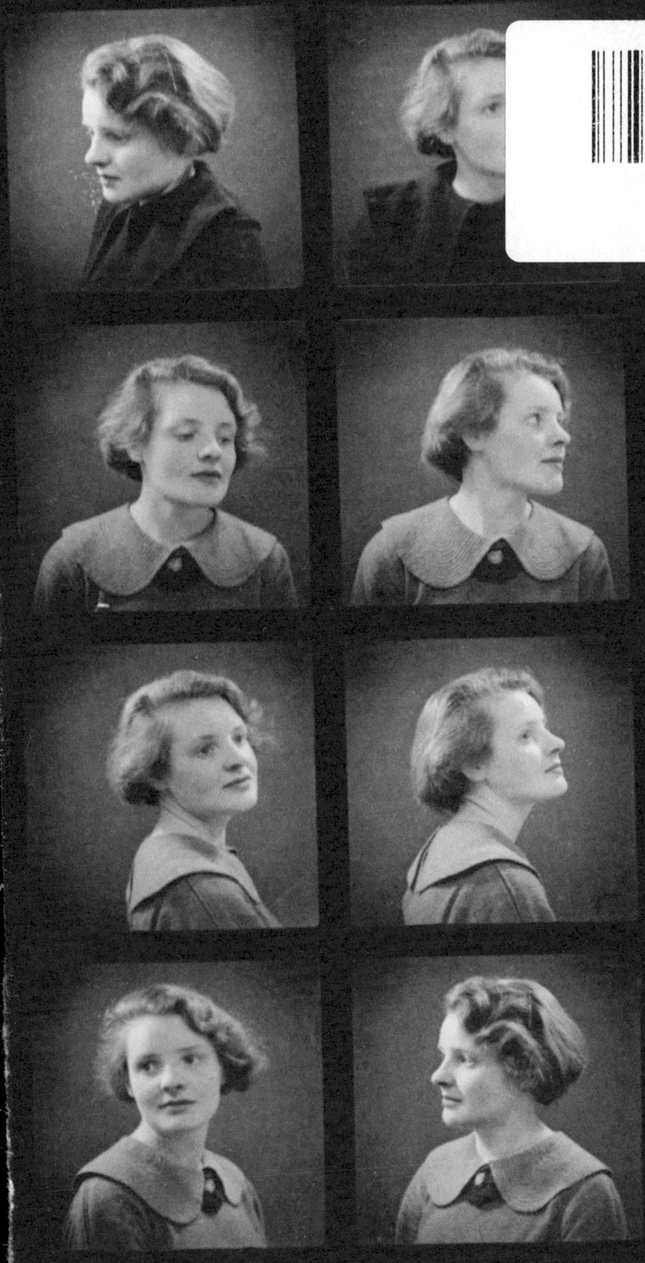

personae

Acknowledgements

This book is published as part of Margaret Tait 100, a project which celebrated the centenary of Tait's birth in 2018, and ran in partnership with LUX Scotland, University of Glasgow, and the Pier Arts Centre, with generous support from Creative Scotland.

The book is the result of many years of work by its author, Margaret Tait. Its existence was also enabled by the various efforts to preserve and champion Tait's work made by others, including her husband Alex Pirie, who gathered Tait's work together after her death and ensured its future security through its deposit in the Orkney Archive. As with previous publications, the Orkney Archive and its staff – David Mackie, Sarah MacLean and Lucy Gibbon – have been of vital support. I would also like to express gratitude to the Margaret Tait Estate, Marian Taylor and Ian Pirie, for their support, and the wider Tait family in Orkney, including Anne Tait, who provided access to the collection of Tait's photographs. I am also grateful to Stills Gallery who digitised the collection for their exhibition, 'Gunnie Moberg and Margaret Tait: The days never seem the same', 27 July – 28 Oct 2018.

I would like to express thanks to those involved in Tait's centenary, including Nicole Yip, Andrew Parkinson, Marcus Jack, as well the team behind the book's production, including Maeve Redmond, Ali Smith, Rebecca Padden (who helped assemble the index), Benjamin Cook (director of LUX, who was the driving force behind the project), Bob Anderson and Daniel Sellers. Thanks also to Peter Todd, Ute Aurand and Lucy Reynolds for their own input in the publication's final stages.

— Sarah Neely, July 2020

Published in 2020

LUX
Waterlow Park Centre
Dartmouth Park Hill
London
N19 5JF, UK
www.lux.org.uk

Edited by Sarah Neely
Designed by Maeve Redmond

Printed by Die Keure in Belgium

All rights reserved

© 2020 the estate of Margaret Tait, the individual authors, and LUX

Images courtesy of the Margaret Tait Estate and Orkney Library and Archive

ISBN 978-0-9928840-7-9

Publication supported by Creative Scotland
LUX is financially supported by Arts Council England and Creative Scotland

Foreword, Ali Smith I

Introduction, Sarah Neely V

Personae 1

Rivers 21

Work 39

Christmas 87

Beauty is truth and truth beauty that is all
we know on earth and all we need to know,
John Keats, 1795-1821 119

Documentary 131

You Must Have Been a Beautiful Baby
(because, honey, look at you now!) 141

The Bravest Boat, selected pages from
Margaret Tait's photograph albums 178

Index 243

Foreword

'In the beginning was the word. What beginning? What word?' Trust the Orcadian filmmaker, poet and writer, the uncategorisable Margaret Tait, to ask the real questions. This book in your hands began in answer to some publishers' readers' critiques Tait received on her novel *The Lilywhite Boys*. This was a work, as yet unpublished, which she wrote over the immediate postwar years about her time in India in the Second World War, when she served as a young medic in the Royal Army Medical Corps – a work concerning her 'experience' there. The quote marks round the word are hers, because everything in this book, and everything in Tait's work across its different forms, asks questions not just about what experience is, but also what happens when you start to call something an 'experience'.

She doesn't just answer the critiquers of this novel, whose characters and story surface and vanish throughout this work like companionable transparent presences. Instead she critiques their critiques, and out of this dialogic urge that's central to all her work, and over the years as she gathers pieces into this open-structure book, a kind of artist's handbook arises, a book of fragments which, in their loose connecting, their ability to shift place and shape within its rough outline as it formed and grew, produced and still produce even in this finished form their own dialogue. This book demands dialogue, its aesthetic imperative. 'What IS a book, anyway?' Her aggregative spatial thinking produces an open and contingent form, something like a chance choreography of lights winking across landscape in the dark.

Wryly witty, matter-of-fact anarchic, Tait is always asking conventional meaning to explain itself. 'Genitals isn't a very lively word, considering what it refers to.' This book, right from the start, deals with the lifeforce that happens in the meeting between self and other, and with human complexity, conventional dishonesties, us-and-them differences, divisions of gender, geography, race and class, and how these lead to racial and national tensions. In the immediate shadow of the war it asks questions about that war in stark terms of good and evil, asks why we care about anything, suggests why we must. It examines every surface response. 'I think if you stare and stare at the surface then eventually something immensely significant happens.'

It critiques the making of identity, what makes you be you and me be me, and demands we unfix ourselves too. Is its title a reference to Ingmar Bergman's film *Persona*? Is its insistence on plurality Tait's own take on what this very different northern filmmaker makes of the woman/women in his film? This fluid text analyses the gender politics of her generation, certainly connected to Tait's insistence on human multiplicity and natural inconsistency, the human as a fluid and changeable being – it is a book by turn irascible, furious, calm, itself every bit as contradictory as she grants that people naturally are and rightly should be. It considers art in terms of magic and very physical healing, the kind a doctor-artist like herself is used to, working in an everyday way with death certificates, 'disease certificates'. In this book she explains her shift of focus towards what she calls *life certificates*, and sure enough, *Personae* is also a kind of autobiography.

'Think in a shape. Think in a rhythm. It is something other than thinking. The sin is to reject the rhythm. The evil is to refuse the shape.'

Her rejection of the kind of Scottish presbyterian thinking that was one of the reasons Tait's own extraordinary body of work was so underrated in her own lifetime is at the core of both her aesthetic discipline and her vital idiosyncracy. 'Everything in the same book from now on. It all has to go together. ... No separation of one thing from another, of poetry from fact, of documentation from speculation, of story from anything that is not a story. It's all a story.' *Personae* becomes a version of the story this artist's life, and in the reading of any story, she says here, 'some of the life must come from the reader.'

Every reader coming to this book, a book full of curiosity, irreverence, calmness, anarchy, and bristling with Tait's good argumentative lifeforce, will find themselves, one way or another, brought alive by it.

— Ali Smith, 2020

When empty the container folds into the size of a golf bag, and it has passed tests for the carriage of solids and liquids, including cement, sugar, oil, wet fish, and potatoes.

POEMS...p
ems...po em
QUENCES SU
SEQUENCES
POEMSPOEMS
POEMSPOem
po emspo em
po emspo em
spo emsPOE
quences s
sequences
nd sequen
s and seq
cts and s
bjects an
ubjects a
s subject
nces subj
and sequer
oems subje
ems poems p
poems poem
equences po
s Subjects
equences PO
S subjects
equences PO
S subjects
equences PO
S Subjects
ems Poems p
EMS PoemS P
ects Subjec
Subjects Su
  poems sequ
quences poe
cts subject
ences sequer
s poems po em
s sequences
subjects poem

ANCONA FILMS

91 ROSE STR
EDINBURGH

AUTO SERVIZI PERUGIA
SOCIETA' PER AZIONI
PERUGIA - GUBBIO
ANDATA

| 1 | 2 | 3 | 4 | 5 | 6 | 7 | 8 | 9 | 10 | 11 | 12 | 13 | 14 | 15 | 16 |
| 17 | 18 | 19 | 20 | 21 | 22 | 23 | 24 | 25 | 26 | 27 | 28 | 29 | 30 | 31 | |

| 1 | 2 | 3 | 4 | 5 | 6 | 7 | 8 | 9 | 10 | 11 | 12 |

IL BIGLIETTO NON E' CEDIBILE

4229

TIP. SINIBALDI - FOLIGNO

AUTO SERVIZI P
SOCIETA' PER AZ
PERUGIA - GU
RITORN

| 1 | 2 | 3 | 4 | 5 | 6 | 7 | 8 | 9 | 10 | 11 |
| 17 | 18 | 19 | 20 | 21 | 22 | 23 | 24 | 25 | 26 | 27 |

| 1 | 2 | 3 | 4 | 5 | 6 | 7 | 8 |

IL BIGLIETTO NON E' C

4229

Introduction

Margaret Tait (1918-1999), filmmaker and poet, is one of Scotland's most extraordinary talents, and yet she was largely overlooked during her lifetime. Born in Orkney, she trained first as a medical doctor and served in the Royal Army Medical Corps during the Second World War, before studying film at Centro Sperimentale di Cinematographia in Rome in the early 1950s. After returning to Edinburgh, Tait established her film studio, Ancona Films, before eventually returning to Orkney in the 1960s, where she lived and continued to make films until her death in 1999.

Margaret Tait is best known as a filmmaker, yet she was also a prolific writer. During her lifetime she self-published three books of poetry and two collections of short stories. She was an avid writer and kept a diary from when she was a teenager, writing with some regularity until her death in 1999. Although some of the entries relate to more personal issues, the pages are also often dedicated to documenting the more mundane aspects daily life; there are notes of television and radio programmes watched, chores to be done, letters written and received, shopping lists, descriptions of the weather, as well as copious notes relating to her filmmaking activities. In many ways, the attention Tait gives to these many different aspects of her everyday experience can be seen as an early indication of what would become Tait's distinctive approach as a filmmaker, which insisted that all subjects within the frame of the film should be treated equally. Tait regularly referred to Lorca's notion of 'stalking the image' to describe the approach, and his postulation that 'An apple is no less important than the sea', that no subject should take precedence over the other, that all things should be considered with equal intensity.[1] This approach is one seen across her life's work, in her films but also her poetry and other writing, including *Personae*.

Personae, was initially conceived of as a 'postscript' to *The Lilywhite Boys*, a novel which drew from Tait's experiences serving in the Royal Army Medical Corps during the Second World War, while stationed in Jhansi, a city in northern India that served as a recuperation point for troops returning from Burma. The novel was written after Tait returned from India, during a particularly prolific period for her writing, which resulted in several scripts and short stories. The novel, which Tait began writing in 1945 and worked on intermittently until the late 1950s, was sent out to several publishers who were, for the most part, unresponsive, citing the current glut of war novels as the cause for rejection. According to Tait, one reader complained that the novel was rather boring. Perhaps in response to this critique, Tait scrawled on the outside of a folder containing a draft of *The Lilywhite Boys*, 'war is excessively boring'. *Personae*, or what was originally titled, *Postscript to the Lilywhite Boys*, can be seen as a further riposte, and was intended to go deeper than the novel – to not simply recount the events and what happened, but to give more of a sense of what the experience felt like emotionally. After writing it, Tait remarked that it would be best for the reader to skip over the earlier novel altogether.

Tait's approach, akin to the poet Lorca's idea of 'blood poetry' to which she aspired, intended to follow a more direct form of expression, perhaps unfinished or unpolished, but more able to articulate emotion through its rawness. Tait also pursued this approach in her filmmaking. When John Grierson, offering his 'support', suggested that Tait edit *Orquil Burn*, her slow and meditative film following the course of a burn which ran past her uncle's house, she refused to alter it. Writing in *Personae*, Tait criticises Grierson's proposal to 'edit it and make it into a tak-tak-tak natty little short film', saying that it is like the 'raw material' of her poetry, but 'isn't that kind of raw material. It's not just footage. It is a made thing. It is a made thing, set like that on purpose, but its form is distant or unfinished perhaps.'

Tait assembled her manuscript of *Personae* in a similar spirit. Although Tait states that the bulk of it was written in 1959 – around the same time her three poetry collections were produced – the manuscript was continued over a number of years, using a seven section 'Severen' folder, which Tait would fill with single sheets of typewriter paper in a variety of colours (gold, blue, green, white), and interspersed with scraps of other bits of paper – newspaper clippings, drawings, tiny hand-scrawled notes. Tait described the moment when she first began working on the manuscript:

> *On this table now there is paper to write on, a cardboard file with seven divisions and elastic at the corners, four reels of thread, three red (one of them silk) and one white, a round brooch of Kandyan silver, needles, pins, a packet of paper tissues, a small round black tin which once contained 100 feet of 16mm. film and now contains hairgrips and hairpins, "Finnegans Wake", a sheet of Ancona Films notepaper and a letter to reply from a young man wishing to work in films, an inchtape, some clean handkerchiefs and a linen napkin with a lotus design, hand made in China, never been used.*
>
> *It helps the reader to understand the work if some idea of the author is given. A few days ago I laid out some paper, the file and a*

ball-point pen on _this_ table, in the smaller room of my studio. I just looked at it there. No need to write, really.

Although this account is absent from the manuscript, the self-reflective style evident here is something that Tait retains in the final work. The folder, now in the Orkney archive, at first glance, is difficult to judge. The fragmentary nature and inconsistency of the contents heaving from the now dog-eared file compartments gives a false impression of what exactly you are looking at – that the fragments do in fact make up a whole. And yet, for the most part, the writing contained on the pages within are what eventually make up the final manuscript. Although Tait produced different versions over the years, very little was altered apart from structural changes involving moving entire paragraphs or sections to different parts of the manuscript. For the most part, Tait left the words as they were the moment they were first written. However, some of the words, including entire paragraphs and some sections, didn't make the final cut – including, the following passage, describing her intentions for keeping the writing in a raw and unfinished state:

Growth. That's what interests me. I like to leave a verse rough and do it again. Repeat it afresh. The small changes wrought by oral repetition are pleasing. I don't see anything as ever finished. Men like to finish a thing and put their name on it. Married to them and preserved in glue. That's not what I mean really of course. I just said it.

I am a little afraid of elegance. It is so _finished_. I am uneasy with things which are complete. Perfection, – and the impulse to smash it. Having got it complete and perfect, then break it to bits and start again. My own impulse is not to break it but to leave it and start something else. I cannot really quite understand people breaking up their own work, or anybody else's work. I like to keep starting afresh, but I don't like to break the things which are made. The need to smash things is probably a more male need. We depend on that male destructiveness to get things out of the way so that there will be room for new things.

People don't look on what's written as a book until it is published. All are completely taken with the present-day convention that "if it's any good a publisher will take it." GOOD. Good music. Good books. We are such judges, we educate people.

What IS a book, anyway? Something written, or something published?

The book in many ways reads as a stream-of-consciousness narrative, starting with a focus on her time spent serving in India during the Second World War, then digressing to a wide variety of topics significant to Tait. Her writing is similarly defined by what Richard Demarco describes an insistence on marrying the heart with the head and encompassing 'in equal measure, the profound truths embodied in both artistic and scientific thinking.'[2] In this respect, Demarco draws comparison between Tait and another 'artist-scientist', Joseph Beuys. Like her poetry, her writing is candid, addressing difficult and sometimes sensitive topics in a direct and inquisitive manner. Written after the Second World War, *Personae* engages with Tait's own mental anguish as well as the wider culture's, struggling to make sense of the horrific events to have taken place and the legacy of trauma left behind. Underlying much of the manuscript, is a sense of Tait's urgency to speak to her own truth, to avoid convention and any form of compromised or disingenuine life: 'Why go through all of this and put your life forward to be sacrificed if you then just live a muted stunted life?'

There is no evidence in Tait's archive to indicate whether or not she ever sent the manuscript off to publishers; however, on a few occasions she remarks that the book would never be published during her lifetime. As illustrated in the following passage, where Tait playfully imagines her own connection with the future, she predicts the potential for her work to be interpreted in the years to come as ahead of its time:

> *Nobody wants any of it. Not now. In fifty years they will and will wish they had more. I seem to have a connection with the future, and I don't mean posterity. I've always felt very attached to the present. Everything had to be <u>now</u>. I do still feel that, as well as the other attachment to the future. The past is something I can take more easily than most people, I think.*
>
> *What silly romantic talk all that is, about past, present and future. The kind of consciousness which is trying to be more conscious than it is.*
>
> *Nevertheless, this feeling of being at ease with a fairly distant future is something new to me.*

Elsewhere, in earlier drafts of *Personae*, Tait describes feeling 'paradoxically both that this book should/would only be published posthumously and that it was nearly complete and while in a way I felt appeased (or something) that it was nearly complete I didn't like the implication'. As with her film work, Tait's interest was in the making and doing.

The 'ongoing' nature of Tait's work proved a challenge for assembling a 'complete' manuscript of *Personae* for publication. Several versions of the manuscript exist in Tait's archive, with the titles *Personae* and *Postscript to the Lilywhite Boys* sometimes used interchangeably. Although, as suggested before, the earlier 'Severen' file seems to have served as a central point for collating the manuscript in full, its fragmentary nature, and use of single sheets of paper, precariously ordered like a deck of cards at risk of reshuffling, means it's unable to serve as a definitive source. Typed versions of the manuscript may give the illusion of being a final or more complete version, but these versions also have handwritten annotations and some pages have received more significant edits by Tait, through a physical alteration of the text using scissors and tape. Ultimately, the most complete version to be found was written out by hand in Tait's fluid cursive script. Unfortunately, the version stops short of the intended conclusion and instead ends with a selection of fragmentary notes as well as a poem. For this version of Tait's manuscript, the text ends by reproducing the final pages from the Severen file in full, including the handwritten pages of the original alongside their transcription. As much as possible, this version aims to reflect the original presentation of Tait's manuscript, including its stylistic features and unique formatting.

— Sarah Neely, November 2019

1. Tait's notes for television profile, Margaret Tait collection, Orkney Archive, D97/1/2, p. 5.
2. Programme notes for the exhibition, 'Interim Edition: The Margaret Tait Poetry Archive', Demarco Archive Exhibitions, Summerhall, Edinburgh, 8 November 2018 – 6 January 2019.

PERSONAE

MARGARET TAIT

PERSONAE

Gwen wanted to marry a Jew. But she didn't really know what a Jew is. (Neither do I, who am writing this book, know really what a Jew is. So how can I get near to my characters?) Does it matter for her in the least what "a Jew" is? Jo is Jo, not "a Jew", not "a" anything, but Jo. There he is. He is hers.

I as author of the book don't really know the other culture. The other outlook. But nobody ever completely knows another person, not even oneself. Oneself is like another person, sometimes. <u>How near</u> is the point. The nearer it seems the truer it seems.

And the last quartet was written six months before his death. QUARTET. For four instruments. That's the title.

The documentary distance preserves objectivity. Gwen and the rest are not in vitro; they are in vivo. That's really <u>why</u> I don't get so very close. In life, you don't. The documentary approach. How do I know she loved Jo, then? There it is. She loved Jo. I say so on page ———.

But what happened afterwards, when they all left, and the war eventually ended? It's all guess-work what happened. I didn't keep in touch with them. I left my characters in that time, there. To that extent, they are in vitro. Isolated and mounted in a section of their youth. I don't know, I can't tell what happened later. I haven't kept up with any of them. I invented them young and they are still young – specimens only.

A specimen of young Briton in wartime – sounds very pallid and congealed. So that can't be what they each are either, because each has moving blood, growing knowledge, eyes, nose, genitals. Genitals isn't a very lively word, considering what it refers to. And all the old words have turned into swear-words. It is not always suitable to use them tenderly. And then, I don't hear them, don't even know them all, and have got used to the clinical words, the correct anatomical terms, not invented as endearments, or not introduced into the English language as endearments. In Latin – when people spoke and murmured Latin – they may have been tender words.

There's not very much in this book about the deeper motives that move mankind. One publisher's reader has said that the characters in my book never really come to life. My idea was that some of the life must come from the reader. For instance, did Gwen and Jo sleep together? I leave it to you. I suppose they did. Others might suppose they didn't.

Incidents don't really change things. That Gwen loved Jo she felt was a permanent thing, unrelated to plans about when they would marry or whether it would "work out" or what his family would say to him or how much he would earn.

There is some kind of perverseness in people which attaches them more to the people who don't care about them than to the ones who do. The whole of morality depends on it.

I wonder if women are more liable to go dotty than men. Women live longer on the average, so more of them come to the age of dottiness. Women have more to put up with than men, I think it is probably true to say. Women certainly have great compensations, but they get beaten a lot. Perhaps it is jealousy of her "compensations" that makes men beat women.

In a way, to be a father isn't anything. Just another relationship. Adopting a nephew or equally close relative might be as much. Being a mother is something additional to that. Ejaculation is the achievement of both parents, speaking just physically! The mother is ejaculating the child at a more viable stage, that's all! Without the father's ejaculation first of course, the child wouldn't be there, but his ejaculation might have resulted in any child. Hers is the child and that child only. So it's a different relationship. After a time though, after some years I mean, when the child is away from her breast and her skirts the relationship changes. It isn't so intense after that and it's artificial and preying to keep it intense. The maternal business can get oppressive and of the "possessive mother" order.

People – or particularly men – seem reduced when they become parents. Maybe something material is taken from him, more I mean than just the semen at the time of insemination. Some afflatus is robbed from him for the children. The mother is robbed of her teeth and her figure but the man of his breath, his life.

It all depends on what you think of as reduction and what you think of as enlargement. Some would say it enlarges their life. So it does in a way, of course.

The evil thing that happened in the Garden of Eden was that Adam turned against Eve. Even now he still says that the wicked thing was the love – that their loving together in their sex was what caused the "fall". But it was his turning against her afterwards that did it. "It was the woman, Lord," and every goddamn bugger has repeated and believed it ever since.

Separation of thought. A life without sex. How can a woman

believe in such things?

You take a section of yourself and set it apart. Inviolable. (To me this seems nonsense.)

They separate the sentiment of love from what they feel about a woman's sex. One they say is lofty, related to honour (a man's honour) and the other they disdain in some way. Their own need is low, they think, and they <u>blame</u> women for it.

Thought is in a compartment apart, say the men-thinkers. It's apart both from their sentiment of love and from the deplorable (in a way, you know) need of their own sex for a woman's sex. Therefore, thought has nothing to do with women in either way. Therefore you can't possibly connect women with thought, they firmly believe. It's nothing to do with women, the way they have set women apart, therefore <u>women</u> can't possibly have anything to do with <u>thought</u>. Women involved with thought are not really women then. This is obvious to the men. Thought is separate, therefore women who concern themselves with thought cannot be connected with either the sentiment of love or the other sex feeling (sweet enough in its way but rather beneath us men really you know). So far as I can tell this is the way men's minds work about women. Thought is not a thing for women – and if, occasionally, a woman shows herself capable of thought then she is not a real woman and though she may deserve respect for her thought she's damn well not going to get the other two things from us. No, NO? (Most women, in consequence, are careful not to show themselves capable of thought. And of course there are plenty of women as there are plenty of men who are not capable of much thought anyway.) If she is going to have to do with thought she must take on the label "could be a man."

There's no end to it. It can go on and on. It goes on and on and on.

Stupid people are often nasty as well. It's a treat to know a stupid person with a nice nature. So unusual.

"You've got to watch them. They're fly from the word go," said a man in Castle Street. I don't know who he was talking about. Somebody or other working for him I suppose.

The stupid ones always win. Because the clever ones <u>let</u> them. <u>They</u> are not cute, they are not fly, and don't believe that "you've got to watch them." Only the stupid are really treacherous. The fly stupid ones are. For they value such paltry things. They commit treachery for the sake of trivia you would think nobody could possible care about.

Men need help from women as well as women needing help from men. They need help <u>as men</u>. Most women only want to break men, for their own purposes. There would need to be some women who <u>won't do this</u>. The men want to be broken. (Many – or most – men <u>want</u> that.) They want their courage broken, so that they won't have to fight but can just jog along seeing to the "missis and kids." It has always been fairly easy for men to break women <u>as women</u>, and they have certainly done so. Men have broken women and turned them into servants, until some men <u>helped</u> women. The men now need help. Maybe a man thinks "If I don't break her then she'll break me" – and I see now at last that this is, usually, true. Or if not usually, then ordinarily. An <u>ordinary</u> woman breaks a man, turns him to her own needs. To some extent men want to think that "women" are just <u>like</u> that, then this makes it that <u>he</u> has to break <u>her</u>.

People do perhaps mostly <u>want</u> to be broken. Be broken to society "It's a pity I wasn't caught sooner," said Hugh Miller, referring to his domestication with the church and "The Witness."

Harnessed.

They break his courage and give him something called honour instead. Honourable cowards.

I wouldn't have thought a man is so dependent on the things that go with being broken. A woman is dependent <u>as a woman</u> on what they refuse to let her have without breaking her. But what does a man get out of it? Comfort – security – cosiness – ? Those seem "unmanly" things to want. Perhaps they are not. They break him and make him head of the family, head of the household. He is the boss. A sort of lord, they allow him to think. It's even a <u>declared</u> womanly wile, "Let him think he controls everything and then you'll get what you want out of him."

I think that after a time some men are very sad under this system. But of course can't get out of it. Wee wifie makes it all so cosy for him.

What it amounts to – if your wants are trivial enough you can always get what you want. Other people are thinking about other things and don't notice you working away there for your small but undermining need.

Men can't <u>really</u> get out of their heads the idea that men are superior to women. The English can't get out of their heads the idea that English are superior to other people, especially to Scots. This goes along with some idea (kindly idea even) that they are providing for the lesser kind, and setting an example. In return for this man women despise the men and break them. It is curiously easy for them. Some Scots work with the English on that sort of basis too. It is treacherous not only to the other person but to oneself – and to other Scots, or to other women.

Social conformity is necessary in a social world. That it is <u>necessary</u> doesn't make it <u>good</u>. Marriage is necessary in a social world. But to the extent to which it is a bargain for possession of a human soul it is degrading. Basically, legal marriage is a business arrangement. Business is necessary in our social, material, money-based world. It is so. I don't know how else it could be, but it's degrading for all that. People want to make servants out of other people. It's a curious need people have. Yet I suppose <u>society</u> is dependent on it.

If you point out the evil, you'll always be told it is <u>you</u> who are evil. And in a way this is true. You wouldn't see the evil if you didn't have evil in yourself to see it with. That is how anyone <u>at last</u> discovering evil is so horrified. The discovery is within oneself as well as in the other one sees it in.

It's no use refusing to feel the pain of the trauma. Suppressed pain splits the sense from the knowledge. Considering the word "schizophrenia" – phren means both mind and heart. Are both split, or is it that one is split from the other, in the state of detachment from the self?

They walked about on the daily earth, and yet it was always strange. To Inez coming to the B.M.H. Mess it was the Britishness of it which was strange, for her. The British, almost without knowing it, made it all a bit British and yet it remained for them foreign, India, exile. For Gwen and Jo it was <u>agreeably</u> foreign, their own in a way, and yet foreign. For Inez and for the Indians there was the foreign-ness which the British had imported there.

Young people newly arriving from a troop-ship had a perpetual feeling of strangeness and they looked half-enviously, half-fearfully at those others there before them who had become familiar, who spoke of

"<u>the</u> mess", "<u>the</u> bazar", and of those strangers by name, able to speak to the bearers about known needs or incidents or future requirements. In the familiar voice. The knowing-you-will-be-understood voice. People newly from home really sounded like it. They were quite different. The quip, "Get your knees brown" meant "I see you!"

It is quite natural that people of one race should think that people of another race are not quite human. Their idea of "human" is what they are themselves. Somebody radically different must seem something else. They <u>are</u> something else. It is not a matter of superiority or inferiority. But they are something <u>else</u>. It then depends on your teaching whether you think something else from yourself is to be despised. Many people despise all foreigners. Many people even despise anyone not from their own town or place. Nearly all Londoners despise people who don't belong to London, and even those who have gone to live there despise people who have not gone to live there. Londoners use a word, "provincial", to mean not-London. They snigger in an understanding way to one another about anyone who does not understand that "Town" means London. A Londoner in Truro was very tickled when at the railway station he asked for two tickets to town and the ticket clerk asked, "What town?" The Londoner thought it exceedingly quaint of the rural person to be asking such a question. He doubled up with laughter at the idea that there might be another <u>town</u> for anybody. He clearly thought that his own notion the there being one Town only was much superior. To me it seemed very ignorant of the Londoner rather than quaint or funny of the Cornishman. I would have understood when the Londoner said "town" that he meant "London", but not because I by "town" meant "London", only that I had already noticed the phenomenon that Londoners carry their localness far afield and that even if they were in Cape Town or New York they would still speak of going back to town, meaning back to London.

It is a thing something like this, that <u>people</u> think that <u>people</u> means people like themselves. Other people are not exactly people.

British troops in India liked the Indian soldiers fine, but they didn't quite consider them as men in the way they considered themselves to be men. Indian servants worked away for British sahibs, but they didn't quite consider a sahib to be a <u>man</u>. Certainly they didn't consider a "mem-sahib" or a "miss-sahib" to be the same as a <u>woman</u>. Whether less or more it would be hard to say, but I think it was probably <u>less</u>. Most of the British soldiers and Indian soldiers and servants, nice ordinary ignorant people, probably considered the other race as almost another kind of animal. It might be almost as great as the distance between a domestic cat and a wild cat. Except that British and Indian are both domestic – to each his own way is just <u>the</u> simple domestic life, just how people live. And then there appear those others, quite different. The colour of their skin is different too, but I don't think that has so much to do with it as nearly everything else about them. It is there, though, – a symbol.

"You're just a ＿＿", just whatever you are, Scot, woman, blonde, writer, spinster, doctor, middle-class person, five feet three inch woman, or whatever it is that you just are and the other person perhaps isn't. Then if they shout it at you the impulse is to retaliate, "No, I'm not!" Defend yourself. "What if I am?" Whatever you reply it sounds as if you were accepting that the epithet is an insult. It needn't be anything wrong with you and it isn't anything unique that they insult you in that way. It is usually something you have in common with a lot of others, so you can be called "one of those". They can imitate your speech and it will raise a laugh among those who speak differently. Somebody imitating <u>them</u> for you and yours would get a laugh too. Imitation can be done in a friendly way or it can be done as a jeer. It depends on who does it.

Inez felt a responsibility for the farm. There wasn't exactly anything wrong with it. She felt guilty about it because it seemed inadequate, and it was India. She felt that in a way she was part of the backwardness she imagined Jo saw about it all. She was angry, and muttered a bit, and that did make her seem of <u>that</u> earth and for Jo at that moment quite distant and utterly foreign. I have seen people look at me in that uncomprehending way when I moved familiarly somewhere they felt alien in, or spoke a few quick words to someone who understood perhaps the language or perhaps the technical phrase or perhaps simply a style of grunt or gesture.

It didn't seem like a place for Europeans to buy milk from. And yet it was not exactly dirty. For Jo it just seemed that it would be impossible ever to know whether the milk from those buffaloes was infected or not. It might be one time and not another time. The people in the place would not understand what was meant by infection and how to avoid it. He felt guilty about rejecting the farm, and sad about it. He felt troubled that he had to go and leave it, not try to know it, but simply advise the parents of Inez's little patients to get their milk from somewhere else. It would be surer. That was all. There was a check on the "military dairy", but none there on the few milking buffaloes of the small proprietor, the struggling villager, the untaught man earning his living as he best knew how. Perhaps the Anglo-Indian families in the married quarters at the edge of the cantonment would change their milkman, perhaps they wouldn't. Most likely they would. But there was no saying for certain that that was where the typhoid had come from.

Penicillin was being discovered at the time when millions of Jews in Germany were being tricked into the extermination chambers by practical jokes. Such a prank for the SS officers, some of whom went away after the war, escaped trial and settled somewhere, led an orderly life, and are only now in 1960 being discovered by Palestinians relentlessly seeking them out. Some of them will be tried now for their incredible crimes. Nothing can ever expiate the evil. There never has been an evil like that.

I don't know why people say it's a book about "my experiences" – all that austere documentary stuff. "She has written a book about her experiences in a hospital in the East." It seems to be meant in a belittling way. To write about your experiences is really something – would be poetry. But the story of "The Lilywhite Boys" isn't poetry, it's prose. It's not about my experiences but about some things. A medical service and its organisation. And so on. About ideas. The war. And war. It is authentic but it is not about me. It is a story, in my sense of a story. It is a kind of saga, but a saga follows the heroes out on their exploit, whereas this variant on the saga sees the heroes going away and waits for them coming back. It is a saga from the woman's point of view. What it is about, all the same, is the heroes. That is what it was all about. The whole of what happened in Gurrumpore was a story of the Chindits.

The whole of the "war effort", London being bombed, queues for cakes and children being boarded in the country was all about defeat in

France, bombing of Germany, invasion of coasts, paratroop landings and tank advances. The whole story was about that and yet the strategy of it means nothing. I mean it means nothing to me and ultimately it means nothing at all. That they <u>did it</u> is all that matters. Not whether they won or lost so much simply that they went.

Swein Asleifson's men sailed with him and took Dublin. That is very interesting. Then they lost it again. That is very interesting too. They got so drunk, celebrating their victory, that the Irish quite easily overcame their conquerors and got their city back. Swein had no use for Dublin anyway: it was just for loot. All he was doing was robbing Dublin, or stealing Dublin, – but he did it. It is not politically – historically interesting that he had Dublin, but it is inherently interesting, poetically interesting. It is a story.

I am trying to get at what I mean by this. If you feel like writing me a long letter or another book about it, please do so.

They were all there, placed there, and they were young. That was their life. If they did not use that for their life their youth would pass and they wouldn't have lived it. To some, certainly there didn't seem anything there to live, it was all exile, they were just waiting to get home. They passed the time. They did their work, they accepted that there was some necessity about it, some felt virtuous, but they were damned if they were going to enjoy it or even live it at all. Not even live mournfully. They just pined, or did their duty, rather.

There were those officers saving their money who wrote long letters home daily. I don't know what they wrote home <u>about</u>, for besides working they only played bridge and wrote home. McIlroy and Fraser were like that. They were quite prim, even grim. They smoked, but never handed round cigarettes. You could see them mentally weighing up the price of a drink before they had one, unless it was being bought for them by someone else. They were a little disapproving all the time of Jo, of Emlyn, of Gavin Ross, of Alan. They saved their money and wrote home and resented their contemporaries who seemed to think there was anything <u>in</u> being in Gurrumpore. They were a little severe with their bearers, like ministers talking to the congregation. They were conscientious about regular hours of ward work, but resented anything extra being required of them. They seemed very ready to stick up for their rights, but they did their duties, and when they did occasionally shirk, nip off unseen to do a bit of shopping in the bazar, they did it in a secretive way or in a righteous way, so that there seemed something terrible about it rather than something simple.

They resented Inez very much. They didn't like there being a woman in the Mess.

It was hard for Fraser and McIlroy. They were separated from their wives and they felt that as a deep bitterness which nothing could sweeten. So far as they knew, they were away from home for years. Four years – later reduced to three years and eight months. "Three-eight" <u>meant</u> that. Everyone knew what was meant by "three-eight". It meant the length of the tour of service in India, three years and eight months. A long time to be separated.

In a way, the story I wrote is all about separation and only about that. The theme I had most in mind was the theme of separation. For not only were young married men like Fraser and McIlroy separated from their wives, but everyone was separated from their "own" and if they made something where they were into their own, they were just as liable to be separated from that, quite arbitrarily, at any time at all. So when Alan said, "There's enough bitter separation in time of war without adding to it unnecessarily," he was speaking from a deep hurt of his own as well as generalising, and wishing Mary and Berry something better although he probably didn't think there was much chance of it for anybody. The huge impersonal "god" or "mammon" which was War made nonentities of people.

But, in addition to their homesickness, McIlroy and Fraser were mean. They <u>grudged</u> any pleasure they might get out of being where they were. They grudged the others being able to make their life of it. They were not able to, and they didn't want it to be a life for anyone. All they could think of about it was to save from their pay and send money home. The pay was rather generous. They got <u>more</u> for being overseas, and they certainly did not want to use any of it up just in <u>being</u> there. It would be a complete waste to use it as any of the others did, to take part, to live there and then. Instead, they saved up. And, saving themselves, they played bridge and wrote letters home.

I don't want ever to have to say goodbye again. There has been too much separation. But it is not a phenomenon of wartime only. It goes on all the time, and is in a sense what life consists of. And what is necessary is acceptance of the separation. Acceptance of the inevitable separation. Refusal of that or insistence on unnatural separation (insisted on in anger or in fear or perhaps in an attempt at logicality) is what causes the inner split, separation of the self from the self.

There is nothing quite like terror. Fear is a relic of our "jungle" existence. People forget or don't realise that we are all still living in a condition of "jungle", for all the streets, buses, post office savings and school hours, hours for work and the rest. In a state of fear you <u>realise</u> things – things that become very apparent, and there it's like eyes glaring at you, you can't get rid of them. The eyes aren't <u>looking</u> so much as – something else altogether. Emitting, or engulfing, I never know quite which it is. They have a terrible blankness in them and at the same time a sort of calculating.

In a way, there was that in the look of the young boy and the oldish woman at the buffalo farm. A look of enmity – but not planned antagonism.

There is nothing else to do except just die, if they win over you, those eyes. They are deathly, eyeless eyes, jellyfish, or amoebae, set in place of the eyes.

I don't know how much of the fear is fear of death and how much fear of other things – pain, deprivation, or even of injury or death to someone else to whom one is attached. (That is the same as deprivation, partly.)

They always talk about folk songs as if the "folk" were somebody <u>else</u>, never us. And what you do is you go and collect them, on a tape recorder, save them from obscurity, protect them for posterity. Even if you ever sang them you don't just sing them, you do this other thing. The Chindits, however, took the old song for themselves, clothed all in green-O "One is one and all alone and evermore shall be so." The troops knew some ancient songs just as songs, not as folk-lore.

He breathed deeply of the warm evening air. "There's another village soon," he said. A smell of it came down to the road to meet them and reminded David of the village to be passed through. He knew the road well, from driving in and out, to Gurrumpore and back to camp. He took the village as it was and did not marvel at it, felt perhaps some slight scorn for it because of the smell and because of the evident poverty and because of the languid apathetic movements of the men on the road. "Out of my way, you black chappati-scoffing bastard!" David's driver had once shouted, and David laughed deeply each time he repeated the phrase for his friends. You couldn't tell from his chuckle whether he thought the epithet delightfully suitable or hilariously unsuitable. David usually spoke in a tone of banter. Sometimes it was difficult to tell whether he was being serious or not. Nearly all of his companions used the bantering tone, but in John's banter there was an overtone of sadness, in Trim's an undertone of coarseness, in Colonel Barron's a permeating tone of pretentiousness. David's voice simply spoke the banter as if it was the only way to speak, or as if he was afraid to drop it and just speak evenly and simply to anyone. Afraid, or had forgotten how. Sometimes a direct appeal to him like Inez's song as they drove out in the jeep would make him nervous and angry. He would splutter, as if to cry, "How dare you approach me like that?" – give a penetrating quizzical stare, and then bitterly talk about other things. So Inez never really got to know David very well, and she could not tell either whether he and John were really very close friends as they sometimes seemed to be, or not. A guardedness about him and about most of his companions kept them at a distance, the warriors, the picked, the brave – the sacrifice. They knew where they were going, and why. There was nothing more to tell them.

    War is a way of putting off doing anything. While the Anabasis is on you can't think about anything except just getting home again and the daily work in hand. The details of what you are really going to do (once you are home) you haven't time to consider, and you <u>can't</u>

consider, are afraid to consider, until there is some real prospect of getting home or perhaps even until you are actually home. If the war goes on for long enough then what you have done in the war turns out to be all you have done. You die in it, or perhaps when you get home you find you have no heart for whatever it was you were going to do. And those who weren't at the war or in whose lives there wasn't a war to go to feel <u>they</u> haven't done <u>that</u>, feel that is something they have missed, that complete absorption in what didn't really concern themselves. War takes you away from doing your own work, away from working for yourself. When there is conscription, there is no question of its being a choice to go to war. Jim Ashbourne was changed by marching into Burma and being flown out again. It all happened in a matter of months. He was trained to be tough, then he marched in with the troops. When he revisited the B.M.H. Mess he was curiously different – a little coarser, a little calmer, and his ambition was all gone. He found he had already enough, or had already had enough. He had achieved something quite different from what he was thinking about when he used to swot up anatomy and surgery and discuss advanced and rather academic surgical possibilities with his colleagues. After he came back, he took things for granted. Surgery he would leave to others. He cared no more about becoming a great surgeon. He was a man – a kind of strong animal who had survived the jungle and who was also in addition to that, "the doc", to be looked up to already as he was. He was the doctor: that was enough, and he had found the sheer business of being a man not so much a revelation as a relaxation. Some physical necessities of living occupied him as they never had before and he was contented as he sat solidly on a bar stool, grasping a great pint glass of beer, he who had been quick, slight and nervous, whose quick fingers had looked always sensitive and alert but had become thickened, and, peacefully laid against the glass, seemed to belong now to a different man. His smile was a little removed, unquestioning and happy, vaguely frightening to Jo and Emlyn as they watched him. He couldn't be stirred into academic or intellectual discussion now; he just laughed. His voice had become deeper too, resounding out of his bulkier frame. He made the rest of them feel a little ashamed and afraid.

The men marching deeply into the jungle met with something which was quite beyond them. The enemy was there. It was <u>all</u> enemy, – the jungle itself, and the Japanese. They were united against all that because they had to be and there was no use questioning it. They were all a nameable thing, they were together, they were "us", they were British, they were Chindits, they were a particular column, a brigade, a platoon. Any solitary individual of them against the enemy would be lost. So they needed their unifying factors. They welcomed a sort of easiness of being obviously a certain thing – British, for instance. They intensified their typifying characteristics, allowed them to coarsen. They maintained their bodily health because it was totally necessary, and even if their bodies were invaded by parasites of malaria, dysentery, bookworm or anything else they fought robustly against the disease and kept at least their health of spirit. Afraid of the enemy, they relied on each other. When they came out again they seemed to have a pervading good humour – an ease towards each other and towards all others. They had met the enemy, and in Gurrumpore it was peace, even if they were ill and in hospital. They liked obvious broad similarities after the subtle alien insidious jungle, and the men in it on the hunt for themselves with powerful firearms. They defended themselves with their Britishness and accepted that the enemy was an enemy and not to be despised. Humility and pride were in them as in all people who do great things.

In Gurrumpore there seemed to be nothing to fight, and yet something was there – inimical. Perhaps it was the country itself resenting their presence, despising them. It was demoralising. There was nothing to respond to, nothing to fight against, but just the huge contempt of the immense empty Plain, and the heat. Just nothing really. There was something morbid about Gurrumpore, undermining them, turning them out of themselves, making them doubt the reality or at least the validity of their own selves and their own ways. There were some who became quite bewildered and gave in to it. They became recognisably ill, but any treatment they could be given in Gurrumpore could not help them very much. Those who were sensitive were forced to examine their own values and they questioned both what they chose to do and what they had to do in a way which, out in the Columns, would have been fatal. Some people disintegrated completely under the self-questioning. The morbidity rate was high, but the mortality rate, of course, nothing like the toll of the jungle or the front.

RIVERS

Irrawaddy and Bramaputra and Anna Livia Plurabelle. Beyond the River. The Jordan. The Rubicon.

The drops that drop out of the hill
Are destined
To run on to the ocean.
But they'll be back.

The experience of following Orquil Burn up to its source was much more than the film I made of it. Strange strange people asked me why I went from sea to source and not from source to sea. Why not, they said, so so puzzled, not the more obvious the more logical direction of source to sea. They wanted me to know beforehand where it all started, what it all is. A river is well known in its busy part. You follow it up. Those puzzled people think you know it all, so you can start with the source, the cause, and demonstrate the issue. All already known.

I didn't know about the origins of Orquil Burn until I followed it up into the hill with a camera and surprised the owl, found the short plants in the wind, was burned and heard the whaup. That's the way it was. I always knew the burn was running past Orquil, and quite early I knew it at the waterfall at Scapa. I was small enough to feel a mystery in the fact that there was a connection, that it was the same burn. The waterfall on to the shore over the Scapa Banks was one thing, a thing in itself, approached along the shore or along the top of the bank, arrived at from Scapa, walking there with grownups, a deliberate expedition.

The burn at Orquil was a thing in itself, there always, – there. Flowing past the bungalow where we lived sometimes in April and passing under the bridge at the steading, looked down at over the high wall with the horse trough in the upper side, the trough supplied from the overflow of the water wheel, it was just the burn, well known. The waterfall at Scapa was Orquil Burn arrived there. Unbelievable. But believed, because my father said it. Believed but still seen as a mystery. Some doubt about it. How could he know? When you're only about three the things seem so very separate.

There was later a time when it was a great adventure just to walk to the burn banks to link those two places. Then further up the burn, bit by bit. I never reached the source until I filmed it, aged 35, I aged 35, the burn aged I don't know what. And I found there wasn't exactly a source, not like the Source of the Clitunnus, but a general wetness of hillside – peat-banks hand-cut and the peaty water dripping out and running off into rivulets. All the overall wetness colliding to be a burn, but at no one point, not any point where I could say now here this is the very first of Orquil Burn.

But all they did was to cross the Bramaputra, cross the Chindwin, cross the Irrawaddy. Something that, though! To get to the far side of the river. And we for them are beyond, as they for us. Indians spoke of going out to England as we of going out to India.

I was out in India during the war. Out. But they come out here. It's quite true. It's so far away it's "out". Out to China. Out to Africa. Out to Canada. Out to England, from Scotland? Down to England, we say, usually. Over to France. Over to America and back. Out to America to emigrate.

Out across the Chindwin. What I mean is the Japanese were out across the Chindwin when they were on the Indiaward side of it. So they were driven <u>back</u>. Burmese would have to be driven <u>away</u>. But the Burmese – tribes of the hills – stayed, whoever else was there, out in whichever direction. For those who lived there it was simply there, that is "here". "Out" would be somewhere else altogether. "Out in Burma" isn't out, for them. It's in.

A huge river rolling down from the Himalayas. The Bramaputra. Immense. It takes steamers. I've never seen it. Only in a film by Jean Renoir, entitled "The River". One has to imagine those distant things, not see them all.

And the water runs down to meet the sea. That's all it is. That's all it is.

A sufficient number of atom, hydrogen, heavy water, cobalt and so on bombs could blow up the whole world, meaning the whole surface of the earth with the civilisations upon it. It's hardly likely we could disintegrate the planet itself, but on the other hand that may happen, may have happened before, may have to happen again. And again and again and again.

It's all interacting witchcraft. Every single human relation. You can tell – something in their bearing, their demeanour. We're all under a spell and all casting spells. Doctor, I'm ill. I can't help you: go to the witch-doctor. I would like to know what the witch-doctor does, to cast out spells.

Away across the Chindwin. That's the other side. And then, once it's crossed, settled, there's the Irrawaddy next. And the Chindwin is just there in the middle. It all seems very strange to me. All those places so very far out, so remote, get conquered and then become bases, humdrum with Naafi and Ensa. And complaints. Once it's all settled there are the complaints. Too many bones in the fish. And serious consideration of sanitation, of amenities, of recreation. Out on a limb you've no thought of recreation. It takes you all your time being there.

Spearheads. Pioneers. Poets.

You can't enter into the social state of things, with amenities, sanitation, family allowances and agreed hours of work. There can't be any agreement, for you're alone, a column, and no one to agree with but yourself.

Sleep is not oblivion. That's the mistake you make, to think that time used for sleep is time wasted. And sleeping together – well, sleeping together, what am I trying to say, sleeping together isn't just another expression for sexual intercourse. Sleeping together is sleeping together too.

There are the evil spell-casters and the good spell-casters, in Kenya. It is a punishable offence by British colonial law to put the evil spell upon a person. The witch-doctors, the curers, cast the spell out. They live in the reservations. I would like to know what it means to live in a reservation. I have lived in a cantonment. Perhaps it is something like that, except that the reservation for you is where you and your ancestors always were before, and the cantonment is the opposite, in a way. A reservation of colonisers. On the other hand, don't we all live in reservations here in Europe, protected by laws, not annihilated by our enemies although we could be, easily?

Edinburgh is a reservation, where the Corporation play with dinky-toys in the street. Brightly painted charming road rollers of newest design. "I would like to try <u>that</u> one."

What was I going to say? It must have been <u>something</u>. You'll never know now, for I seem to have forgotten it. Nevertheless, it will probably come out later in some way or other. Or has already been communicated, straight from my mind or thought, or straight thoughtless out of myself to all you others. Or I took it out of the blue at the same time as the rest of you and the rest of you all got it too at the same time as me.

Is that what you believe?

The black-coated ministers of the General Assembly believe that there's an individual out there called God. He's everywhere they say but indivisible and a downright personality into the bargain. He's good, they say, and they talk as if they understood this Goodness, which is God, they say, who is nevertheless not a which but a who. What do YOU think? Is God a which or a who, and, if either, then a thing or being we pick up or a thing or being we emit? Invented or discovered, and what is the difference anyway.

Mathematics an invention or a discovery. Music an invention or a discovery. Words. Language. Made? Found?

In the beginning was the word. What beginning? What word? W.O.R.D. word. I could hug it. Sentimental as a Saroyan. And what's wrong with that? Sentimentality is a falsification of emotion. Sentimentalism is dishonesty about feeling. But whatever is ever anything else, I'd like to know. You too, you'd like to know, if you're reading this book, I suppose.

It's a ghastly, hideous kind of greed, wanting to know everything. One I'm very guilty of. It's impossible to say such a thing without commending oneself as well as reproving oneself. We all think we are so marvellous. I used to be so objective, too. Everybody said so. I knew there was some mistake, but could see what they meant and began to accept it as a characteristic of myself.

    Until I split into two.

    Dementia praecox.

Palm of my left hand

You may see what I mean or may not.

I went out of myself so far I couldn't get back. And there I was and there was me, the two of us quite separate. The subject separate from the object. Subjective separate from the objective. That's what they mean by schizophrenia. And yet I wasn't exactly psychotic, – or was I? I wasn't so far removed that other people had to come and take care of me. I "managed". But the others <u>couldn't</u> help. No one could help, except by loving me, enough to fuse the two together again. It happened in the end.

Love.

It's just the thing it's not really possible to say anything much about. And yet the whole of everything is an attempt to say something of it, or about it. Or say it. The one thing that doesn't express love is to say, "I love you", although I don't mean to say that saying it means the opposite. Just, the saying it has very little to do with it. Yet <u>something</u> to do with it.

We don't really have the words. But that's not all that it is. The words have to be used in other ways than for statement. Statement is what is out of place. And yet, apparently contradictorily but not so, statements are what must be said. Not the final statement, I seem to think, but contributory statements. Trouble is, people seem to think you think you are stating the whole.

As if I could be so stupid!

"Roses are red,

Violets are blue:

that's not sayin what Ah'm thinkin about you.

Oh you

don't know my mind,
you don't know my mind."

The blues. As sung on a gramophone record by Mildred Bailey. Long ago. I remember it. You see, I have to present you these little facts, dig them out of my store-house, present you with the information, the reference. Scots are such workers, such knowledge-seekers. Do you believe any truth in that? They're a lazy lot the Scots. We Scots. Oh, but part Scandinavian, part Pict. I'm not a Scot, I'm an Orcadian. (What's that? Said the London publisher's reader, and, later, the London critic. What do we care about Orcadian or not Orcadian, Scot or not Scot! And we're not allowed to say Scotch it must be Scots or is it the other way round. Oh those foolish barbarians! And they resent being called English. <u>Resent</u> it! Can you beat it? They actually resent being called us. Whatever next? Some people have no more gumption than to refuse the greatest honour available.)

Some people!

"It's all right for some people." We've never had it so good. You mean you've never had it so good. I mean we're all better off than we used to be. Who is? Me? You? All of us. I'm not "all of us", never was. Think of the poor; they're not poor now. And the amenities we have! A-men-ities. Long may it be so. Oh, the crying shame of being called a welfare state – as if we cared about material things. WE! <u>They</u> may, but <u>we</u>!

I love little matter, its coat is so warm, and if I don't hurt it it'll do me no harm.

I am the peaty burn you see arriving at the sea. And I will be in the sea. I will never be virgin again and yet I am always virgin, as everybody always is. And you can follow upstream, not in time, but in some connotation, climbing through the barbed-wire fences. Whirlpools of bubbles seem to be just whirling on and on forever in perfect formation (in a dance). And "What are those flowers?"

Upstream

Into.
      On.
          Up.
Drops   splash.

In the deep river it is difficult to
recognise a drop.
In the dark river it is impossible
to see one drop from another.
In the resounding river I cannot
tell drop from drop. Unless they
are flung off by the heaving water
hitting something there is no sign
of drops there.

Upstream
The water collects in drops.

Upstream
You see the rhythm of water running over land.

The bulk of the river is full of drops and rhythms.

The heave of the river is a multiple rhythm of many coalesced drops acting as a great mass with momentum. The thrust of the river is dark and whole and heavy.

The deep moving water dark with peat or dark simply from being deep liquid unlit is an entity – a river, a burn – not just drops of water. Any handful of it can be scattered in drops. The drops are there, visible, upstream, elemental water.

How lightsome when there is sand at the bottom of the river, when the water runs over sand and is lit by reflections from it. Then the river is pale, sparkling, yellowish, light blue, clear water-coloured, iridescent. It splits the light back at us into rainbows.

There is a sound like a gurgle of water only, and above it a sound like light rapid voices. It is a sound heard nowhere else except above rivers, burns, streams, rivulets, any kind of water channel with the water moving down it.

The water comes from several sources. The tributaries commingle. Going upstream leads you in many directions. There are multiple streams to choose from. Who can say which is the one with the name? The water for the river comes from everywhere. Only, just over the brae-top it goes in the other direction for the other river. The Clyde runs west and the Tweed runs east from their beginnings on either side of the same ridge. I saw a deep river running through the Vale of Kashmir, thousands of miles from the sea. It was the Jhelum and would go into the Indus. The Ganges, the Indus and the Bramaputra seem on the map to beginning quite close together, and when they go their several and distinct ways and become their immense selves. The Ganges and the Bramaputra meet again where they go into the sea. They begin close together on the high plateau on "the roof of the world", one runs south of the Himalayan range and the other runs north of it, both going eastward. Their journey takes them to the same low point. They meet, they explode into a delta and their water runs into the sea. But this going, this journey, this meeting, this entering the sea is going on <u>all the time</u>. Water moves on down the channel but as I watch from the bank I still see water there and it is the same river. The river has a name and is itself.

The Indus goes in quite another direction from the other two. It runs south and gets to the sea on the western side of the Indian peninsula.

Disproportion is what worries me more than anything. This includes making too much of things, making too little of things, and every kind of "bad art" there is. Proportion is what form is. I don't like the grotesque German thing, like Hoffnung's drawings. That is the same as the SS and the <u>fun</u> they had with the extermination camps.

The river is a river even before it is a river. In that sense it is great, and also in the sense that it is itself. The stream, the trickle, even the drop of water. All real things.

It's their potty <u>creations</u> that people make too much of. They are so astonished at themselves for having invented anything at all that they try to make the slightest invention equal to the maximum invention. So it is, <u>in a way</u> – so long as it is recognised as invention and in scale. But what they try to do, maybe, is pretend that their invention is the whole of everything. I know what I'm trying to say but I don't know how to say it. There is a kind of disproportion which gives me a feeling of great distress and even of evil if it is insisted on.

I could think of menstruation as a kind of river. My blood has flowed for so long, and always been renewed. New blood always. The same river. Like a river in a difficult land, still wild.

The holy Ganges seems connected with the sacred cows. Placid, pallid, fluid-delivering eternities.

ROSES
R O S E S

Deep red
and a <u>deep</u> scent

heady purple tinge on the outer surface
of the petals

Petals
Rose petals
Transparent
A translucent colour of many colours
Sheer red.........
Never just sheer red.
Colour like this is colour which
is never quite like colour put on.

Paint
Rose
The difference is irreconcilable is the shuddering hope of the artist

— ! — — ! — !
  CRIES
(Hear!)
      No one can write a cry.

A smell of a rose
Presence

R O S E S
  Roses!

Oh the bloom the bonny bonny bloom
the buzz the buzzy buzzy buzz
The smell! (THE SMELL!)
    Particles
    Scent
    Organs
bee at flowers
    (HONEY)
Honey?
Some have a smell and some haven't.

THOSE now.
   Those ——

Warm sunny smell.
The colour of the petals.
The form of the flower.
The style of the bush.
    Juxtaposed and interpreted and referred back and
re-brought forward, instantly
    and KNOWN
WHICH rose
    and WHAT scent

but, physically now SMELL IT I SMELL IT IT IS THERE I KNOW IT IT IS THE SMELL OF A ROSE
It is *that* rose
    Which?
    Smell!
    See! (*Look!*)

(The very colour of the very rose, the very shape, the very smell, the very day of opening to the sun, the very bearing, the demeanour of the rose.)

I want to write spells.

℞
Recipe

Thou shalt take so much of so and so, grains of powder minims of liquid and a sufficient quantity of flavouring, a suitable amount of excipient, and then mix a mixture, form a pill, make a powder and dispense the quantity I here enumerate. Then label it, in readable language, a simple explanation of how to use it. And write someone's name there, the name of who it is for.

Are you a pharmacologist, a dispenser, a chemist's assistant? Do you measure out the drugs, the powdered herbs, the lakes, the tinctures, and count the encapsulated dust of spores? Do you know the secret of how to write upon a box? Can you fill a bottle, cork it, write a label for it and stick it on securely and clearly? The label is the continuation of the spell, the bottle or box and its contents are part translation of the spell. The label must be there.

For those who cannot read, what solution? All must be dissolved, for them, given them to ingest there and then, or injected or administered in whatever is the appropriate way. They don't see the magic spell. They would need incantation. They like to hear the words. Over their heads the words waft, from the chief in the white coat to the nurse in the slim striped dress, crisp white apron, trim prim head-dress, – a little stiff cap or handkerchief pinned over her hair.

Those words!

Awesome that the uncomprehended words have a precise implication, contain your healing. Are you sick and can't read, and hear the words, magic words, barely recognizable, which you clutch at hoping to save a few to take home and REPEAT.

"He said it was ____."

"No!"

"And they gave me, what was it now? ____ something like ____."

Imprecise, with some of the magic syllables, known as clinical words by the very sound of them. But the meaning? Ah, the meaning is that <u>they know</u>. And the meaning of the spell is that I will be well.

WORK

To provide work for people: that's a funny necessity. Something I learnt in the East is the validity of not working. Jo was fascinated by an apparent passivity which he felt must nevertheless be the face of a way of living. Deep in, and positive, but not positive in the doing doing doing way he was brought up among.

Honest labour.

The myth of the happy workman. And yet you can be happy working. Just work itself, the effort of it and the accomplishment of it, can make you feel quite blissful. The mistake is to consider it virtuous. "You're doing too much." Purr, purr. "Yes, I'm afraid so. But what can I do? I have to." They won't stop their miserable unnecessary this and that. Or they STOP. Stop everything. But still expect it all to be done. Somebody else has to do it. Somebody else's turn now. Oh, it's got to be done. Never do to admit that just the work itself was unnecessary. No, no, no! It was I was so good I did it all myself. No help. I kept on. Died with my boots on. Continued in harness. I'm not one to shirk. Not a one to admit it's all a lot of rubbish which nobody need do anyway, ever. Or even that I did it because I liked doing it. The doing was fun. For social reasons it has to be presented as a necessity. The working rather than the work done may be the value of it.

It seems very hypocritical of people to say there's something wrong in getting something for nothing. Surely everybody gets something for nothing, many things for nothing. To get everything for nothing is impossible. To hope to get everything for nothing is what is vicious, but that doesn't mean that to get something for nothing is wrong.

I don't believe that there is right and wrong, although I believe that there is good and evil.

I was usually in a great hurry to get things finished – a piece of work completed, sealed and set there. But nevertheless I am going to go on writing this book for as long as I go on writing it. So don't be surprised if it is inconsistent. There will be a sort of basic consistency, a dough of Margaret Caroline Tait. But as I am inconsistent in my opinions from moment to moment, from year to year it will be even more noticeable. As it is, "The Lilywhite Boys" has been on the go, one way and another, for nearly fifteen years I do declare. In 1945 I began writing it as a screenplay for a documentary film. That was in Ceylon, perhaps about November; certainly some of it got written in November at the Rest House, Weligama. Later, in Singapore, it acquired a title, "Brave Thunder", from my misremembering the line

"Oh! the brave music of a distant drum" as

"Oh! the brave thunder of a distant drum."

Later, in London, I changed the title to "Brave Music", but I didn't like it and then I noticed another book with the same title. It was just some trivial novel or other and I was quite glad to drop the title. I tried "A Distant Drum" for a time, but that whole notion was beginning to appear too ordinary and hackneyed altogether, and after a time I got the brainwave of "Lilywhite Boys." That may have been about the time when it changed from being a screenplay to being a book. (A novel?) I seem to remember hawking it around as "A Distant Drum", but maybe that was to film companies. In 1948 in London and 1949 at Holly Cottage, Windlesham it was all written out as a book for reading, later typed professionally and sent from time to time to different publishers. In 1957, I attacked it again. Re-typed it completely, myself, re-writing large tracts of it, intending to add a great deal in the form of dissertation but not in the end adding so very much. But it changed, and became a little more appealing to publishers. In 1959, I wrote the Post-Script, fairly rapidly. And now and from now on there's all this.

And of course I could be asked WHY? Why still this book? To which I can reply WHY NOT? Or give the infuriating answer slightly bigger children used to give to slightly smaller children, – "Because I thought you would ask."

I worked well for a time on a small overdose of coffee (writing "Dark Water", in 1952, and, in recent years, books of poetry.). Quite possibly there is something inherently abnormal about work, especially artistic work. It is even more abnormal for me not to work. I mean, not to work in art. Poetry, film, painting. It is a kind of suicide for me to allow myself to be absorbed in activities which preclude it. Activities, relationships. States of affairs where I am taken to be a sort of person suitable for some other people's social purposes.

I _cannot_ be used according to what other people think I should be used for. So I am not really a social being, I suppose. And yet I _am_. Only, the initiative has to be mine. This is the fatal, the suicidal role of the artist. I can't join in. In a way I can. And yet, never. I'm really joined in with them all more fully than any one of those who complain about me is, or can realise.

They always manage, or at least try, to get at you through money. It seems to have so very little to do with anything yet there it is, they get you through money.

When people prey upon you I think it often means that they feel guilty towards you.

If you give in to somebody's claims upon you which seem in a way just and are in fact justified, say, but are nevertheless against what you would choose for yourself and not <u>really</u> essential or important for the person claiming, then you feel quite evil to have given in and the whole arrangement or transaction is quite profoundly wrong.

As I walked through the gardens and smelt the roses I was thinking about the relation of words to the senses. Is smell the only sensation we don't feel impelled to put into words all the time? Manufactured perfume is only used to decorate women, not really used for any art. It couldn't be used for an art constructed in time, such as music, literature or film. Nor can it be entirely in space, as a picture or sculpture. It is definable in neither space nor time, although it is material – <u>at</u> a place – and evanescent – <u>in</u> a time. The control of it in time and space has been worked out hardly at all. There are absolutely no <u>records</u> of smell. The sweetest smells are still natural smells, and a perfume-maker hasn't produced anything which can affect anybody profoundly like the smell of a rose.

People now and again talk of using smell with film. I think they usually mean naturalistic smell, produced at relevant moments. Its use in the theatre seems more possible, because a stage production uses actual things whereas a film is all recordings and there are no recording smells. Certainly if any kind of rocket or squib is let off in some piece of action on the stage, then the smell of the gunpowder lingering afterwards has a very special effect. I think that this kind of extra effect could be used more often to advantage in theatre and possible in cinema, but not chiefly as a naturalistic accompaniment. The gunpowder smell continues on into subsequent action as a memory of what they were trying to do. There's a shooting episode and a bang, and you know the bang is just a stage effect, that they're not _really_ shooting, but then, a few moments after, this lingering smell of gunpowder which comes wafting out is _real_. A real smell allied to a patently stagey effect, and a syncopation of rhythm caused by the smell continuing as an undertone for action proceeding at stage speed.

But there are other ways in which a suggestive or nostalgic smell can be used, not exactly fitting any seen action there at the time, but related to it. Certain houses have a certain smell. And certain _kinds_ of house have a certain _kind_ of smell. Flower smells could perhaps be used something in the way I used or tried to use bird song in "A Portrait of Ga".

A garden is a composition in sight, smell and time. And sound, in terms of the silence of it and the birds. Bees too. There are specific garden sounds. A garden which is a work of art is a different thing from the usual house garden. Gardening as a hobby. Well, – the work of it is useful in its small way to the one who does it. And the product might be sort of admirable, that he has "got things to grow", but it is the MacNib stuff really. It would need a great deal of restraint and deliberateness to make a work of art out of the garden patch. A council house garden, for instance. The house itself would ruin any whole. Such gardens should be used only for crops. They often are, and that is the best use for them. The gardener who gardens for crops cannot "see" the concept of the garden as a whole. A "whole" garden would infuriate him, and make him want to dig it up for _crops_. And I think he's right in regard to most gardens – they _are_ best used for crops. The rare thing of a garden which is a composition should be kept rare – or allowed to be rare, rather. Poky approximations to it are worse than simple cropping.

The simple pleasure of getting something to grow is very great, but it's not the same thing as creating a garden, and that, I think, is very very rare. Professional gardeners are often entirely taken up with achieving difficult growths and with keeping things neat. They are technologists rather than artists. They don't consider scent and buzz and atmosphere. And what hobby gardeners do I've just been mentioning.

I have thought of gardens that I once wanted to create. Gardens like forests in that they could be left untended or almost untended – just cleared a bit now and again. Bulbs planted deliberately for an effect of colour, especially as seen from a distance, (I even thought of doing a whole island, such as Damsay for the sake of seeing it from Wideford Hill and from the road at Quaterness and so on) which could be left to proliferate and have a more or less predictable slightly different form each year. Not relying too much on "sheer colour" as in the bulb nurseries of Holland and Lincolnshire, but using more subtle colour combinations, and using the slope of the land and its quality, for light and shade, for depth of growth and so on. Some utterly amazing things of this kind occur naturally, and it seems in a way quite hopeless to think of <u>making</u> anything that could be as wonderful. But it's not, for the control and the feel of control of a made thing saves one from a wild feeling of madness there is about natural beauty. Or haphazard beauty, say, for in the countryside there is very little that has not been made even though it was not made to <u>look at</u> so much as for other purposes. The tearing and breaking effect on one's heart of some naturally occurring beauties is different from the comfort of the work of art. I suppose if you don't feel one you don't feel the other. The people who don't feel broken to bits by certain things which are just there don't feel either the terrible magnanimous soothing of some music, some pictures, some poetry.

Disruption. The terrible intimate split, the fission, the blood-eagle effect of just everything – the particular blue the sky is and its variations, sound of voices on the wind, meetings in the street, everything. From our limited vision. From the seeming un-wholeness of it. And then the inherent order there is really. The movement which is every movement. Human expression, in art, of a control there is – uniformity, wholeness, FORM, say. A form in it all, but not a meaning. A meaning is beyond me. But a form there is. It is the same as the form of myself, and of every atom-orbit in me. Infinitely varying reminders of this are in the infinity of <u>works</u>.

In a way all this can be expressed simply in living. Living is enough, if it is enough. Why do some of us feel we <u>have to</u> do the rest too, make things, be artists? I don't know why it is at all, but it is a necessity and part of the necessity of living, for me. It isn't a substitute, or an expression of failure. It is the elemental essence of the whole of living. All of living is in the work and the whole of what the work is in living. There is no such thing as one without the other.

All the poetry I have written up till now is folk-poetry or blood-poetry. It is the raw material of poetry in Paul Valéry's sense. In the same way, "Orquil Burn" is the raw material of a film rather than a film itself. But that doesn't mean that some busybody of a Grierson could take it and hash it about – <u>edit it</u> and make it into a tak-tak-tak natty little short film. It isn't <u>that</u> kind of raw material. It's not just footage. It is a made thing, set like that on purpose, but its form is distant, or unfinished perhaps. It is raw material in the sense that working from that one could now set out and make a real film of Orquil Burn. In fact, I was more correct before when I said my films are sketches for films rather than films themselves. Except maybe "The Drift Back".

I am totally non-didactic. I don't want to teach. I don't want to be a missionary. I don't want to "do things for people". I have complete faith in other people being who they are. The phrase, "education of the public" to me implies the most terrible impertinence.

I put my poetry and films out for other people to make something of their own of. They can sing it to their own tune. In spite of all this I am accused of (i.e. commended for) "reforming zeal" and other rubbish which I feel myself to be quite alien from. If people want to use my poetry to <u>reform</u> with, well they can, but I don't know what they will re-form into. Maybe "reform" <u>is</u> partly what I offer my poetry for, but not with the word in its usual, political, sense, i.e. with the reformer being very sure of the results he wants to obtain. Political results, I mean. I suppose one has a sort of sureness about the poetical results one is after.

THE SHAME OF THE UNIFORM AND THE GLORY OF THE UNIFORM

Using the strict forms of poetry so far unearthed is like wearing men's clothes. School uniform and military uniform for girls and women is shameful. A nurse's uniform is a different kind of thing. It expresses an almost frighteningly feminine kind of uniformity or FORM – frightening and sweet at the same time, something as the soldier's uniform is one FORM of the utterly male – arrogance and fatedness together. Marching, team spirit, flamboyance, rigidity, all in a male way expressed in those extraordinary uniforms – regimental, naval and air force.

Women are possibly less inclined to find a FORM for themselves than men. However, fashion, dance, movement are used by women in feminine FORM. The sari is a dress form as the sonnet is a literary form. There can be great variations within this strict form. Maybe this dress I'm working out, part sari, part kilt, such as I've made with Saulat's Indian silk is a Scottish <u>form</u> of dress which will –"come out" – "work" for women in this part of the world.

It is necessary for me to be anonymous. That is why I put my name on everything. The name is there. So they don't wonder who it is. They just take it. It means nothing. It's just a sort of identity disc. "Oh yes, her."

S. P. E. L. L.

Whole. WHOLE.

Life certificate.

17th June 1960. I resolve (resolved two days ago and still resolve) to write no more disease certificates. Only life certificates, life spells, life prescriptions.

Poetry is a spell, is a life certificate.

Whole. Healing. Healthy. Sane. Wholesome. Hale.

So I cannot be a locum any more, can't certify disease.

Poetry is the most live art. People use words all the time, keep them vivid with the help of poetry. (People use music all the time, use clothes all the time, and shapes and forms, people use buildings all the time so architecture is a live art.)

"It's time something was done about it."

I never know what people mean."

"How in the world could you give up Medicine and go in for Cinema?" People are so dense they don't see connections. And "give up" and "go in for" are only what they think anyway. "Do you like this better?" Of course, I don't know how to put it either. Why don't they just wait? Multitudes wait and there's something for everybody.

Men call the Anabasis glorious. All those bitter sad experiences – the futile fate of an Army. Those men and their adventures are the very epitome of an army, with all its meaninglessness. "Army" is a sort of art form too. An expression of life as a fight. Robbing, making provision, capturing women and boys, seizing animals, fighting battles for somebody, fighting battles for somebody else. Always some killed, wounded, dying incidentally of something like some fatal honey they found or an unlucky medicine somebody took for a fever. And trying to get home all the time. What was the difference from being at home? They had a life, women, beasts, goods, but they were away from home. They didn't even want to found a city anywhere that they came to rest. They wanted home. At home, they would be fighting too, likely.

I don't know whether those Greek soldiers fancied themselves as coming home full of glory in order to settle down in lasting peace on their family homestead, or what. The soldiers in Burma and in the Echelon were thinking towards home, just of getting there. I don't know how they thought it was going to be once they had returned. They probably didn't think of glory but just of welcome, and then of familiarity. Things they were used to, accents they were used to, paths they could follow like a homing cat.

Exile. You see, I couldn't understand about exile, when I was young. It seemed to me a thrilling pleasure to go away to distant places. People do it on purpose. They emigrate. They travel. How can it be painful? What was that terrible punishment, of exile? Surely any place could be made into home.

For I planted bulbs round the Nissen hut in Derby, put up curtains in the stone room in Jhansi, scrubbed clean the bathroom ledges in Jutogh to the eternal shame of my plainsman bearer, kept a white kitten in Katugastota. With it all there was a pain – a terrible nostalgia, of myself looking for my own. It was not Margaret I mourned for so much then as Margaret I sought, searching in the pricking light of the high mountains and in the downpour of the tropics and in the fog of England. Leaving anything behind and breaking a continuity was a pain, and taking things with me was an equal pain. Out of the tin trunk when I opened it came the same old things I had put in it. Only me, nothing of mine really. The Jhansi curtains hang here in the Rose Street studio now – but they don't give me pain. I seem to have come to rest at last, to accept what is for me.

People describe a feeling they have, as if of having lost something. I don't remember ever feeling it to be that. I was seeking, but not for something I had lost. For something I had never had. Something of mine – something that would be mine. And I its, I suppose.

I keep thinking of a poem which comes in lines and constructions. I keep thinking of some sort of thing which will take its form in the formation on the page. But it's probably a film I'm thinking of, really. Will film survive the holocaust? And will they perhaps have to invent projectors again, to show them with? Discovering the right rate per second, all those things.

Think in a shape. Think in a rhythm. It is something other than thinking. The sin is to reject the rhythm. The evil is to refuse the shape. When it comes, for you, seize it. It doesn't do to take something else instead and hope to make something of it, believing it will be more yours because you <u>decided</u> to make it. It's other. It's when it comes, take it, it's not pick and choose. It's, simply, reply – respond when it <u>is</u> yours. Leave the rest alone: it is there all right, it won't waste and it's even related to you in a way. But your own rhythm is <u>for you</u>. If you are a poet it is for you to reverberate, drum, relay, send messages with, write life certificates with. And love with, whether you are a poet or not a poet your own is for you to love with. Woman, man, place, light, flower work.

I would like to write a poem carefully laid in place like the table in candle light with rowan jelly matching some other browns. I would like to lay it out square and simple and set in what is needed, completing it in a roundelay. The eye goes round and round it, receiving. The mind reads. Hear the soft sound of the flame of the candle, watch the exact formation of a word.

I like carelessness too, if there is such a thing. I think I like it. But not carelessness in what needs to care, that is <u>not</u> slipshodness, <u>not</u> triviality and unseriousness about a poem. There is a kind of poetry which is <u>essentially</u> incomplete. Any attempt to complete and form it to known ends ruins it. It is not slipshod to revere that incompleteness – that PROMISE. It is the substance of poetry rather than the made thing. It is not really literature: it is the raw magic. It has to go on as it came in, be relayed <u>whole</u> (that is, incomplete) for it is food and will be sustenance of growth.

The more life the more pain! The more you are able to live and to feel poetry the more they will kill you, daily, or expect you to commit suicide. The raw poetry which is the sustenance of growth leads to PAIN. The delicately formed, the strong, constructed poetry, might give you SOLACE, out of its perfection (the form, the exactly placed). The mad poetry, the substance of poetry, the folk-song the cry from the blood perhaps is <u>always</u> grief, ship-wreck, loss. The more you take poetry to grow with, and grow, the more terrible it will be for you. The more you grow, the more poet you are, the greater the pain. And the more they will kill you. Daily.

<u>Extinction</u>

The kings and queens were expected to
    walk into the extermination chambers
    without flinching.
Any show of tears would have gone against them.
Some thought
That nothing could be more against them
    than it was already,
And one young woman let out a wail
So terrible
That if they all had done it
The massacre of the kings and queens might
    have had to stop.
But she was one of the last to go.
It so happened that all the others had gone quietly

To their unseen death which took place
    at the turn of a switch.
She had to be pushed in by horrified attendants,
And through the small round thick glass
    window of the chamber
The two nearest saw but could not hear her screams.
The few remaining victims
Then went in quickly, terrified of terror,
Terrified of allowing their feelings out,
Terrified of terrifying themselves more than
    they were already terrified.
They went in quickly,
Half-choking in anxiety to get it over.

I wrote so much that was all just blood-song. I tore it out of myself. It all came charging out, a precipitate birth. It all came heaving, surging, covered with blood. Before I put it into books I wiped some of the blood away. This wiped wound I call "interim edition". But my discovery had been discovery of, my sorrow was soul-sorrow, root-sorrow. Hatred. It was all there raw before I edited it. The lymph and the corpuscles shouted aloud. It was madness deep in myself, as my split self re-united; as my soul and my mind found my heart again they all roared aloud in grief and madness.

    A madness which is not a "psychosis". A madness which is profound and vital response to injury.

    (The iron kick which the ordinary deal to the tenderest tissue! The gash they smash open, draining the innermost fluid! The laugh they laugh!)

"Nobody knows the trouble I've seen
"Nobody knows my sorrow.
"Nobody knows the trouble I've seen
Lord, hallelujah!"

So sang the negroes. They knew! They sang with their blood.

The poetry that is blood-poetry (blood-song) is responded to in the blood. It is not exactly a solace, but a saving for an instant. A donation of other blood. A saving drip into the vein, if it is of the right group, if it is compatible.

There's never an end. And the poetry itself is simply an instance. It is instantaneousness, that is, only a middle, with no beginning and no end.

I don't hold with prolonged virginity.

I don't care about chastity, one way or the other. Be chaste if you want to. If that's what you call it. It is of course less painful to stay dead than to come alive again. Could I make a poem of the balance between the madness and pain of being fully alive and the sunk awful deadness of non-participation? Could I? I don't want to give in to the bleakness. I don't want to starve myself.

If you expose yourself, they all laugh at you. Unless they think you have emperor's clothes on.

Edit as you write. That is <u>work</u>. That is what work is. I belong to the future. I don't mean posterity. Not just my spirit, and not just my verses, but myself. I am my own child, or my own grandchild. People will see me leaping over dykes in two hundred years' time.

Polygamy is a good idea. And purdah is a good idea. A woman shouldn't have to devote her whole attention to a man. Especially a woman who is an artist (a poet). I'd much rather be a concubine than a wife really. A concubine can get on with her own work and needn't forever be mending socks, cleaning vegetables, doing the shopping. Probably polygamy is the only condition under which a woman can be a poet. So that she needn't be a man's only wife and yet have the comfort of being his, him being hers. He can't be married by law to more than one wife, and there are probably very few legal wives who would feel a system of polygamy or concubinage suited them, so the legal wife might sue for divorce. Should she agree or be deceived? Of course, what a husband could do would be to have none of his wives legal, but men seem to like the business of having conferred a great honour on somebody by making her into "married woman". So he'd want to have his legal wife that he is "responsible for", who can claim things from him and so on. Then let the others be "unmarried wife". I'm not being frivolous about this. I think it would be a good situation to be in. Most men and most women want monogamy, and there's no reason why they shouldn't be monogamous. Nobody will be against them for it. But there shouldn't be guilt about a life allowing something different. If you say this, they say you are "advocating promiscuous intercourse". Nothing of the kind. Promiscuous is another thing altogether.

    I really hate that kind of cynical undiscriminating promiscuity. Coitus as a sort of lark, – "naughtiness" and all that. Thing where people get a bit drunk at parties and go disappearing into bedrooms with other people's wives. All on a level of a sort of naughty daring, or contempt, or despair perhaps. Or just idle curiosity. It all thrives on the convention of monogamy. There's a ministers on the spree element to it. Even the so-called orgies at fertility celebrations are not like the sort of poisoned modern thing, I'm quite sure. I think that ritual kind of intercourse although promiscuous and public is just as real as marriage. "Licence" is quite a correct word for it, but I don't think licence should imply the other kind of "wild party" promiscuousness. Licence – i.e. that they have actually licence, for the occasion, which is a particular occasion, with a meaning. I don't think this has anything to do with "hot under the collar" "sexiness".

Probably those occasions and feasts of public intercourse and licence were very valuable and healthy in a community. (No fear of a lack of sex education in the young.) They see it all and everybody sees everybody else seeing it all. But it's only for the occasion. Privacy is returned to and kept except for the feasts, the meaningful feasts, the healthy sane joy of the public sex feast with everybody taking part, not just sitting in a dark auditorium hotly resisting masturbation. Sex in public isn't a good idea except under those occasional conditions of licence. When I say "sex in public" I'm thinking of rolling couples in public parks, and some films, "sexy" newspaper photographs, and so on – all of which are just a sad substitute for an occasional, i.e. unusual fertility feast with licence, for a purpose.

What I am writing now is less imaginative than what I was writing. It really seems to be all ideas now, and I don't believe in ideas. But I have to give my imagination a rest for a time. This work with ideas has to be direct. I don't like ideas disguised as fiction. Fiction has to be something else, something in itself. (A great many of my poems have to be read as fiction. I would like "The Hen And The Bees" to go on the Fiction shelf, not on the Poetry shelf in bookshops) (And even such a poem as "The eyebright was for you" is of value to the extent that it is fiction. The feeling is true. The event is partly fiction.) But this working with ideas, now, with thought brought to order, could lead to the other kind of poem. There's less affection in it; it can be rather bleak. Or it can have the classic solace – of Paestum.

The real feat is to have the blood-image and the thought-image perfectly united. That is major poetry. Less endearing than folk-song, and not so handy for pompous critics to lay forth about as the all-in-the-head kind. <u>They</u> like stuff that's all in the head, because they can <u>talk</u> about it.

To what extent should all poetry be orgasm or to what extent should it be completely NOT? I'm speaking of the minutes beyond excitement, when it's all movement. It's related too to the bliss I speak of in the poem about matching the sun's movement to the movement within oneself, although I wasn't thinking then of orgasm but of interstellar space, as Cocteau has it. The stars in the blood.

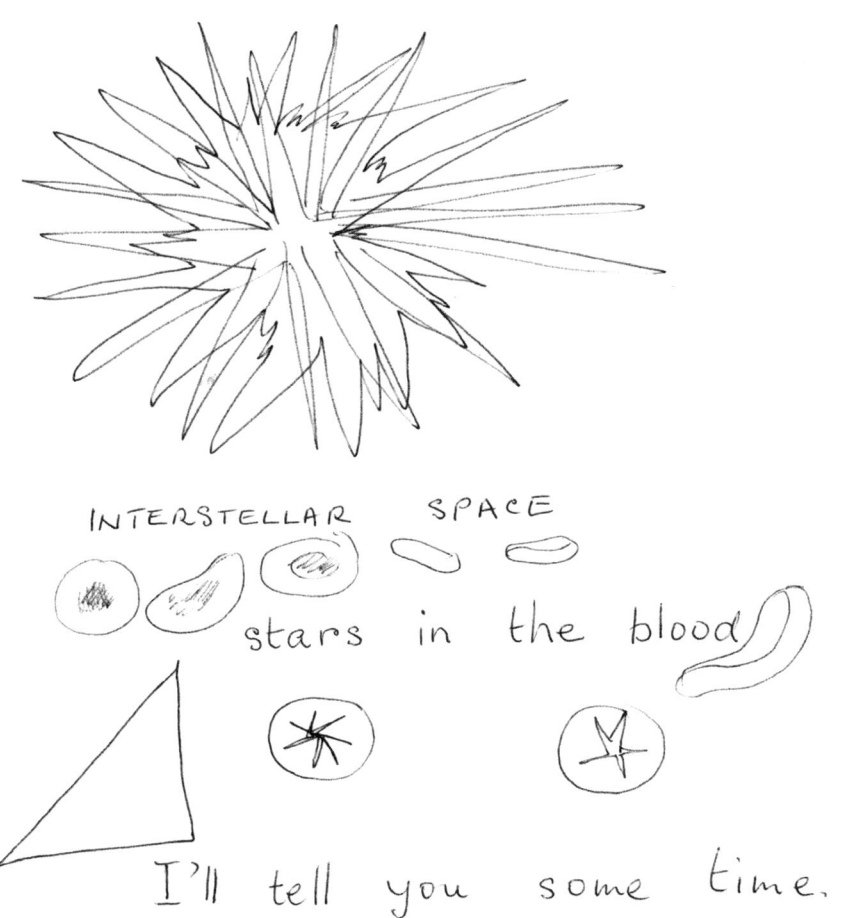

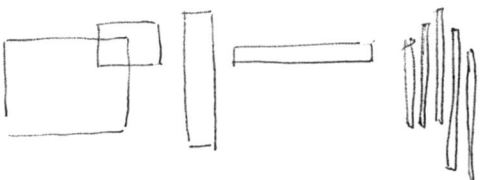

"I'll tell you some time." This is the ineffable promise which is the whole of love and the whole of poetry.

Going among people. Inter-orbital. Inter-stellar. Paths and poetry. A perfect ellipse. Jocasta's mask was a perfect ellipse. And the girl chasing pigeons is so wee that the pigeon just <u>runs</u> away from her, doesn't get up and fly.

Everything joins with everything else, and when this is felt as pain it is called nostalgia.

Can you get excited by reading a scientific description of something? Exactness of factual (physical) description is something venerable. Relation of precise facts, – that is, indication of precise identity.

What do all those people think a woman is anyway? "The feminine touch." They are thinking of knitting hints for thumb-cosies. They'd have us knitting penis-cosies. Embroidered condoms with a fleecy lining – that's what they'd like to be coddled in, by US, despicable us. They think we have nothing else to do but toddle. To and fro with shopping baskets.

After a time a certain smell comes to be connected with a yellow rose and could be called a <u>yellow smell</u>. Because I associate the smell with the colour. All yellow roses if they have a scent at all have some variant of the yellow smell. And there's a smell of deep red roses. Some quite different varieties of deep red rose have strong heady perfumes, different from each other and yet more alike than any are like the perfume of a yellow rose or a pink rose. The yellow rose smell and the pink rose smell come together in pinkish-yellow roses. There is a particular smell of the creamy white roses which I know in advance as I approach them. There is nothing in the world like the scent of a wild white rose in Scotland. There are wild roses without a scent, and little pink ones with a warm brier scent. There are cultivated roses with no perfume whatsoever. They are recognizable as a kind of rose that doesn't have a perfume, even some way off. It may be partly simply that the outer aura of perfume isn't there, so that one's perceptive self walking into the area meets no element of it.

All round the rose there is a cloud of perfume, and even as I come into the penumbra a little of it reaches my perception, but not enough to arrive at my consciousness. So I know a little beforehand just what the scent will be. A little before I can smell it to the extent, of Ah, I smell it!, it is there, affecting my senses. And since I don't smoke or anaesthetise myself regularly my senses are quick. Perceptively quick. Translation into opinion or diagnosis may be slow. Reaction might be slow, but the perception itself is alive. So that I sometimes seem deaf to words, but I can hear very faint sounds. I can hear the faint rustle in the lungs, but sometimes I have to listen for a long time in order to identify it.

If you want to read my work you have to understand about the value of fiction as I use it. In Orkney they understand about the story. What I mean by a story. What a story is. What I feel about a story.

Even a poem would go into the same book.

I get no blood-poems now. I wrote the blood-song all away. The next poetry will be thought and blood together. No differentiation. Or yes, differentiation, but no <u>separation</u> (this sort of mention <u>about</u> it differentiates, separates). I think the next poetry will have to be on film. A poem like a film, with the flesh there and the voice. In a film the flesh is actually there, the voice is really heard. Accents, and cries. (Pain and grief are not the same thing.)

    I am not really a writer. Something which involves <u>performance</u> is what I feel my fingers are grasping at, my mind embracing. That is, I would like to write for performance – for film, particularly – or else to <u>tell</u> stories, using my voice. I don't like this society I live in in Edinburgh where people don't tell stories. In the north they understand about stories. Here they only want to listen to the gospel, and whatever you say they think you are <u>reporting</u> something. The journalist's "story" would be less harmful if taken as a story and not as a "I saw in the paper that – " etc., as if it were <u>the case</u>. Those clinically presented stories in fiction (in literature) – presented as a sort of case history, or evidence of own eyes – are false, in a journalistic way. I wrote a very bad one like that myself once called "Top of the Mountain". I always get a feeling of evil from it if I re-read it. There is a quality of fiction in most of what I write. Everything should be read as fiction. Everything is fiction once it is written.

    I hate Sundays, when nobody is working. People are too bare and uninteresting on Sundays.

    Some of the poets every now and again have the idea of using the typography in the construction of the work. The next best thing to an ideogram. I think you would need to see a whole lot of proofs before you got it right. Perhaps even print it yourself – but I have an idea that what can be commercially printed is <u>more</u>, in that line. But it would mean understanding the printer's resources, working with a compositor, trying out a good many things before you got it right. Another kind of thing, to be done entirely yourself, would be to work with pencil, pen, brush, on a lithographic plate – stone, zinc or aluminium – making the poem in shapes on the page (i.e. on the plate). This would be nearer to an ideogram and it might be possible to get a heightened effect from the addition of appearance to meaning and sound and other qualities of words.

I like the formal Italian gardens like the Giardino Boboli at Florence. And I love the Nishat Bagh near Srinagar, set in terraces, with fountains and pavilions to grace it, its flowers and its trees graceful and alive while growing in the particularly chosen area, the precise location in the map of the garden. Height, extent, colour, perfume, shelter, relation of stone to growing things and of water to plants and to constructions are all formalised and placed on a slope of the mountain rising from the lake shore. You arrive by water. There is a stone terrace, gates, a pavilion. The mountains slope up for thousands of feet. The huge garden lies there on the mountainside, wealthy, adjusted.

You can climb by stairs, by paths or by grass slopes. Women in silk saris visit the garden, with men in white dhotis and slim Kashmiri coats. Children play. The gardeners are working. I do not remember any uniformed park attendants except for someone at the gate to take the entrance money. The extent of the garden is great, and it is a whole. More formal centrally, at one side it has a small forest, almost wild. The highest terrace of all is tended, but remains more like a field surrounded by hedges than a garden. It is bounded above by a wall and beyond that the mountain is for grazing. A herd boy sat on the wall and watched us. High above are the peaks, hiding from view even higher peaks deep among the Himalayas.

The Moghul gardens were made in the Italian style, except for the Shalimar which is rather more in the style of an English garden. It is on a lakeside too, on level ground. There is an Eastern pavilion, painted and carved, and fountains, but something about the landscaping, the subdivision of the garden, is English. I felt a little uneasy in it. There were more English visitors in it than in the Nishat Bagh. They seemed to like it best. It was a little more pretty, less splendid than the other. Less perfect, more nostalgic. It made the British soldiers feel homesick.

In a way, the garden which affected me most was the Nasheem Bagh. It was made entirely of chinar trees and grass, on the flat shore on the opposite side of the same lake as the Shalimar. There was no stone terracing, no entrance money, no wall, few foreign visitors. Jolly boatloads of Kashmiris were picnicking there. There was something adventurous about it, something distant, something impossible.

High up a mountain, well away from the lakes, a journey by road, was a jewel of a garden, quite small, the name of which I have forgotten for the moment. It is like a condensed Nishat Bagh, terraced, formal, having square ponds set round with flowers in pots, steps, straight paths, a central pavilion, high sunny walls, fruit, and all the light flowers lit by the rarefied mountain light, shielded from the wind by the high walls, a warm place with a magic of sound in it. The gardener was singing. He laughed at us coming there, I think.

The English landscaped gardens make me feel very unhappy. Some of the flowers are so much in place that they don't seem fully alive any more. They are placed with a pretence of seeming "natural" and so their inalienable naturalness is somehow destroyed, or negated. But there is something else, something of it all having been smoothed over, or moored. Edges trimmed. It is the growth which is controlled in English gardens more even than the placing. I like the placing to be precise and then the growth to be free.

Ah, how I envy you being a doctor, said Fernando, for you have known "la morte". But one doesn't know death by witnessing it. For it is absence. I thought to say but didn't that the much greater mystery of that kind is "la nascita". Then you are aware of the arrival of life in a way that at death you are not quite aware of its departure. Or – I have been aware of its departure, but that's it: a departure is nothing. You become aware of a sudden absence. Listen with a stethoscope, and so on, but you KNOW. "Is he gone, doctor? Yes, I thought so."

People don't know what they are doing when they go in for Medicine. They think it is an interesting study, or a job. They may feel some kind of aura connected with status, which they wish to have. But I didn't know what I was doing. I didn't know what I was going into. It isn't possible to leave it. It isn't possible to stop doing it. But I couldn't ever have not done it. It was the whole of me that undertook it, the same me the same I as knew I must some day be a practising artist of some kind. I didn't then know whether writer, painter or what, but I knew. Cinema was invented at the right time for me to find it when I was ready. It seems strange to me now that I am prevented from working at film. I am effectively prevented, just now, but perhaps this won't be permanent. Perhaps it's when I'm older that I'm to be making films, not now at all. This does seem strange, because cinema and I reached a compatible stage of maturity at the same time, and yet I am now being effectively prevented. It may be that this is some provision for me (by myself, I suppose) so that now I must simply live my life, not do and organise in a producing way. It may be that something is to happen here, and I have to be here for it. I must live just now, and I can write, like this, but not organise film production. That would take me away, and I know I have to be here just now.

I don't see how anyone can be an artist without being a doctor first. All the studies involved in the study of "medicine" and then the practice of it seem to me absolutely necessary. It only seems funny to me that they don't seem to be necessary for other people. I could never have been an artist without my study and practice of Medicine.

Suppose I had not done any of it, but had reared children instead. Would that have been better? I don't know, I don't know, I don't know, I don't know, I don't know.

Those of whom a lot is expected have quite a hard time really. They are looked on as having greater capabilities than others, and this is doubtless so, but nevertheless their capabilities are not infinite. They are expected to protect the others all the time as well as looking after themselves, and never to need protection themselves. If they are given protection, it's only on a basis of slavery, and they are unsuited to be slaves. I see some of the young children being burdened like this already. Those who are so certainly full of capabilities are always expected to give in to their weaker sisters and brothers. Give in because you are strong. I'm not so sure that that is altogether a good lesson to teach children. Teach them the possibility (and wisdom, kindness, use, pleasure, at times) of doing such a thing, but not that they should

<u>always</u> do so. If you are always to give in because you are strong then it's stronger to be weak. It's true the weak are very strong: they get the strong to do things for them <u>all</u> the time. The strong have to work for both –themselves and the weak ones – and they may not have as much strength as all that.

If you allow any sign to appear that you have strength or capabilities, then all the weak ones try to seize on you – "Ah yes, <u>you</u> work for <u>me</u>."

People sometimes expect too much of you, if you are good at things and good-natured too. If you have anything specific to do, or even if you feel non-specifically that there is <u>something</u> you should be doing which is not what anybody tells you or asks you to do, then you must use some of your strength in resisting them. There are situations where it seems to be taking all of your strength just to resist them, leaving you none for what it is you have to do. So then you feel your strength is being entirely wasted and you might just as well give in and work for them. But if you do you feel as if you had committed suicide. A lot of people who seem strong are not strong enough to resist <u>and</u> do something. So they don't attempt to. I suppose they just <u>know</u> that they are not capable of <u>all</u> of it. A lot of people are happy having given in. I suppose it depends on who you give in to. The worst thing it is to give in to somebody who is only pretending to be weak in order to get you nobly to give in. Some who are quite strong see how easy it is for the weak to win, and decide to win too by being "weak". And if <u>they</u> get you, then that <u>is</u> evil.

It's not necessary for a man to be so aberrant, in order to be an artist, as it is for a woman. The world has been ordered by men without considering women very much – except for considering their own need for women and women's <u>demands</u>. So within their own, male, pattern there might be a way a male artist could live and be. For a woman it is more difficult. She is forced to be further outside, more aberrant. The women understand what she is after, in a way. Possibly for this very reason, that she is forced to be more aberrant, she <u>can</u> be clearer about it. Not many women ever manage any of it at all, though. They are not prepared to be so far out of the fold. They try to do something within the fold – do something and be within the fold too. But they can't. They can't be a genuine womanly artist under those conditions. It's in those ways that the "feminine touch" is born – false femininity. All a bit arch. A man, however, within the fold might easily do a lot as an artist. So long as he is genuinely within and not pretending. Perhaps even if he is pretending; I don't know.

I don't think I am making it at all clear what I mean by this.

A woman more completely has to <u>find a new way</u>. A man can still do a lot with an adaptation of the old way. It's still all right for him, I mean, up to a point, but it won't really be all right until he finds a new way too. A new way for both, which allows <u>both</u>, doesn't necessitate one kow-towing to the other. Everybody thinks this is just impossible, of course. Perhaps they are right. I don't quite see how it <u>can</u> go on as it is. Women can be <u>not</u> all the other things they have been trying to be this century, but they can't be not artists. They probably shouldn't try to be the <u>kind</u> of artists men are. It's something different. Nearer to folk-song and to <u>told</u> story, probably. Maybe many of the unknown folk-artists were women. It's men who like to put their name on things.

Women <u>have</u> continued to be artists all the time in that anonymous way, but in most recent times there has entered the business of being the "amateur" kind of artist, which is a poor thing. Not the same thing at all as a folk-artist. For the amateur it is a hobby, and he may spend a great deal of time on it, yet it remains not serious. It's an attitude of seriousness rather than a matter of payment, or "full time" etc., which distinguishes the genuine artist from the amateur. There is an element of play even in most genuine art, but that is not the same as playing <u>at</u> art, as the amateurs do. All the terrible solemnity about art doesn't help any, of course. Toffee-nosed critics and "teaching appreciation".

I don't know what writing is. I don't know what it is I am doing, exactly. I still have to find out. I <u>have</u> to find out. I have to keep on writing until I find out. What I say it is isn't what it is – not yet. I don't altogether mean that I believe I <u>will</u> find out. I'll have to keep thinking about it.

Thinking about thinking. And working at work. Those are the ultimate pleasures of the intellectual and the poet. Intellectual-scientist-poet. (I can think of it as a sort of hair style.) (So you'd say I'm not serious. But I could equally think of it as a garden, as a hair style, or as a formula, or as a mathematical equation, or as a piece of music.) The way a person walks is related to their way of thinking. You see it in their eyes too. "One of the roving kind." That's me, I suppose.

There's a sort of gaiety about sheer thought that is not equalled by anything else. It is like the scent of wild thyme on the bank of an old grassy road. There are cart tracks indenting the grass and the short sprouting heather, and the road runs between two dykes built at a distance apart suitable for a sizeable road. It used to be a principal road but now simply leads to some fields. It has an air of being something, although the logic of it is far-fetched by some standards.

The old pack road too, in Derbyshire, where they had donkey races. A fine place for blackberries. Long, straight, a route, a walk, thick with grass.

The road to Babina was quite another thing. It led away out somewhere, far away, across the hot jungly plain. Rocks and thorn bushes and stunted teak trees and dry hard ground there. Snakes and lizards and scorpions. The road was similar in colour to the dry ground, and dusty, but distinct. Hard in the centre, with softer dustier edges for animals to walk on. Jeeps and trucks went roaring up the centre. Long trains of bullock carts came slowly through the dust of the edges dangling a lantern at night, carts and bullocks white as dust. The white bullocks of India are beautiful animals.

"The Tiddim Road" was one of the names we heard about, from the distant front. It was where the men were fighting or what they were fighting for, away out in the Kohima far from anywhere. "For your tomorrow they gave their today." But our today now is not much concerned with the Tiddim Road. It's not a road any of the relatives of the dead men of the Fourteenth Army every hear very much about now, I'm sure. But all that fighting out there, and the Columns, the eastward-directed warfare, "the road to Mandalay" had some effect on our today and tomorrow, I suppose. The suggestion in the inscription (on a monument in Kohima) that it was worthwhile is what I question. Was it worth it to have those men killed, for anything we got out of it? I don't know at all. It is impossible to know how much is due directly or indirectly to their death. Certainly the war has had certain <u>results</u>.

Death of the fighting men is part of the cause of the results. It is not easy to say whether the results are good or not. <u>Our tomorrow, for which they gave their today</u>. I think they died for the Jews, if for anybody. The war stopped the extermination camps. That is its one positive wholesome result.

People don't know what they are doing when they carry out their plans. There used to be an island in the Orquil Burn near the Bungalow, where the children used to play. It was big enough for two or three small children to stand on together and near enough the bank to jump across to, or to scramble across, for the trickle of water between it and the bank was so shallow you needn't even get your feet wet. There was another flatter island further out which was sometimes covered and sometimes not, according to the fullness of the burn. A good many years after the time when my cousins played there and brothers and I played there, my Uncle Ernest decided to make what he called a "wild garden" at that part of the burn. It meant planting willows and other plants and deepening the burn by means of some sort of partial dam; so that the two islands were covered and lost and the shallow pebbly dancing stretch where we once caught a very small trout by hand was also lost. Instead of being a stony noisy bit of burn with boulders sticking up and islands you could step across to, it became a deep slow gurgling burn there, shaded by willows, the grass beside it growing long and lush, and exotic plants transported there from catalogues flourishing. My uncle was very pleased with it and proud of it. It only made me feel sad. Now it is wild in a way he never meant it to be, for nobody takes care of it and it is quite rank and overgrown. Both the "wild garden" and the sunlit shallow burn with islands are lost now. But there are always some children about the farm, and I've seen boys there using for javelins the stems of the pampas grass my uncle put in his wild garden. To them and to other children coming there now perhaps there is something irreplaceably wonderful about the illogical growth of willow and unnameable horticultural plants, and the dark shadowy burn there, unlike all the rest of Orquil Burn. I missed that stretch out of my film of Orquil Burn, not quite intentionally but it happened like that, perhaps because that part to me doesn't seem to be really Orquil Burn. I don't quite believe in it.

The University is extending into George Square. It would be all right if the new buildings they are putting up were likeable, but the plan is for heavy Mussolini-esque lumps. The medical building at the corner which is already partly up is not unlike some appalling new insurance buildings in George Street which depress me every time I pass them. Most of the recent building in Edinburgh is quite appalling. It seems to be all derived from a New-Town-gone-to-pot style. A more genuinely Edinburgh style of building has quite an airy grace. Even in the superbly smug "New Town" the backs of some of the buildings have a lightness and liveliness lacking on their street front. There are certain features of building which appear to me almost uniquely Edinburgh – far more Edinburgh than the New Town really – but no architects take their inspiration from them. Instead, they heave up ton weights of degenerate New Town, which in any case was already degenerate Roman and Greek. I think it is high time Edinburgh stopped calling itself the Athens of the North and thought of itself simply as the Edinburgh of the North, that is just as Edinburgh.

Why does no architect take a good look at the back of St. James'

Square, happily left revealed by the lowness of building at the bus terminal or at Buccleuch Place or at Nicholson Street or Bristo Street? There is no need to copy the quaintness of crowstepping any more than there is to re-perpetuate the Bank of England quality of the New Town. If only present-day architects would develop something new and of their own out of those deep semicircular bays set with three windows or out of the extra tall gable going up unexpectedly but supremely logically above the roofline, features of building which seem to be right for the stone and the weather and for the shape of this city!

As a graduate of Edinburgh University I had a brochure sent to me showing roughly what the great lump of stodge is to be like that they plan to plonk around George Square and need money for. It really seems a pity it has to be so ugly and old-fashioned. One of the nice things about Edinburgh University used to be that there wasn't any "campus" or integration of the university as something distinct from the town. It may be that the University wants to be more extraneous to Edinburgh now that it is planning a campus and integrated University life, and prefers to stick up something quite alien, nothing to do with Edinburgh.

"Life itself is entirely East-Lynnish", a correspondent in "The Scotsman" says, and Marjory that of Mrs. Dale's Diary events "are what life consists of". A level of observation – And a level of experience. Most people do just want diminished experience. The man gives in and marries the girl, and she is pleased. In fact, political results are probably all produced by means of false emotion. False emotion rather than illogical thought is what makes people unhappy, but, nevertheless, good results – "progress" – can be effected through false emotion. People who are so imperceptive that they do not even notice that some other people are starving may be persuaded by the equivalent of East Lynne to give money or open a club or whatever the rector's wife recommends. Nevertheless, "Look Back in Anger" is observation on the "Mrs. Dale's Diary" level only. Some people do certain things. Jimmy Porter "protests" by thumping <u>The Observer</u> with his fist. But the playwright is accepting something about <u>The Observer</u> and something about Porter's environment that it is by no means necessary to accept. Gwen Dale wins a prize in a raffle and puts it up for auction at the next sale of work. Those are the unnecessary ordinary things that people do – not significant except as very outward symptoms. It is certainly possible to make some kind of concoction out of those things, for a play, radio programme, film, novel, and it is quite likely to be remarked on for its "realism". Those works always seem to me to be pointing out something so obvious that it is incredible that there should be anybody who hadn't noticed them before, and yet there are always some who see them as a revelation.

    Observation that So and So does so and so can be very fascinating. But then to say that is just what life <u>is</u> – is that enough? No examination of it. I think it is all right simply to <u>present</u> something with no examination of it, but it cannot like that be presented as a profound analysis. You can present something as a surface pattern and it can be full of meaning or beauty or lots of things <u>as</u> a surface pattern, but it is not really revealing. Well, it is in a way, especially as to most people even the surface pattern has to be <u>revealed</u>, for they just don't see it. But what riles me, I suppose, is on-the-surface being claimed as revolutionary for the way they get below the surface, which is the thing they just <u>don't</u> do. In fact, the "Look Back In Anger" kind of play doesn't even <u>stare</u> at the surface. I don't even feel sure that it is a real surface. It seems a bit like somebody getting angry about something which is not there anyway.

I think if you stare and stare at the surface then eventually something immensely significant happens. Like watching Loch Ness until one day you <u>do</u> see a monster. Or like any kind of scientific investigation or observation. That's not what John Osborne is doing though. He <u>starts off</u> with an argument. He isn't really watching anybody, but nor does it seem like a real invention, a real work of imagination, a story. It's as if he was pretending that he just observed this "Slice of Life" as it happened. But it isn't at all a slice of life any more than "Mrs. Dale's Diary."

Or IS "Mrs. Dale's Diary" a slice of life? Is it just that the kind of life it is a slice of uncritically, is a life I abhor?

I think it is that those works accept a standard of false emotion as being a maximum. And what do I mean by "false emotion"? It certainly is very difficult to define what I mean, although I dare say you know really what I mean by false emotion. I mean a kind of laziness about feeling, too. Readiness to accept some kind of approximation.

"News for Scottish Farmers" and "The Fishing News" give me a feeling of relief. In a way. Though it's all part of it. And Roche Laboratories send a brochure about a new drug they have developed, the "successor to the tranquillisers", which even tames wild animals. It makes wild cats less aggressive, and domestic cats become more playful under its influence. And in children with "behavioural disorders" low dosage produces a general reversal of unacceptable behaviour. Aggressiveness is dramatically reduced.

"For the rapid, safe control of

> Tension – Anxiety – Agitation
> Phobias – Obsessions"

So they say.

People do such terrible things to other people and to animals, and then they want to be commended for it.

Goodness, all the <u>information</u> people want, and get! Much of it is presented in ways that, it seems to me, must be incomprehensible to anybody who has not studied the subject.

Then, people think you want solutions. They think you want it made easy. So they solve your problems for you. And they write those plays which will "move" you to start a club for ex-miners or invite drunkards to tea on Sundays or else which just smoothe you and say everything is all right, this is just how it all is, so nice, and we all have our troubles and the doctor's wife will get you to poach an egg, occupy you, you know, and that will do away with your grief.

Don't try to impose an order on it, for there will be an order in it as it comes, in an eventual way. Write it out and set it down, and place it in a bunch like picking roses. I always make the bunch in my hand as I pick the flowers, ready to set in the jar so. I don't like to make later "flower arrangements." There's a horrible hobby among housewives these days, called "floral art". I pick a bunch and then put it in water, in a jam jar or bowl or bottle or book or jug or pail. The selection came at the stage of taking it into my hand. I select when shooting. I edit in my mind while I shoot. I use most of my material. I am not really a writer or a student of literature, at least not in the usual male way of writer etc. All I am saying is that I am not male. The male standard isn't the only standard. It is neither higher nor lower but it is different.

The story of Gurrumpore started off by being written or starting to be written as a script for a documentary film which, it seemed to me, would be a useful one to be made about the War in the East, for the information of people elsewhere, especially in Britain, who thought that when the war was over in Germany the War was over. That means it must have been started between May 1945 and August 1945, at that time when Great Britain seemed to us to be happily relaxing, thinking it was all over, while in S.E.A.C it looked as if it would all go on for a very long time yet. It looked as if "at home" they weren't even bothering to send out any help for the Forgotten Army. I imagined that a documentary film about the actual life of units connected with the other war, out east, would make people interested. If more troops were not sent out it looked as if the war might go on for ever. "For ever". Years and years anyway. I thought I would write the script first and then offer it to the Crown Film Unit or to somebody concerned with making semi-official documentary films. As it now appears, the reason they didn't "bother" to send more troops out east after the surrender of Germany was perhaps just because the powerful people already knew about the atom bomb and that sooner or later the war would be ended by that. We out there of course did not know. All of us just working at one thing and another that we had been sent out to do could only see the war progressing in the same bitter way as before, going on and on and on, our friends preparing themselves for desperate attacks, entering enemy-held places by parachute, by glider, by long-range penetration in infantry columns, by sea. We were not preparing for the blank horror of the "atomic bomb" nor for the shameful relief that two of them finished the war at least for that time being.

In the fairly frequent local wars since then no one has used the Bomb.

The "Great Powers" keep it up their sleeve as a "deterrent", and practice with it in deserts and at sea and underground, developing it all the time. The two bombs that were dropped on Japan are quite old-fashioned now. The thing has gone beyond all sense and feeling.

It seems inevitable. What can people do? They go on. They keep trying for something more than before.

The rather journalistic documentary I had in mind as a stimulus to action was not necessary. I'm not sure that I even <u>wrote</u> any of it, but perhaps only thought about it. After the "victory" and the "liberation" everything and everybody seemed to be in such a muddle and there was such a mixture of bitterness, disappointment and ignorance about both the war itself and its results that I felt that a documentary record of one complete part of it would have a certain value and interest. Since the events were all over by then, and there was peace, it could not be a contemporaneous record but would have to be a work of fiction. Fiction of the kind called in cinema "documentary", with a set-up as near as possible to what actually happened, but nevertheless "acted", specially organised. The longer it took to write, the more the actual conditions were, naturally and obviously, changing, and the more fictional it had become. All the characters, the dramatis personae, were of course fictitious from the start.

As a screenplay the thing had some character and charm, but it was done without any professional knowledge of the cinema. So far as the subject is concerned, it led me to redeveloping it as a book and eventually to this dissertation. So far as cinema is concerned, it led me to writing more screenplays, to studying cinema, working out ideas connected with it, going to Rome to the Centro Sperimentale di Cinematografia, working in film myself, founding Ancona Films, making some short documentaries in Scotland, writing more screenplays for fiction films and meeting with fairly strenuous opposition to anything I have tried to do in cinema in Scotland.

Although I thought of Damsey as a garden I wouldn't really have made it into a garden (supposing I had had the possibility of doing so) because it is particularly wonderful as it is. I think now I wouldn't. Or I think sometimes now that I wouldn't. It's unusual green-ness is vivid in the Bay of Firth and it is perfectly in place. Gardened as I imagined it, it would be alien. Perhaps another type of garden would be more suitable, one that would be more of a surprise when you landed on the island. It belongs to Mr. Scarth and he keeps sheep on it. I may yet buy it, if I ever have the money, and make a garden of it. If it was left untended there would be sure to be people who would land and maliciously destroy as much as they could. It would be important not to have any fruit on it or anything that would tempt people to raid it for its produce. There are many types of garden it could be. The maximum might be to make something which could even after deliberate destruction still be something remarkable.

People have made "natural gardens" here and there in Orkney, for instance in the Hammers of Syradale. The effect is pungently nostalgic. There is this private place which is nevertheless open hillside, a burn up which anyone can walk. It gives me something the same feeling as a deserted house, but sharper. More painful, more deeply disturbing in some ways – but without a feeling of irritation, of resentment

I sometimes get from the croft house which has been left empty or from the closed-up mansion only visited for a month in the year. The maker of the garden left it there for me. The householders rejected their house. They should have pulled it down. It creates a bitter or sad wish to fill it up again and use it.

The you is sometimes quite an impersonal "you". It means "I" in a way. This is the "you" that teachers try to teach children not to use instead of "I". But people keep using it. Patients use it a lot. They say to the doctor, "You get a pain right there in your back", and they dunt the doctor's back to show where. But they don't mean the doctor gets a pain they mean they themselves get a pain. Perhaps they hope to transfer the pain by that "you". Or perhaps they hope to make it into a fictitious pain. (My "you" of that kind is fictitious, in a way.) They don't quite like to say, "I get a pain in my back" – perhaps for fear of tempting the Devil to fix the pain there as they say it. Perhaps they are trying to make the doctor understand it subjectively by saying "You get a pain." Perhaps that is what I am trying to do with my you – trying to make you experience being me. I don't like it when patients do it to me – when they poke me and say "that's where it is." You may resent my using that "you" that isn't really you.

Sometimes it may be a kind of modesty that makes one use this "you". "I know I'm not the only one with a pain." The English overdo it, and they overdo "one" used when they should say "I". It can be false modesty and used to put your opinions on to somebody else.

The vocabulary of the stonechat he wanted to study. And so he had to learn about sound recording. He has kindly brought some of his bird recordings for us today.

Having studied <u>any</u> subject, then at least you know what is involved in studying a subject. "They have so much energy", he said, of the Americans coming here to study or collect. Implying that we haven't. In a way it is quite lazy to go abroad to study and collect things. It may be a preparation for a later concentration of energy and actual work, but it is not in itself very energetic but is rather passive.

Whenever I feel fully that what I am for — what I am here for — is to write, and when I realise that, well, here I am anyway, I have this paper and pencil and table and I <u>can</u> just go ahead and do it, so long as I remain alive, and I needn't think too much of the economy (money economy) of the situation, but can just do it, then I have a weird feeling like happiness, which isn't quite happiness really but a kind of acceptance. It isn't that nothing else matters, but I have to do this anyway, <u>whatever</u>, and there it is, whatever else matters has to matter as well as this. Writing of course is <u>about</u> all the other things that matter, and that is how a kind of circular confusion may sometimes disrupt the acceptance or sometimes go with it. So long as the circle is in the desired direction so to speak. I'm all right, that must be it.

— *To Sit Down At A Desk And To Work* —

Some writers set themselves at it for a certain number of hours per day, and presumably they write for all of that time and then, when it is time for something else, stop. It may be that they are the real writers. I can't imagine myself writing like that, working like that. I think probably that kind of routine is dependent on being a man and having a wife or somebody at least to look after him. I have spent days, weeks, months, loafing – in a sense – but germinating, gestating, and then when I worked I just worked on and not to any timetable. The way I work must appear to be very lazy to an observer but it's the only way I can work.

In the short stories I wrote in 1956 the "plot" is something you infer. It happens outside the story, so to speak. You know about it from reading the story but it isn't told there and then, exactly. Something the same could be said of "The Lilywhite Boys".

People <u>all</u> sell their souls for a mess of pottage. All but the very few. It's probably the best thing to do, for it isn't really possible to be happy without the mess of pottage.

The terrible, evil thing perhaps is to sell your soul in order to provide a mess of pottage for <u>another</u> person. For that person wouldn't do without just because <u>you</u> didn't provide it for them. They'd get it all right, if that was their need. If you are one of the very few who need your soul, you must only have the mess of pottage if you can have it as well as your soul. That <u>is</u> possible, if rare, and I think it is necessary to go for that, that is to go through all the unhappiness and doing without until you can have <u>both</u>. Whenever there's a choice, choosing soul, until in the end you do arrive at the circumstance where it's both and there doesn't have to be a <u>choice</u> any more.

So perhaps people <u>are</u> stating a modest need when they say all they want is to be happy. They mean they'll be content with the mess of pottage and are quite prepared to hand over their soul for which they have no great need, for it, or even that their soul is small enough to be contained within the pottage. I used to laugh myself sick at that phrase which keeps cropping up in novels, of the young heroine (or hero) saying, "I don't ask a lot. I only want to be happy" – rather plaintive and meant to be very touching and innocent. For I felt well that's a hell of a lot to ask. To be happy!

But they mean they can be happy with mess pottage only, so why should anyone take their mean little can from them. If you can't be happy with that only, it's no use selling your soul for it. You may feel you'll be bitterly unhappy whichever you choose, because of doing without the other, but if you always choose soul each time it can't be both. I think you probably do or at least can reach both in the end. (So long as you don't mistake for soul what is really just pottage.) But if you sell your soul I don't know if there's any kind of trading where you get it back again. I don't know.

What artists in Scotland are suffering from is starvation. There is a giant leech sucking our blood. Everything the artist has to give – and not only his art – is gulped up regardless, into a great vacuum, all into the huge gut of those who go to the theatre to laugh uproariously at every "bloody" and "damn" and at "all the funny Scotch words" (-just for a giggle-) or who want pretty paintings for their drawing room walls. It's all a drawing-room and a gut and no work is of any value.

Nobody here has any curiosity about what's going on. All they want to do is collect antiques. They actually think they are being progressive when they say, "Scotland should sell itself." And then when I think about what all the writing is for – apart from the pleasure, or necessity, of just doing it – it only seems to be for all the ordinary people, to help them with their very ordinary lives. In a way, it leads to nothing. Is merely a sauce for the ordinariness.

Or else it is the only communication among the extraordinary.

There are so few that only through the poetry have you any chance of meeting the others. Those before and after as well as those present. The interstellar space is so huge, the distance is so great. Poetry brings the other and the distant into the present and the here.

Why do people always want it to be as it is somewhere else? I don't know. "There's no tradition of theatre in Scotland," they complain – meaning that therefore you can't do so-and-so and so-and-so that they do somewhere else. If there's no tradition, then you can do anything. That's how I feel. The scope is terrific. I like it that there is no Scottish film tradition. It has to be made yet – will come imperceptibly from the particular films which do get made. Those who want to work in a tradition should work in something there's a tradition of, in the country they belong to. There are traditions in Scotland that can be worked within and developed – in building, song, story-telling, dance, games events (gatherings) and other things. People all think it must be done in the form of somewhere else, that a theatre must be like a theatre, a concert must be a concert and orchestral symphonies are the only "real thing" in music. And pictures must be in galleries (or drawing rooms). Everything already at a museum stage in fact. Nowadays people want to begin with the museum.

All poetry is coitus. All writing is a life certificate. When it's real, I mean, not when it's fashionable. Fashionableness is the enemy. "Are you one of us?" Has been truck-driver, dish-washer, etc. etc., as always used to appear on the "About Our Contributors" page in magazines. Students (and then the English) have so much of that unreal fashionableness. Such a look they give you – like cows. I don't like false magic and false mystery; it is the insult to real magic and real mystery. Of course I used to get those mad impulses towards fashionableness too. The difference gets more and more recognisable. Anyone could lapse at any time, I suppose. Most people just get more and more fashionable or moral or whatever they call it. Their "lapses" would be more real than their usual behaviour.

People say that I say so and so or that I think so and so. This is dangerous. Somehow, when people get a second-hand opinion of what somebody else thinks I think, they believe it. I don't mean that this is true only of me. Somebody says, "So-and-So says such and such and thinks that it should all be done just so, as I'm telling you," and you get the impression that that is what the person says and thinks because of the importance given to it by repeating it. But the speaker may be quite mistaken, may even be lying, but more likely has just misunderstood and is passing on what he (she) thinks So and So said, making it maybe extra definite in order to express either a contrary or a similar opinion of their own.

Other people's interpretations of what I say or think are nearly always wrong. Quite mistaken. I don't mind them making their own interpretation and passing that on as their own, but that they pass it on as mine – that I don't like.

I wonder if by going to the Congo it would be possible to learn anything from the witch doctors about how to deal with evil. They seem to know about good and evil in a way that we don't. I wonder if it would be any help to know what they do. It's probably not so much doing as knowing. That is true in Medicine too. It's the knowing that counts. A different kind of knowing – but not altogether different. The patient pays the doctor for knowing, not for doing. The knowing whether to act and how to act is what matters. However, even "masterly inaction" must be performed with an appearance of "doing" or the patient will not believe in you. It is not necessary to feel false about pretence of that kind, because it is not ultimate pretence. Apparent, or superficial, mumbo-jumbo for the sake of ultimate precision. Drumbeating or anaesthetic to distract the attention while the precise treatment proceeds. It is necessary to be honest in your ultimate treatment, and not insulting with your drumbeating mumbo jumbo must be respectful to the patient, anaesthetics administered in humility to the conscious being.

I think there is no master, no authority, about the poetry to be written by women. It is no use consulting anyone or having it "criticised" by men or even male standards. Women critics tend to apply the male standards even more outrageously (to show they are not just women, so to speak). Men write the most utter bilge about Emily Brontë and about Emily Dickinson. They apply potty little standards and fail to recognise the immensity. Or they may recognise it and then demur, "but no, look at this and at this; it CAN'T be" and work out that because it is not like male poetry it is wrong. "Undisciplined" is one of the words they use, but they don't know what they are talking about there.

GO ON.

Growth. That's what interests me. I like to leave a verse rough and do it again. Repeat it afresh. The small changes wrought by oral repetition are pleasing. I don't see anything as ever finished. Men like to finish a thing and put their name on it. Married to them and preserved in glue. That's not what I mean really of course. I just said it.

Perhaps my reaction is a reaction against a whole modern trend about the sanctity of the written word, the written note. "What the author 'intended'". Nabokov and Menuhin were talking about improvisation in music and seemed to regret its passing. (But it's coming back, they said, hopefully. The influence of jazz on modern composers makes composers value improvisation by the performer.) All this ballad-collecting and notating of folk-songs destroys the ballads and songs because it cuts out the improvisation which is always done by the transmitter of the ballad. Pipe music is composed, I believe, with allowance for improvisation by the piper.

I used to believe in the other way, which I am now calling the male way. I used to think that even a film script should be written completely and precisely on paper before beginning to shoot. I was brought up in a very male manner, at least so far as my "education" was concerned. There was some self-defence involved too in undertaking a rather male kind of learning. If you didn't do that it was because you "couldn't" and made you <u>only</u> a woman". There can be a completeness in the script which yet allows for improvisation. Certain improvisations are inevitable if a performer is involved. No two performances can be exactly the same. If you can trust the performer it is better to be generous in allowing freedom within the framework.

It's lonely to be a woman writer. There isn't anyone to discuss it with.

I am a little afraid of elegance. It is so <u>finished</u>. I am uneasy with things which are complete. PERFECTION: the impulse BEING to smash it. Having got it complete and perfect, then break it to bits and start again. That isn't really my own impulse. My own impulse is not to break it but to leave it and start something else. I can't really quite understand people breaking up their own work, or anybody else's work. I like to keep starting afresh, but I don't like to break the things which are made. The need to smash things is probably a more male need. We depend on that male destructiveness to get things out of the way so that there will be <u>room</u> for new things.

The piece of paper should be as large as the floor, and the poem come on to it. On the floor is where to write. It has to come in words, word by word. In film you can have gasps and harsh sounds, any kind of wordless human noise that fits, as well of course as the non-human sounds, natural ones and unnatural, from musical to electronic. There's no electronic device for use in a poem on paper. The poem is further from the elements. It is another kind of formalization – simpler, in a way.

Political and moral movements can only lead to disaster of one kind or another. A "movement" through poetry is different. It is secret, and healing. This wholesome, anti-political and un-moral effect comes from ballad and song and dance and story as well as from highly developed literature and other art. Political and moral reformers may be well-intentioned, but they don't allow for the soul. They don't allow for either good or evil. All is just right and wrong in their minds and they think that on principles of right and wrong things can go forward.

DISCIPLINE

I might begin by finding out what it means exactly. Has it something to do with "disciple"? Its dictionary meanings are a bit removed from the sense I have of the word.

(People steel themselves against me. That's a kind of discipline too, I suppose.)

Discere, to learn. The words come from that – that is, both "disciple" and "discipline".

CHRISTMAS

And it wasn't a Christian country. It hadn't a tradition of Christmas from that point of view either. Neither the heaped fire and blazing log nor the church bells, the recurring legend of nativity, the gift-giving in honour of the Child. The carrying of gifts. Christmas presents. The Mess servants knew about Christmas presents in a way. They got tips at Christmas.

The gift-giving of Christmas is connected with a religion which extols charity. Charity came in with Christianity: that's how it appears. In any religion and in any art, only very few appreciate the real meaning of anything. Charity got corrupted, fouled, debased, like everything else. So that Christians <u>use</u> charity. It has become a sort of bribe, not what it really is or was. As a concept, charity is not a bribe. But Christians are people who like things cosy. The gifts are to buy favour of a very subtle sort.

The Christmas giving! Jo who was not a Christian saw the Christmas giving and geniality as something he hankered after with a "nostalgic" wish to possess that other tradition and at the same time an impatience with it for being so unquestioningly accepted as the right way to spend "Christmas". Mary saw the giving as a real token of love. Mary believed in love. Yet Mary was stern, could even be sentimental. Emlyn saw the gift-giving simply as gift-giving, with nothing behind it, a custom simply. Emlyn didn't examine the gift-giving, he took it as part of Christmas as a child does. Mary's mother used to save the more useless gifts she received, store them, and send them away again to somebody else the next Christmas. Mary laughed at that when she was home with her mother, but didn't quite like it, and she used to tease her mother that some year she would send a silly gift back to the person she got it from. It was all a sort of game to Mary's mother.

To Emlyn it was not a game or time. But he did not in the very least think of Christmas at the B.M.H. Gurrumpore in the same way as Christmas, just <u>Christmas</u>. Christmas at the B.M.H. might be something in itself, something different. Emlyn missed his home, but the B.M.H. was something too. He was twenty-four.

"I'm looking forward to a wonderful day of overeating," said Mary as she came in to breakfast.

"Merry Kismmiss," said the abda.

"Merry Christmas, abda," said Mary.

"Over-eating!" said the C.O. "I hope you have time for it."

The British Empire was founded on the Christian way of life, on gift-giving as bribery. The belief in charity leads to bribery becoming hidden. Without that belief, bribery is recognised and open. A recognised method. But the British believed in freedom from corruption. The Eastern people were perhaps wiser. They realised simply, without saying it, that gifts are bribes. All gifts are bribes. Acceptance of a gift is acceptance of a bribe.

All soldiers should be mercenary. It is more honest to fight for money than for someone else's cause. Fight in anger or to fight for money. To fight for right is very evil.

In writing about Christmas you could write about everything, as if it were a golden bough or an Irishman's wake. For it's all there. Some sort of information about the origin of the festival would be in order.

Research. And then it comes out of the lore deep in one's own mind too. As well as early associations, memories of the festival as played in one's own infancy. Christianity brought in something new. It was charity. Of course Christians have misinterpreted it. The giving they all use as being a form of bribery. I didn't exactly see it like that when I first wrote that chapter on Christmas. I said their liberality with gifts was a symbol of the giving they truly believed in. It's true it's right there in the religion, belief in giving freely. But most Christians are not religious Christians: they are Christians for a "Christian way of life". A sort of policy. Honesty is the best <u>policy</u>; that's what they think. If they give, they think, then they'll <u>get</u> in return. Giving for getting. That's their kind of giving. And it would be all right if they didn't make it out to be something else.

There's a fundamental mean-ness in certain people. Such people are never religious, I think, though they may be Christians. I think the world is infected with a pest of un-religious Christians. Faithful Christians, unwavering in their way of life, but nevertheless fundamentally un-religious. I am perhaps using religion to mean something it does not mean. I think really it only means what they make it mean, a way of life, a form, a creed, a policy. I don't know that there <u>is</u> a word for what I mean beyond that. <u>Morally</u>, charity need only mean do-as-you-would-be-done-by. Give, so that you can receive in peace of mind. Give to the poor so that you can feel morally comfortable. What about the poor, then? What are they supposed to feel? Grateful? Because you have given for the sake of your moral comfort.

It all seems to me very much deeper in than that. Giving freely and the response of free acceptance is more what I mean by charity.

The gift that is accepted with gratitude, or with a cheery sense that it is only one's right after all, is an article of trade, not a gift. Trade is all right, but <u>call</u> it that. It is not the same thing as charity. Charity is quite rare. Perhaps very few people are capable of it. Perhaps nobody. It is a manner of receiving as well as a manner of giving. A manner – but more than a manner. A magic.

A magic of receiving and giving. Magic is perhaps the word I intend, more than <u>religion</u>. The magic is what people refuse to have, refuse to believe in. They use the word for jiggery-pokery. A poet ought to be able to accept charity without having to feel <u>entitled</u> to it. My own religion consists of nothing more than saying IT IS SO. "So" being whatever is. Not that it is <u>so</u>, as I say it, but that it is so, however it is. It is so. It hasn't always been quite like that with me. I tried to deny things or to change things, morally, and when I write about the Christians and others I'm really only vociferating about my own faults, past, present and feared.

I hate smugness. I hate self-righteousness. Saying so makes me smug and self-righteous. Am I then smug and self-righteous?

These questions are unanswerable. And what I really mean, now, is that they do not matter. Everybody is, everybody isn't. And yet – NO. For that is my older, tolerant way, I mean my younger tolerant way. Older, I see I have to admit that some people are just <u>awful</u> – for me. Saying so doesn't condemn them, for I am not God, not even a judge. They are all right, they can live their own lives, but they are not for me.

Well, there's no need to be rash in your opinions, lass. You can take twenty more years to finish this book. It'll all come out slowly and won't exactly make SENSE in the end, but listen, reader, heeder, just read it, just listen. Any magic there may be has not much to do with the sense. There again, what I mean by magic is not what everybody means. But there's no such thing as everybody meaning the same by a word or phrase. Sometimes a gesture.

The Italian hand gestures are a language. You <u>learn</u> the gestures. Certain ones mean certain things. Not like the vague spontaneous hand gestures I make.

Travellers' Tales. When I was in India. Oh, you were in India during the War. Did you like it?

Mi dica, signorina, non sono molto freddi. Gli uomini inglesi? Di quale religione, Lei? Sposata? Fidanzata? Perché non? Di quale città viene? E gli nomini inglesi, non sono freddi freddi? Mi dispiace per le donne. Per Lei mi dispiace. Se non è cosi, meglio! Quanti anni ha, Lei? Va in vacanza? Le piace Italia?

Non piove mai. In Inghilterra, invece, il cielo sta sempre coperto, sempre coperto – vero? Ma si, si, mi l'hanno detto.

Caffeine, ephedrine, benzedrine all have a rather excessive effect on me. Constrict my arterioles noticeably, causing trembling, edginess, headache, chest pain, nosebleeds. I depend on tea and coffee for stimulation. Yet I do all right without them too. It could be just habit. Yet I wrote a lot of poetry, sustained at high doh by black coffee drunk frequently and not very much to eat. After some months of it I felt exhausted. Ill. Extra systoles and tired out. And fear. I was terrified. Of the witches. And with good reason.

People don't look on what's written as a book until it is published. All are completely taken with the present-day convention that "if it's any good a publisher will take it." GOOD. Good music. Good books. We are such judges, we educate people.

What IS a book, anyway? Something written, or something published? A tale told of Shem and Shaun. A treatise on the excretion of 17 ketosteroids by rats under conditions of controlled radiation by nuclear waste products.

A story can be resolved or analysed into subjects and each subject written about. There can be a written work in the manner of a documentary film, full of authentic detail. The story part, about some people, might be used as a way of stating some generalisations; the same thing is done in a moral tale, or a play of ideas. People can be used to give life to certain mechanisms which are only of interest to the extent that they affect or are used by people. In ordinary conversation you keep saying a thing in a small variety of ways and the sum of it gives some notion of what you mean.

And then at a certain point you get up and go out for a walk.

Some of them felt they couldn't really know what it was unless they had been there. Unless they had Been There they knew they couldn't know. Been in action. Been at the front. You can see from the front what you can't see from the back. On the stage, in the limelight, you see what is going on right around you; you are part of it. From further back you see the whole action, in a way, in a non-participant's way. You can say that you see it in perspective. This means you see it a bit smaller, down those parallel lines gradually meeting towards the horizon.

– What you know as an experience and what you know as an observed fact. –

Some people just live. They just simply live, accept things and live it all out. This includes grumbling. Grumble about the immediate discomforts. Bones in the fish. YOU put it right! Somebody else do it. I grumble. I live. I'm here. Where else could I be?

In that simplicity of living, death is all part of it. Nothing is tragedy, or everything is tragedy.

We write stories about our ancient homeland even after fifty years trading in Africa. Harald the Webbed and the boatload he met off Anglesey Diamonds and in the Veldt. Buttons. Kettles. The African Story, of exploration by the white man. I've never heard an African African story. I suppose there are stories, unless stories are all an Indo-European phenomenon. Dance. Song. Statuary. Dress. There must be stories too. Or maybe not.

The story of a man out in a Column in a jungle is simply his day to day existence. There's no story at all. The story is that he went and he came back. They didn't even achieve anything. But they went and they came back. From war to war it will be much the same. Unless it's all left to long-range missiles and the nucleus-disintegrating bombs. Long-range meaning thousands of miles' range, and the bomb splitting the intimate structure of the infinitesimal particle.

And what is the glamour? What IS the glamour, exactly? For there's glamour, no doubt about that. It's in the very word, Chindit. I feel it yet.

And in another twenty years of writing will there have been another war? It seems so certain it seems a stupid question.

"Love your enemies" is nonsense. But it is necessary to be sure who <u>are</u> your enemies. There are not so very many of them, but undoubtedly you have enemies. Anyway, I have enemies. You know them when you see them. I think if we were to get clearer to ourselves exactly what we mean by an enemy and then begin to get clear what we are to do about enemies, then this might have some effect on what wars are and even on whether there are to be wars or not. The furthest people have got so far is a concept of "avoiding wars". We must avoid war. So they say. There's war, but we must avoid it. That's what they say. Something like that. Just a political manoeuvre. Avoid war.

Politics is a feeble pattern of life, I think. That's what I think. We have to get something beyond politics. That's why I find it necessary to concentrate, to be here, simply, that is to be engaged in poetry.

Poetry, magic, witch-doctoring. These are the only lanes of approach to people. I don't believe anything can be done by politics. Or, at least, things can be done on a sort of plumbing level, but world wars or not world wars should not depend on the state of the plumbing. I like plumbing to be efficient, of course.

The playwright, say the critics, has not given us a solution to the problem he poses. In tones of gentle reproach. He might have put a solution into his play, the mean thing! He failed us, he didn't give a solution. Shaw's weakness: no solutions. And why can't the doctors cure so-and-so, I frequently hear people ask in peeved tones. You doctors, you're no good, you haven't got a cure for this disease I'm taking the trouble to mention because I happen to know someone with it and the doctors can't put it right, they just can't, now they ought to be able to do that, <u>surely</u> to goodness. What are they for? – But I'm all against all experimentation with animals, what's called vivisection. No, they must not do any experiments. But they ought to know the cure for everything or they're no good. What do they want to experiment on poor helpless animals for? They're doctors, aren't they? They should know.

Well, I mean, just <u>know</u>.

Like knowing you in bed, my dear? Should I know how to cure tuberculosis like knowing your erect self deep in my dark cavity? When all's said and done, it is not unlike that in a way. But there was at some time the saying and the doing, staining of the spit, manipulation of coarse adjustment, fine adjustment, oil immersion and, long before that, culture, sub-culture, post-mortem examination of dead humans who had been sick and yes, experimental animals deliberately infected, deliberately killed.

I don't know what witch doctors do. I wish I knew. Perhaps they have had to at some time drink lion's blood or eat human flesh, to give them strength. Strength is needed, for healing.

I have to calm down and be twenty years about it. I have to calm down, concentrate, emanate aphorisms from a hidden cave. Euphorisms, more likely.

Try making coffee over a wood fire in the open in a small blackened pot given to you long ago by Captain (Miss) A M. Woods R.A.M.C. in Simla, and you'll feel oddly isolated, spinsterish and euphoric in a detached way. Sadly euphoric. The sad euphoria of cave life, of yogi existence. Not what a woman would choose at all at all as her idea of heaven. This is the male nirvana the ministers want to force us into. I don't like it. I don't want the black coffee elevation, levitation, the spiritual absenteeism. I'm here, alive, responsive.

I think the witch-doctors are wiser. They do it with blood. Blood must be there. Full-blooded. For what the evil witches try to do is to suck our blood. They suck your blood and swallow it, only to drain you and destroy you. The doctor needs power over that. Enormous strength.

Dr. Jenner of Liverpool noticed that milkmaids' faces were rarely disfigured by smallpox, at a time when the disease was common in England and most people had pockmarks. What was eventually understood was that girls working with the cows got from the cows the lesser illness of cowpox and this made them immune to the smallpox. Infection with the one disease gave them immunity not only to it but also to another similar but more severe disease. From this knowledge he devised the technique of vaccination. Lymph is taken from a calf with the cowpox and is introduced into a small wound less than skin-deep in a human arm or leg or anywhere else; the person gets a miniature localized dose of the cowpox and, from the body's reaction to that, immunity to smallpox. The techniques used in this cycle have been refined considerably since the time when it was first proved effective. It is now more precise and, also, leaves no scar.

Smallpox (variola) is very rare in Britain now.

A few calves, however, have to be given the cowpox (vaccinia).

It is not so bad for a calf to have the cowpox as for you or me to have the smallpox. You could go into this more fully, find if that is really so. Finally it is a matter of opinion. Do you say so or don't you.

Christmas Day means a very definite thing for most people. It is seen in a certain pattern, and no other pattern will do. Until, as sometimes happens, it is discarded whole, and after that Christmas never matters again.

The food is important. The constituents of the ritual feast should not vary very much. Certain elaborations and refinements only. An art practised within specific limitations.

There are certain old winter festivals – Bacchanalia – Saturnalia – in which the social order is reversed. There is something in old English custom too, a play where there is a Lord of Misrule. It really emphasizes the order to have it all turned topsy-turvy as a game, or at a feast. It wouldn't be funny, it wouldn't be fun if you didn't believe in the order. The Army, for Christmas has the men being served by the officers. In a sense, the men are always served by the officers. The officers are not called "the men", although they are men. There is something quite loving about the words "the men" as applied to soldiers. The rulers are in the public service. All in authority are servants. The postman. The judge. Poets even – suicidally, <u>serve</u>. Not intentionally, not purposefully. BUT. The higher the more complete the service. An absolute king is an utter servant. To escape the state of serving, of being bound, we try to escape our function. Attempt to <u>abdicate</u>. Or abdicate, in fact. It's useless. It is impossible, and therefore it is useless to try. Royalty is unflensable, not to be sloughed off.

How, even, did the word "royalties" come to mean the money compensation an author gets for his book, a playwright for his play performed? Did some clever rascal of a word-inventor see the association of ideas? There's not an exact analogy, but an undercurrent of association, quite sly.

Flattery of royalty. "Truly regal", they said of the queen in the dowdy humdrum new dress she wore for her sister's wedding.

The poet in his ultimate service, which is service not to the order as it is but to the next order, is a rebel, and the rebel is a servant in the manner of rulers not in the manner of obedient followers. This doesn't matter except just that it has to be seen and allowed. But allowed by poets themselves only, perhaps, I don't know; it may be that <u>allowing</u> of poets prevents the existence of poets or prevents the development of poets. These are things I don't know how to work out and I don't know if it is possible to work out. We just have to go ahead and DO it. It is not even possible to know what the new order is that is being worked towards. Political reformers invent a theoretical system and then try to manufacture it with <u>people</u>. It never works. You don't know what your children will be like, however carefully you may choose the other parent and however judicially you may "bring them up". They are themselves. It's impudence to be proud of them or to be ashamed of them. Inevitable, but impertinent.

 The poet's poems are part of a new order which he doesn't know about yet, and once that order is, it will have to be broken of course. The value of it is in its evanescence, even in its futility.

 Abstract words are so handy. You just set them down and there they are. You can say anything you like with them, speak seeming rubbish which contains science or make solemn pronouncements which are rubbish.

 Why should anybody grudge having got any particular thing from somebody else? No need, on the other hand, to be bound by it. Give and take is trade. Give and take is also response. That is more. It can also be quite absentminded, thoughtless, just <u>given</u>, just <u>taken</u>. That is charity.

 Every year there is a record for Christmas parcels and, worse still, for Christmas cards. Everybody thinking up large lists of people to send tokens and symbols to, and the Post Office coping, all very proud of it. A record. Meaning more than ever before. The thing has got out of hand. I've known people who have to be very careful in their selection of article type "Christmas present", not to send back by mistake to the same person they got it or its replica from last year some little monstrosity or obscenity of powder puff in special container, or novelty notebook. The fun is the sending. The fun is the unwrapping of parcels. The getting of rubbish through the post. All a jolly game of Post-man. The shops are full of the seasonal tumours. Buy it, pay for it, parcel it up and send it away. It's from YOU. A PRESENT. What is this article? That? That's a Christmas Present. Don't you know a Christmas present when you see one?

I wish I didn't.

Even the toys seem monstrous nowadays. There are no real toys any more. The children get scale models, working replicas, and "educational toys" like I.Q. tests.

But you can always give books. Or money.

Money is the most Christian present of all, for money seems to me the most Christian present of all, for money seems to me the most Christian thing there is. Money might have been invented for Christians it suits them so well. Christians love money. It makes them feel pure.

In the tropics, the solstice is not in itself so noticeable as it is in the North.

Midwinter

Where the sun sets in midwinter
It shines up the south-pointing passage of Maeshowe

And enters warmly at ground level the big stone chamber
    so deeply dark for the rest of the year.

The single standing stone in the field out there is a
    little to the west.
West again is the group of huge standing stones,
And the sentinel,
And the Ring of Brodgar, great stone circle.

No wonder the early inhabitants of the young islands
Raised monoliths.
I would have set up stones too
For such an event
As the sun going down behind the hills of Hoy
And then, while it's away, turning,
So that next day it sets a little further west,
And day after day a little further west and
    a little further north,
Until in the long midsummer days
Which have only twilight instead of dark
The sun going down almost in the north
Merely dips and rises –
But turns again,
Rises always a little further east and south,
Sets a little more west and south.

Oh, anyone at all would have made a circle,

Trailed new-cut heavy stones from anywhere
– From far away –
Monstrous stones needing many men to lug them,
And have raised them upright, pointing to the sky,
To stand with shadows sloping
And signify
The mystery of the sun's progress.

A calendar is a religious object. It shows belief in the repetition of certain natural events. By observation of what IS, there has been devised the calendar. Nowadays, numerals and month-names and names for days of the week. At one time, circles of tall up-ended stones on a flat plain, – objects of veneration, marvels. A kind of church, or calendar. We know when the moon is going to rise again and when it will be full, by looking up the paper. We know how long it is till Christmas. How many days. We know how many years old we are. We know by knowing a child's age when the child should go to school and when school is no longer compulsory by law. After a girl reaches the "age of consent" she may marry. Before that, it is rape for a boy or a man to love her "carnally". It can only be called sexual intercourse and rape before that. Assault. But she knows when she is sixteen and then it is all right. That's in this country. In other countries girls may marry much younger, have children, and it is not rape at all. Nothing of the kind! It's marriage. Then again there's the age of twenty-one. You know when you're twenty-one, and at that age certain privileges come your way. By the law of England, the law of Scotland and the law of many other countries we call western countries. For all these things it is very important to know what a year is, how it is counted, and to have made a count of the years that have passed between such and such a previous time and this time now.

Before all reckoning there were the geological eras. Since then, in "pre-historic" times there was reckoning, by all appearances, but not the sort of records which we nowadays understand. So we don't know just for how long exactly who did what, and those are the things we do so love to know about ancestors and enemies. A tale told of Shem and Shaun. With dates and references. It gets a form about it, becomes a "subject", an entity, this story, the knowledge of the facts and the times.

Christmas is the northern festival. Christmas is the family festival. In the Mediterranean lands Easter is a more prominent feast. Death and resurrection. The turn of the year. It's the equinox, the spring and the sprouting that they notice further south. Here in the north, the days just <u>beginning</u> to lengthen is what we watch for and rejoice about. The light is coming back! Unto us a child is born. The star moves on. In all the snow and ice, there is birth, and a new year. The days are getting longer. It is already noticeable just two or three days after the solstice.

Protected together against the winter cold and dark there is the household. There is a religious significance in surviving the winter, whatever your religion may be. In the long hall of old Norse establishments there wasn't just father, mother, two children and a Christmas tree, but uncles, aunts, foster-parents, grandparents, servants, warriors, an idiot or two and a great many children, brothers, sisters, cousins, half-brothers, half-sisters, chosen sons of exceptional servants. The men seem to have spent a great part of the winter being drunk.

That's them off on their spring forays

The equinox excited the Vikings out of their winter stupor,
Made other lands seem desirable,
Made the roving sea and the turning world all a prod, a
    birch upon them, an unknown waiting welcoming motion
    to receive them:

And in they went
With the prows of their vessels high and proud,
Their weapons clanging against their shields,
With the swift sides of their long ships entering between
    the lips of the water
And at speed rushing –
Yelling off to fight the Irish.
Off they went:
A voyage with life wagered, death won, by many of the company.

And what of Ingebjorg at home? – is what I always think.
What of the women digging, ploughing, sowing, reaping through
    the months of their pregnancy?
I always think of them,
With their men away all the summer,
Fighting,
Raiding,
And the farm to mind, calves to rear, sheep to clip, the
    scanty grain to tend and harvest, ale to brew

And a baby to be born.
The level day and night
Was too much for those exploring men
And the dream of the deepest sea in their eyes
Took them spinning down the coasts,
Ripping out into the ocean,
Conquering, drinking, raging, singing and composing verse,
While they sought in the motion of all the earth and of
    the sea upon the earth, –
The sun's swing and the moon's swing and
The vivid gales and the flooding tide of the time of even
    days and nights, –
Some secret
Or some prize.

I think of the women's eyes seeking too, as they waited,
In the movement which was all around them and within them
– Limbs stirring in the lower abdomen and lengthening of days –
    of days –
Something else besides anything the men could bring home.

In the very midwinter they had a feast – Yule. Even before the Vikings raided and settled in Scotland there must have been a feast then. Jews and Moslems can enjoy all the fun of Christmas without it having for them the any religious significance for them. Like a European attending an Indian puja. Or those American folk-tourists making sure they <u>mustn't</u> miss Puck Fair <u>this</u> time, in County Kerry.

In India the soldiers felt there was something missing at Christmas. It was the dark. We of the North need our annual retreat into the dark, because we are used to it. We live on a swing. Away out into the light, away back into the dark. We develop manic-depressive psychological states, perform wonders and then relapse into the deepest depression. Towards the poles you feel the "stishie o' earth in space". Near the equator, there is simply steady revolution under the sun, monotone of sunshine relieved at regular everlastingly equinoctial intervals by the cool hours. You can be so sure of the sun that you can sleep through the sunniest hot hours and keep some of the cooler time for being awake. Northerners don't sleep in the sun when they are in the north. Building of buildings to keep the sun away seems a wonderful thing to have to do instead of developing architectural ingenuity to build "sun traps". "The delightful courtyard of this charming house is a perfect sun trap." To think that there are places where such a construction would be positively deadly!

The whole conception of "cosy" belongs to the bleakness of cold and not to the bleakness of heat. The scorched dry plains are bleak. Sympathetic magic. The candles on the Christmas tree. Nowadays they never use candles, they're too dangerous, but small electric bulbs called fairy lights, sometimes fixed so as to go on and off automatically. It would be hopelessly out of place in the regions where the sun is as terrifying as the sea. The sun is to be placated in the sizzling centres of continents. It is as powerful as the wind and the cold and the ocean are here. A festival with little spouts of water and gentle manufactured breezes would be unnecessary in the winter here, for we know we can be sure of rain and cooling wind. But the manufactured lights, the fire, the table of harvest meats are needed to encourage the light and the heat back again, so as to give us another ripe harvest.

The time will come when they'll be desperately collecting the lore of the witch-doctors for fear of losing it forever. These years, now, however, they are still busy trying to stamp it out and supplant witch-doctors with hospitals. After a time, they will realise that the witch-doctors really know something, perhaps about good and evil, which modern medicine hardly takes into account at all. I think that doctors take it into account, but Modern Medicine as taught in teaching hospitals and medical schools doesn't quite. It's there, and they acknowledge it's there, but it's not quite mentioned, or mentioned only with a laugh. Not always an irreverent laugh. The great chiefs in the huge hospitals acknowledge its presence and transmit the secret knowledge to those of their students who are capable of it. But if it is a secret knowledge, not spoken of aloud, referred to only obtusely and with silence.

The "spiritual healers" who specialise in laying on of hands seem like only cranks, and so they are, for that is by no means all although it is part of it. Do they think we doctors don't "lay on hands"? An examination is in part an examination and in part a laying on of hands. Not consciously such in a willed way with pious eyes to God, but nevertheless a transmission of health, sanity into the struggling tissues. But they expect you to do it ninety times in a morning. That is just out and out impossible. It is too exhausting. In a careful examination of a patient by a doctor there is a great deal besides scientific assessment of phenomena; but you can't possibly do it with everyone who comes in. So we hand out the old routine. That's all that most people want anyway. I don't know why they go so often to the surgery. It's like smoking. They have a need for the non-intense attention, the handing out of what they request. And you get your money too for the many who have to, to satisfy the law, come in and get the small note, the signed certificate to say yes your knee is still swollen and it is reasonable for you not to work yet.

"The shaman pupil crushes and eats the sun-bee."

I look forward to the time when the negro races will be dominant. And I don't want to try and pretend to be one of them as some "whites" seem to want to do, impossibly. I'm all for the Africans taking over and having it their way. I imagine they'll leave us to be Scots here in Scotland, but even if they don't, even if they try to impose their religion and their ancient African laws upon us that's OK by me. It only makes me sad to think that the ruling Africans are likely to be "westernised" ones, Christians and what not. Marvellous men, these recently arisen African rulers, but it's a pity they are Christians. (No doubt the mission schools helped them greatly in their early education.) Why does everyone want to be "coloured"? I'll stay as I am, for I can't do otherwise. Allow the negroes their simple superiority. No need to try to be one. You can't.

Indians, Malayans, Chinese, Japanese, – the Africans will beat them all, and we'll all be non-blacks. But I'm not jealous, only wistful. I am what I am. It would be nice to be an African inheriting Africa. But it's all right in Scotland too. I'll stay here. (Stay here where I belong.)

It is time I am interested in how my mind works. It may even be my chief study. But I'm not so sure that I hold study to be a main part of existence. Not the main part.

Existence itself.

Existence itself is what is the main thing about existence.

You see I marvelled at those women in the long white tents attached to a cap on their crowns, with only an eye-slit so that they needn't trip and fall. How <u>could</u> they do it? How could they tolerate it? How <u>possible</u>? And yet, how, it seems to me, perhaps purdah is the ideal condition of life for a woman. In purdah a woman can develop herself. She is not at odds with the world. She is kept, in secret. I think, if there is love then, purdah is ideal. Without love it must be intolerable. (But then, with love <u>anything</u> is ideal). The security and peace of purdah. The convention. The form. (I defied convention. NO, I didn't. Convention was never offered to me. It was decided BY OTHERS from my earliest infancy that I was unsuited for convention. I was set outside it. It must have been something in <u>me</u>. And were they wrong or were they right? I became terrified of security – or terrified, I suppose, of an illusion of security, knowing security itself was not for me.) (I was seen to be at odds. It did not originate with me. The elucidation of it did not originate with me. Every suggestion or confirmation of it made me angry.) It would be so sweet to be within purdah. So sweet to concentrate and develop. <u>Solitude</u> is no good for this. There must be the man. The essence of purdah is that there is a man. A woman alone is worthless.

In English, "Machiavellian" is used to mean "diabolical". In Italy, Machiavellian is presented as a great political thinker and writer. He is presented as part of Italian literature. He is not cynical. It is English to say that to remark on the things he remarks on is cynical. He simply points out certain things, certain inevitable results of certain actions, but not <u>cynically</u>. He is no more cynical than Freud, for instance. But people will use "Freudian" too as if Freud was a cynic and not an earnest student. Neither Machiavelli nor Freud was saying "Look how rotten people are that this is what they do!" No, they were simply pointing out how relatively constantly certain events or actions led to certain results. Machiavelli observed how political manoeuvres took place: he wasn't either advising them or condemning them. Freud observed rather how occidental events affect human behaviour.

Has Christianity been a good or an evil influence on civilization? This question would take a lot of debating, would be impossible to decide upon. It is not possible to know how things would have gone if there had not been Christianity. Anyway, it was inevitable, an unavoidable development in the countries it developed in.

China. India. Japan. What has it meant to them not to have Christianity so rife as we have it here? Their civilisations do not seem so very different. Africa is different, and Africa we persist in calling undeveloped, un-advanced, as if the only advance, the only progress must be to be more like us. Parliamentary democracy was a good idea compared with what went before, but it seems to have got into a dead end. There may be some more real some more human way of managing things, which perhaps Africans may yet teach us, if we allow them. Sixty years ago they hadn't even got the wheel, she said of Kenya, meaning to point out how backward. Mechanisation is a sign of progress. But there may be other people than us who will develop in a way more wonderful than mechanization. Who won't need mechanization.

I work with a camera. It's mechanical. And I transplant on to a screen images which seem to move and perform, because of the physiological state of affairs called persistence of vision. By selection of subject and of recording material I get variation of colour and movement on the screen which amounts to a dance and a drama and other things as well, and the doing of all this and linking it with recorded and reproduced sounds too to emphasise the dance is one of the many things people do which is called an art. It is something made. It is a new creation, or creature, say. An entity. I made it. Or somebody made it. It is responded to. And in responding to it you respond to whoever made it.

The most I can do is be here. What people are is more important than what they do. Nobody ever forgives me anything. Except the children. They do. The thing that's really wrong with present day society is that it makes it very difficult to accept charity. I believe in charity, from both sides. Both in receiving it and in initiating it. How can you say that there is any difference between a civil war and any other kind of war? Or, rather, that every war is not a civil war? There isn't any kind of war that is not a civil war, certainly not <u>now</u>. At the time the people from somewhere else might have seemed altogether different. It is all a question of what you mean by an enemy. What is an enemy? Who are enemies?

There ARE enemies: I used to think there weren't.

Anything about military strategy bores me. I wonder really what Christ meant when he said, "Love your enemies." We Christians have taken it to mean that there are no such things as enemies. But that is not necessarily what he meant. Whether or not, I have to decide and you have to decide and politicians have to decide what to do about enemies.

A <u>command</u> to love is in any case a bit beside the point. Love me! Will you? Love thy neighbour as thyself. Go on, love him. Covet not. As a commandment, that is out of place too. Kill, steal, commit adultery are all acts – dependent on feelings, but in themselves acts. It is possible to command against the act but it is useless to command against the feeling. Thou shalt not love. <u>That</u> is what is so ridiculous. And equally so is, Thou shalt not hate. Thou shalt not act upon thy love and Thou shalt not act upon thy hate is what they really mean.

I think that what people inwardly believe is that the crime is in the act but that the sin is in the feeling.

Sinful hatred. Wicked murder.

Sinful love. Wicked adultery.

I don't think that either love or hate is ever sinful. Adultery is by no means necessarily wicked. I believe murder is wicked, but it is by no means always judged to be wicked. Judicial murder seems to be more deeply wicked than angry murder. That is that execution is more foul than passionate killing. When a murderer, murders, his crime is more terrible when he does it judicially. Judgement is in itself a crime, whether it leads to punishment or reward. The kind of murder which is done in "cold blood" because such and such a person has to be eliminated, for a purpose of other people's, seems worse than murder done in anger or hatred. The kind of murder that Peter Manuel committed, killing quite unknown people against whom he had no feeling whatsoever because he had a grudge against the <u>police</u> is something the same kind of thing as political murder or war murder, but brought in to a personal level.

Duty and honour. Those words dog me. I am not very fond of duty or honour, whether done to me or extracted from me.

To do something out of duty.

To do something for somebody's honour or for my own honour.

Neither thing seems to me very much of a thing. It's all right;

there are worse things — but it is by no means the most. Lofty ideals — honour and duty. So they say. But I don't think so. NOBLE. It is the idea of service again. The noble patriot, dying for his country's honour, killing out of duty to his country. Gentlemanly behaviour. Honour of a gentleman. Duty to society.

Aristocracy. The selected few. You see, I think there is an aristocracy. There is a best. And eventually, in a way, the best rule. And to the extent that one is "best" or has "best" in one, one mustn't allow this to be overcome and beaten by demands for duty or, worse still, silent expectation of duty.

And in the end everyone serves.

What I must not give in to is the people who want me to serve them exclusively. They want to make a fool of me, as if to say, "Oh yes, you, you're doing nothing, you could be very handy to me," and then get me to "help them out." What a damned cheek! Presented as them being fearfully generous to "offering me a home" and all sorts of other things that I don't want, lovelessly proffered like that. "You could help me out," they say in their patronising tones, conferring a great favour, "it would please me." And then if you don't help them they are even more patronising. "Oh well, of course, I can manage, even if it half-kills me." So you're then made to seem the kind of person who will allow them to half-kill themselves and not raise a finger. And they are puzzled. For they think you are "not like that really." And they can't make it out at all. So you get a cloak of dishonour. The worse, according to them, because you "needn't be" so dishonourable. You really "know better". I think I just have to accept this dishonour. In any case, I prefer it to honour. There are some things about honour that I like and purr under, but it is disabling. It disables me from doing and being.

Honour gets into you and you adjust your whole being and action to it. Yet, people know what you are, really. In some sort of way they know.

Whenever it is made reasonable it becomes meaningless. The only thing is just to do what you know about, without calculating the future or worrying about honour one way or the other. Know in the inherent way of knowing, I mean. If I "justify" this for other people it's to satisfy them, not to satisfy me. <u>They</u> want an "explanation". There is none, but sometimes a justification suits them not so bad. It is not a scornful thing to give them either, because I know they don't take it as a full explanation but just as something said, something to say. It doesn't leave them in the lurch, they feel, like saying nothing.

Everything in the same book from now on. It all has to go together. It is all for the same book. No separation of one thing from another, of poetry from fact, of documentation from speculation, of story from anything that is not a story. It's all a story. History loves those notebooks and jotting-lists with the price of salt cod in 1763 or the hour at which Mrs. Thrale took her dinner. The story of just exactly what some individual was doing at the hour and minute when the disaster took place is enthralling for later generations or even for people at a greater distance. (Time is distance, size is distance, says Jean Cocteau.)

What exactly are "future generations"? I won't see the benefit of this, but you all will, said my grandfather Isbister. What a nerve! My mother thought it very touching of him. But he didn't know about the whisky fire which there was to be in February of this year. Perhaps it won't affect my dividend, perhaps it will. There would be no dividend at all for me if it wasn't for my grandfather's actions in his lifetime. If he hadn't done what he did he would have done something else. But he didn't know there would be me. He was thinking of his own sons and daughters and a legacy they would get from him, or thinking of a firm he was founding, as a thing in itself. He was thinking of the future, but not exactly about me, because he couldn't know there would be me and that I would in my middle years become dependent on an income from the fees paid for the storage of tobacco in Glasgow. It's all just chance. Here is this money and I can if I choose simply stay put and WRITE.

There are tugging alternatives – duties, and speculations. BUT. There is this possibility that I CAN now be here, just be, and write. For future generations.

I don't know what it is all about. I haven't a clue, really, to that, but what it is I can try to gather, or point at, rather, so that the orbit is illuminated, the form is illustrated by a form, and the assurance of all being one and at one comes from the similarity of the poem to the atom, of the galaxies to the sun which is nearest to us, and of any one construction to any other construction. Some people find this depressing – that "it's all the same." That I can construct a poem and it is like a blood corpuscle – then that is God. Not "I" am God, but just that there IS, there is a state of being, and this in itself is what I mean by God. They always get it right from time to time, and then it becomes corrupted and made extraneous. Jehovah, the great I AM was momentarily utterly all of it, but all too soon he became Jehovah the Just God. He became He. Is it a he or a she? Well, it's a dud.

Moses discovered a God and it was a revelation to him. But in no time it had to be used for politics. You no sooner discover God than you are tempted to use it as a political leader, tempting people to be "good" or "evil" as the case may be.

I believe in good. I believe in evil. But I don't believe in right and wrong.

There was a woman who for me was the explanation of evil and became for me an embodiment of evil, but really she was no different from practically everyone else in the world. Just an example. An example of utter ordinariness. Almost any utterly ordinary person can be seen as good or seen as evil. It depends how you take them, how you meet them. But everybody is not utterly ordinary. I think not. It is all a question of size. And size is distance, Jean Cocteau says, referring to the material size of material things. All is matter. Or nothing is matter. "All is flux", somebody has said, famously. Tides and ionization and love. Worship and business and government.

I love to see the edge of the sea washing in wave by wave, wetting a little more of the rock each time or leaving a little more of it dry. Each wave being of a formation, recognisably similar and yet completely different each from each. You can sit watching the sea for hours on end, as people sit fishing on the bank of a river. They are not really fishing, they are listening to the river. And golfers go round the course, making a calendar or sundial of it. The golf course is the degenerate descendant of the standing stones. Nowadays everything is turned into a "sport". Sport when it is an art form is valid. Or when it is pastime. But what when it is moral? Sport is made so moral, like money. It begins to seem wicked and obscene because of that.

I never learned much of what ayurvedic medicine consists of. I mean that poetically speaking I learnt nothing of it. Just that an Indian A.D.M.S. admitted as a patient to the military hospital, as well as receiving the conventional treatment for whatever his illness was, insisted also on a goat being led three times round his bed by a holy man, some prayers said or spells cast, it's difficult to tell the difference when related to other people's traditional religions.

It is possible that in twenty years' time the world will be a very different place. The great centres (what are they great centres now?) may be all destroyed, and life and living will be revived again from the periphery. The barbarians will renew things – the lively barbarians. Scotland will survive, and especially the peripheral Scotland. The Celtic-Viking- Pictish fringe, where the life keeps coming from. Africa will have been relatively untouched by the self-exploding wars – by the – what is it the Italians express that gesture of puffing out their cheeks? Gonfiato! Bored stiff! Like a great cazzo. And self-explosive. Bursting itself all for nothing, just for a giant boredom and an overblown restlessness. Final war which is not for lust, not for anything but just for a huge swollen masturbation and self-destructiveness. So in twenty years it may be that "civilization as we know it", as the pompous fearers say, may be all blown up and gone. And this which you are reading is from the other days. It will be all different. The old cities will be empty and everything will be new. Not <u>new</u>; it will still all be coming direct out of ancient ancient lore, through generations of Africans, Scots, Chinese, etc., etc., etc., Chileans, etc., handed down (traditionally and genetically, deep in the germ tissue, old).

Am I to care about "future generations"? <u>Generated</u>, how? (By this too.)

God thought Mary was holy because she was bearing God's child. The usual.

God must be very conceited, I used to think sometimes secretly to myself as a child. The way he goes on about himself!

People are not so sure that they want a lot. That's what it is really. I don't want very much really, some will say. They <u>don't</u> want very much. What you offer them is too much for them. They don't <u>want</u> the poetry or any of the rest of the much <u>you</u> think life is or being is or the world is. They just don't want very much. You are too much for them. So if they refuse you, that's all right. It's when they accept you, or take you and try to make you into the little they want that you feel traumatised, belittled, shamed. You feel you are being squashed and damaged.

Christ has been knighted and given an honorary degree. Sir Jesus Christ, Ll. D.

The impudent nitwit is the most powerful kind of person. The bitch. The cocksure fool. Only with those qualities can you counteract those people who are wholly that, so in defeating them you defeat yourself. You become ashamed of defeating them. But you must defeat them with what you have in you of bitch or cocksure fool, then not let those qualities in yourself go on predominating. I don't know if this is possible. It usually fails. The nitwit wins in the end, leaving the non-nitwit feeling both bitchy and defeated. The nitwit bitch just <u>is</u> a bitch, so doesn't feel bitchy.

I think that Africans know something more than we do here about good and evil. "Good" and "evil" have been relegated to what is called religion in Christian countries. But I think it is a profounder thing than that. Morals are much more on the surface than good and evil are, and the word "religion" is usually used to mean mere morality. Church and Religion are taken to be the same thing – a sort of scheme of morality for people to live by. Morality is the use of good and/or evil for political purposes. "Political" in quite a general sense, I mean, of course.

> BEAUTY IS TRUTH AND TRUTH
> BEAUTY THAT IS ALL WE KNOW
> ON EARTH AND ALL WE NEED
> TO KNOW JOHN KEATS 1795-1821

Of course if you try to write everything down it quickly becomes obvious that the task is impossible. The urge persists. Go on, write it ALL down, every bit of it. It doesn't all go into words. Some would have to be done with kisses, animal cries, smells and physical pain. "Physical pain!" What the hell. Most kisses in films are not really functional. It's just the Hero and Heroine kissing. There may be a pornographic effect or sympathetic magic, but not often is the kiss essential as the wail of the mother is essential in "Pather Panchali". The kisses in some "experimental films", about Love – or "the love act" they call it – are the most unkissing kind of kisses ever.

How to say it, how to say it, how to say it? That's all we ever write about.

How <u>could</u> Casanova write the truth? I don't mean how could he want to, but how could he remember, at 70, what had really been the truth even if at the time he knew? When you are acting directly I don't know that you can know afterwards what happened. You might be able to say what you actually did but probably not what you thought (because at the time you weren't exactly thinking) and very possibly not what anybody else did. In any case the words don't describe it, because they can only be read flavoured by the reader's moral judgments. So that even if you don't feel moral about it yourself, if you have any experience at all of the moral way of looking at things you cannot help wondering, How is this going to be taken? And you might overweight one aspect not so much because of your own bias in that direction as because of your presumption of bias to the opposite side by readers (heeders as James Joyce said).

Writing "The Incomers", I had both opposites about equal, and then I began to fear people would think the story meant to make a fool of the fisherman, so I made the husband and wife slightly more fools than just had to be. Yet, some do read it simply as "never the twain shall meet" sort of story. When anyone reads it thinking I mean so-and-so they get a not entirely intended emphasis in it.

If you describe afterwards what you did even if at the time you weren't thinking in the real sense of thinking it sounds as if you were thinking, as if the doing were all as deliberate as the telling afterwards. And this is what gives the "cold-blooded" effect of the narrative. I don't think the use of the present tense gets rid of this. Some people try a kind of subjunctive "So then what would I go and do but...". "I walked up the stairs" sounds very deliberate, and sure enough it's a voluntary act to go upstairs. But how often one is up after being down, without any clear consciousness of the act of ascending stair by stair or two at a time or how can it be remembered how one came, thinking ahead or thinking back at the time, a composite of thought and action and absentmindedness which can hardly be described by "I walked upstairs". "I came upstairs" might be a trifle better, for it does say, "Well, here I am" – but the description of more subtle actions, actions with repercussions and multiple motives, needs more multiple, repercussive and subtle language. And that, that is what writers are trying to write with. Writers.

Writers.

WRITERS.

You see, there I go repeating that word and you don't know why, do you? Children at the tea-table do it. Suddenly pick on a word and repeat it, and all the children <u>say</u> it, and keep saying it in different tones until it becomes ridiculous, meaningless, and they say isn't it funny if you keep saying a word it just changes. Doesn't it seem silly now, the word? Yet shortly we'll use it again just as usual.

What do YOU think? What do YOU THINK? – I mean. Even with a typeface you cannot get all the variations of meaning you could with holograph if you really tried. Meaning. The artist must work within his/her limitations. That is the art of being an artist. Work within the limits of the word and work within the limits of the printed word. Does this mean you have to be thinking of all the print even as you scrawl? Which is the book, the written pages of the author or the printed pages of the publisher? And then hard covers or soft covers.

Nobody knows me at all who hasn't been to bed with me. And of those who knows me? I don't know whether I want to be known or not, that is, in any other way than known in bed. Knowing <u>about</u> me isn't knowing me, is it? So whom do I know, then? Lovers all left something with me. I suppose I left something with them. I never think it makes any sense talking about lovers in the plural. They lose their identity, and a lover without an identity is not to be thought of.

GURU. Have I a guru? The whole of India is my guru. It would be wrong to return. Having learned, then go on. REFRESHER COURSES. Two weeks for bringing your medicine up to date.

The Lore more ancient than anything in a refresher course. Magic. Medicine men.

The more I write it <u>as</u> a statement the less I mean it as a statement.

There are too many Societies for the Prevention of Grief. Denial of things is just as bad as pretence of things. People aren't even allowed to feel grief any more, or to accept the charity of their neighbours. They have to be beneficiaries of a fund set up for their relief. The Czecho-Slovakian father of the drowned boy asked me for a pill to control his grief. They started a fund for the bereaved widow of the murdered man, in protest against the wealthy business philanthropist who awarded a handsome sum to the pregnant mistress of the murderer provided she married him in the death cell. She married the man, got the money, he was reprieved and is serving a life sentence.

When you say that war is futile you haven't said very much. Its futility may be the one thing which is good about it. Then again, everything is futile. The evil thing about war is that they assist progress.

Acceptance of happy futility is the only way to live serene. If you want to be serene. I get a bit tired of serenity, or would get a bit tired of serenity. As soon as I say I'm serene I then say, No, damn it, I'm NOT serene. YOU be serene, if you want to. Not only do I live backwards but I do everything upside down. That's why I seem grotesque and blind. I was looking the other way at the time.

I get the idea that different people dream in completely different ways. Are dreams at all alike? "You know how in dreams – etc". And yes the "how in dreams" method is recognisable all right, and yet what other people say about their dreams is often totally inapplicable to my own dreams. And I am totally at a loss to describe accurately any dream of mine. The memory is inaccurate, for one thing, and then it is difficult to find anything to relate it all to in the telling.

Women really are completely mystified by fighting; and it's for that reason when there is a war they try to get near to "active service" to see what it all is. To watch the men at it. But it is an all-male mystery really, a more-than-masonic rite. Women by going near it make it a little less than it is. It becomes softened and not war at all, with Florence Nightingale there. Or if the woman is a warrior, decides to be herself a fighter, she can only be it truly by becoming less of a woman. This may be true of other things than fighting. Men have tried to make it so of anything they wanted to keep women out of, and, of course, women incapable of the preserved enterprises are pleased to have it assumed that such women as attempt those enterprises are out of the running as women. I don't mind agreeing that a fighting woman is not very womanly, but I don't agree that a thinking woman is unwomanly. Anybody agrees with excluding the thing they don't want to be anyway. Bitchiness is a necessary quality. Men like bitches.

The more it can be told the more you want to know for yourselves, but there is no knowing, either way. Either told, or learning the hard way, still you don't know. Nobody knows what it is. War isn't anything more or less than anything else. War feels like a time separated off. It's all part of it, though. What's the difference? "In wartime." We used to hear stories about the discomfiture of the conquerors, repeated with a sort of glee – how people of "occupied countries" found blameless incorrigible ways of insulting, at least, the Germans who occupied them, without actually contravening the regulations. And "Orkney isn't Orkney any more" said the returned WAAF revisiting her one-time camps and haunts, after the peace.

It isn't easy to know what anything is without having been in it, and even then you don't know. "I was there," they said, until it became a joke. "Kilroy was here," the Americans used to chalk and paint and scratch as they passed by. Everybody knew by that time that we were all just clocking in on War. War as we know it. War is as we know it. But it isn't really – not anymore than anything else. Anything can be anything <u>and</u> it's all the same all the time. Whatever you know by being there means you don't know something else because you weren't there. I have felt terrible greed and nostalgia of wanting to know everything, but I'm over it now.

To know ordinariness – or to know extraordinariness. There's a choice to be made, and yet you can make no choice really, for you are as you are. You <u>cannot</u> choose to be ordinary, if you are extraordinary. Ordinariness, in a way, consists in not choosing but in just going ahead according to the convention, thinking maybe you've chosen but choosing just an example of the <u>sort</u> of thing. Quite a superficial choice, as of turnips or cabbage for veg. So if you deliberately <u>choose</u> ordinariness, so as to know it, then you will never know it, for you never can be it or be part of it in any real way.

When publishers' readers say I have written about "my experiences" are they right after all and is my book simply a long-winded "I Was There" boast? It certainly wasn't meant to be that. It may, however, have been meant to take you there too so that you could have been there. Be to war, without war. Would that be a saver?

For God so loved the world that he gave his only begotten son, etc… Piece of damned cheek that was!

People can't be saved. All the lemmings go head-first over the cliff, they are all so busy thinking they are going somewhere. Only a lemming that might stop for a moment and wonder why all those fools were going hurtling into the sea might save itself. But it would save itself alone. It would be all alone, the only one that didn't become a rhinoceros. Very few people are equal to being left alone on the cliff-top having saved themselves. They go leaping over too, thinking that in that way either they save someone else who might be watching or who is yet to come or else at least they are with the others. Not ALONE.

People used to say (I thought rather smugly), "Oh well, at least it's an experience, you know," about something or other that had happened to them. There <u>was</u> some awful smugness in the way they used to say it. And older people would say to me when I came home from India, "Well, it's been an experience, hasn't it." I always felt like sinking through the floor. Some sort of suggestion that I had been plopped there and got a free experience, that it had cost me nothing and that but for that there wouldn't have been "experience". God, I experienced everything because I was I, not because of what it was, specially. And later, when Margaret became split up, my self from my self, my soul from my mind, I became unable to experience anything no matter what it was. I was not participating and could have gone through any adventures untouched.

One of my discoveries recently has been about hatred. Not that there are certain people who "should" be hated – but that if you hate someone you should hate them. Not suppress it. "They" hate, all right. It's quite a treachery to respond by being "nice" about them all the time – well, I mean, usually one doesn't hate back except momentarily. But allow it for the moment. Don't pretend it wasn't there.

I have an absolutely horrible nature. So has everybody, perhaps. I don't suppose I'm any worse than anyone else. People are all horrible and all wonderful. Evil comes between two people when they are incompatible in size and pretend not to be, and then if you hate the other one you should do so and not be mean about it.

Hatred is quite a salutary thing while it is hatred. But to work up hatred, or try to reconstruct it, or keep it alive, that's evil or bad or something.

The element of reconstruction in art even seems evil sometimes.

You try to remember back to what it was, and then in saying it you change it. In part self-protectively and intentionally, and in part because there aren't the words or there isn't the way of saying it to say just what it was. But it is not possible to be silent. It is necessary to use language all the time and to go on using language to the best of your ability, saying what you can say, allowing that people take (or can take) what you say as something said and not as it itself. That is perhaps why the more constructed poem is in a way truer. It is clearly a poem, a thing made. There is no pretence of it being simply the raw material, what I saw presented to you to judge for yourself. Reminiscences, Casanova's mémoires — well, you must accept it that he is making a story of it. There is no such thing as leaving nothing out.

It may be that in "The Lilywhite Boys" I left too much of it out. Or left it all out, as some considerers of it seem to think. Whether is it "refreshing restraint" or "lifeless facts"? I wrote things, meaning to imply a great deal else. In those days I used to write like that, to be read slowly, the words weighted and examined for their implications and allusions. That's what I thought I was doing, or meant to do. But there has to be something there to make the reader notice all the things you mean. The stories in "Lane Furniture" are like that too. Someone may read one through, find it very moving, and then read it through again to find what it is that's there and find it all very bald, and then wonder where they got their picture of quite a complicated story from. You have to get the words, though, which will make people assume things or invent things for themselves. And you probably have to publish the work yourself, because an editor or publisher's reader even if allowing that <u>he</u> can read a story in it won't allow that the public can, for he'll know he provided half the story himself and he won't believe it's the story as written that caused him to supply the other half and that it will have the same effect on other people.

Nowadays I am trying to put it all in. In some ways this is lazier. In some ways it is more difficult. But it isn't exactly a choice, that I do this now. I just do what I have to do.

I have no ideas or opinions. Anything that is written down as an idea or opinion is not so but is given you as something to play with.

The "you" in what I write, particularly my poems, is not exactly a particular person, nor you, the reader, nor you all, but is a fictitious character spoken to by a fictitious "I". The "I" is I <u>and</u> a fictitious I, the "you" you and a fictitious you. Norna (aged 2) invented two boys to play with, called Jack and Jock (Check and Chock), and when asked who they were said in a tone of voice of her own, "It's <u>me</u>." The you in many of my poems is <u>me</u>, in <u>that</u> sense, me a fictitious character not me who I am. But the you might switch from being one kind of you to another, I think sometimes even within the same poem. Well, people used to be more explicit (in a way) about this, and they made it into a dialogue between

Venus and Adonis, say. But that's not quite right for me, either. That kind of organised fiction is a cheat. My fictitious characters must be wholly my own fictitious characters – my own invention, or creation.

The roses smell differently at different times of day. They smell differently according to how far out they are. A rose just coming out has a certain scent and the same rose when it is fully out has a different scent. As it is getting past, withering a bit, its scent, the actual rose scent, is mixed with the smell of its petals, which is different, a smell of vegetation, a smell of petals as they smell even when plucked off the flower and laid in a bowl to make pot-pourri. This is rose smell too but is different from the scent of the live rose. The volume of scent varies as the weather varies. When the sun is coming up warm on a morning which has been a little moist the roses smell very fresh. On a hot afternoon you are aware of quite a palpable cloud of perfume you feel you might rise in, and float. It is substantial enough to support a body off the ground, I headily feel sometimes.

The autumn roses have very little perfume. They look more fragile, they last longer, fade and fall more slowly, and they have a less strong scent than the roses which bloomed on the same bush in the summer. The scent of the earliest roses of the year has a quality for which the word "fresh" seems appropriate.

Some scents seem to come out best with a strong sun. Others need coolness. There were flowers in the garden of Bungalow 39 which had little perfume in the day, but in the warm moonlight their perfume seemed to be pouring about the garden. Glossy white temple flowers sat solidly open with a fixed impassive Eastern look and their scent was opaque. The air near them stopped moving and the moon's light which fell on them seemed to be of their colour or to make them that colour. The other flowers took their colour from the sun; all the phlox, petunia, hollyhocks, cosmos, blue, yellow, red or white, vibrant and transparent in daylight, by the moon's light seemed asleep, less vivid, gathered away into themselves. The thick-petalled white flowers slept by day. In garlands in the sun or set in offering in the temples they had an absent look, something false about them. Only in the evening their soul came into them again and their strong perfume came thickly out. It was part of a thick, still atmosphere, to do with moon, stars and a velvet blue, and with the heat steadily increasing with the year's revolution.

A certain number of days till Christmas. A certain number of days till it rains. The old hands were sure. What was predicted came true. The year lasted a certain length of time, exactly as prophesied. By the same time next year it was a year later.

And to think there are people leaving school who didn't know that war at all! Not even as babies. I don't know whether they will want to know about it or not. It is all just old rubbish to them. Everything that is past is simply your heritage. Ladies, wear my book as an heirloom!

They came dressed in roses and in leaves of books. The maids came giggling to the door, wearing only rhododendrons. The lady teacher was charmed and subtly shocked. The pupils were blind. The lady teacher remembered it as something scandalous that once happened to her. (The girls in long blue nylon stockings wore leaves phrased by Dylan Thomas in their hair.)

The tourist's eye view is sometimes valid.

Sometimes it is too painful to turn to some chapters. Some days I must leave some investigations alone.

I don't think enmity ever starts from me. I meet it and then it develops in me too, but I don't think I initiate it. I don't think so.

Reading the Bible seems to be a very dangerous activity (dangerous to the reader, I mean). People can prove anything to themselves by consulting the Bible. It is written so metaphorically that you could think up any theory then refer to the Bible and find a proof.

All those proved theories are quite true in a way. But they are not the only truth. Truth is multifarious. Truth is innumerable.

It is quite salutary to hate. But sustained hatred would be poisoning, I think. Pretence of hatred is as bad as pretence of love. "Bad" in the sense of damaging. Hatred is not the same as dislike, any more than love is the same as liking. To pretend not to hate if you do hate is bad. To have it pretended upon you (so to speak) that you still hate someone you hated but now only dislike is harmful. The dislike may flare into hatred now and again, I suppose, so you cannot really state what you feel as a permanent feeling. Love is mixed with liking, and the love is not to the forefront all the time in full intensity.

You have to accept your own grief. There is no "easing" it. Sometimes it will not be there, but it is not either eased or gone. Just that it is part of you and there are other parts of you too. Any emotion which seems to take up the whole of the personality must be, in part at least, false.

Very stupid people with not much complexity but a lot of cunning are evil, in a way. If you let them be. And you feel as if it's yourself who are evil. In a way it is, for letting them. Having children doesn't make them any less evil. There are plenty of evil parents about. The children themselves may be quite different.

DOCUMENTARY

Sometimes I think it is downright impertinence to call anything – play, film, book – "documentary".

Do you perhaps care absolutely not a hoot who the Chindits were, what they did, and what sort of life people led in a hospital in the Plains because there was all that going on out there? Does it just all seem to you absolutely and completely boring? I can understand that perfectly well and sometimes it seems to me quite unreasonable to try to communicate what it all was, as if there was some secret to be found in it. It can seem sometimes like just as much gratuitous information I am handing out, of no consequence.

"Things have returned to normal: shops and banks are open." That's what they said about the Congo, a few days after "independence" began.

A girl patient in Hull, suffering from a mental disorder, told me she wanted to get back to normal and be able to work again as a stenographer in a big busy office. I told her that it was not quite logical to consider that sort of activity "normal", that it was just as normal _not_ to want to be one of a lot of girls banging away at typewriters in the big brightly-artificially-lit brassy office she told me she had had a good job in. She was a bit of a liar. I tried to persuade her it was just as reasonable to want to go and milk cows or something peaceful. Of course she would never _want_ to do that, but it suggested a new point of view to her. I doubt if she'd get much from it, really. She was too stupid and too "cute", and too sure that "normal" was travelling in a bus to a job in an office. A confirmed liar, and a moral one at that. She was surprised when I said I didn't think the buses and typewriters and all those things are specially <u>normal</u> (i.e. that it was not she but the typewriter that was abnormal) and she was grateful in a way, but at the same time I could see her putting this into her mind as something she could use for herself perhaps in some not very nice way. She lived at home with her mother and never went out, she said, and was a "perfectionist", she said. I don't know what would become of her. Nothing very much, I suppose.

There's a kind of person who is very zealous, and who might be a scholar, but not a scientist and not an artist. They are interested in proof and in right and wrong, but they have quite closed minds really. There's an old gentleman, for instance, who has "proved" a whole series of what he calls "facts", mainly by reference to the Bible. At least, I haven't seen any sign of any other kind of proof he has. Now scientists think they have proved a thing when they find references and counter-references to tally with what they say. He is completely sure that he is right. He believes, he said, and then corrected himself, "no, not <u>believe</u>, I <u>know</u>," he said, I've forgotten what it was, something God had imparted to him about the Universe.

You see, I think it's all right just to <u>know</u>, and not know where it's coming from. There are things which can be known in this way which might even eventually be "proved", objectively or scientifically. I mean, a scientist might know a whole scientific solution of some series of things, know it as a whole before learning it in detail, and it might all come out as scientifically correct in the end. (This is more or less what is popularly called proving a theory!). He was grasping in advance. But he doesn't exactly say it is so as a fact to begin with. It is so as a conception, and that is a sort of fact, but I think a real thinker can keep in mind even contradictory conceptions of this kind in his mind as really existing in their own way, as being facts of a kind, or hypotheses, possibilities. I think most facts are just possibilities, really. But the tight-minded zealous thinker who is maybe quite intelligent checks his idea with a set of closed "proofs" and proves that he is right, without really <u>investigating</u>. He may think that this is all a scientist does in "proving a theory", but a scientist isn't exactly looking for proof so much as examining to find if it is so as he has imagined.

Of course, as soon as I start to write about it, proving without investigating seems to be what everybody is doing, what I myself am doing, that it is just the mistake we all make if we think at all and that therefore the best is to be NOT a thinker, and so on and so on. But that's nonsense too, because if you are a thinker you can't be not a thinker, and I suppose if you are that kind of half-thinker that's all you can be. They are demoralising, though, the sure-they're-rights. Because I am not prepared either, or not able to think all the way through some things. I have to get to a certain point and realise I can't <u>think</u> beyond that, and accept it as so, not thought-out beyond there, but nevertheless with possibilities beyond there. In other words, I don't think the universe or whatever it is is limited by <u>me</u> and what I can think about it. Nor do I think that anything or <u>anybody</u> is limited by what I can understand or think or know about it or them. People say, "But I don't understand how – etc. etc.," implying that if they don't understand it just can't be. On the other hand, other people are <u>too</u> willing to hand over and say, "Oh well, I don't understand, but they know what they are doing." Those are irritating to me when they say this to me implying that because the speaker doesn't understand I don't understand either and we must leave it to the other "them" (who might in my opinion be much less capable of understanding than I myself). And so on and so and on.

People are unequal and unhappiness comes from the difficulty of recognising size. Undersized people cannot see many degrees of size greater than themselves, and people also fail in seeing degrees of size smaller than themselves. For any kind of peace one must recognise a continuous gradation in it and not be contemptuous about other levels above or below.

An artist also just "knows", and puts it down as he or she knows it, but does not then set about to prove it.

Perhaps everybody of any calibre should have some scientific training nowadays, at least enough to let them know when they are not being scientific, so that they needn't waste themselves on the nonsense of thinking they are "proving scientifically".

Some priest, too, has written a book called "The Phenomenon of Man", in which he claims to have "proved scientifically" that all evolution has tended towards further development of mind. Of two scientists discussing it on the radio, the Catholic one was convinced by the writer-priest, and the other, non-Catholic and non-Christian, pointed out that all evolution has quite definitely not been for the selective development of mind and brain, but only the evolution of man has gone in this direction. And because the writer described as "scientific" certain observations which were not scientific but were rather expressions of faith, therefore he considered the book to be dishonest.

So if the old gentleman had said, "I don't know, but I believe," it would have been more honest than to say as he did, "No, not I believe but I know." All he meant really was because it was he who believed, therefore he knew, – because he believed he has been chosen by God, i.e. he knows he has been chosen by God.

Of course, I know too that I have to do certain things, because I know that I am a certain sort of person, I have this sort of power or ability, there is nothing else I can do but what I do or try to do, and I don't know WHY, I have no proof of it, and I don't believe there is any proof other than just doing it and when it is done, there it is, that's her life, that's her art, that's what she thought, here it is for us; and I have a feeling that in spite of all the evil in me in the end it is in some way good, or wholesome. There is some tendency to wholeness in what I am doing.

I don't like exclusiveness, and I have only realised after a long time and much injury that there has to be a degree of exclusiveness – and I think I have at last accepted this, even without regret.

Images of sadness. A fire that nobody is beside. A table set and no one coming.

It is absolutely necessary to live. People just die. It's a great mistake they make. It is traditional that the most rebellious men get caught in the most abject domesticity. It is necessary to live, but it is made very difficult. People like things so very dead. People want things finished, complete, not alive and taking place (taking time). They want it all parcelled up and criticised, labelled.

You can't understand it by marrying a cruel person and watching them all your life. You'll never understand them except to the extent that you yourself are cruel. And it's no use trying to understand the cruelty of the Nazis. It's there. It can only be observed – believed. If you try to understand it you won't believe it. But it's true. It WAS so.

The need to suffer is what is, in a way, false about artists. At least, it makes us <u>feel</u> false. But it's a real enough need – a need to know. It makes us feel false because we tend to create situations in which we suffer, or suspect ourselves of doing so. I don't know that anyone does, though, in fact. One just does the inevitable. It's a feeling of gladness to be suffering so much that sometimes startles me. In part it is a feeling of relief that I can stand it, maybe a feeling that there can't be worse than this and therefore, etc. etc. But it's possible to be jealous of another person's suffering – a very strange thing. Emotion can only be experienced by suffering the cause of it, say. One feels the need of all the range and will even seek out unprofitable situations for oneself, to experience the misery. It's not on a very deliberate level, but on a deeper level it is intentional, or, perhaps again, just inevitable. Who can tell? So long as you don't seek <u>all</u> misery and only misery! The upward range is necessary too.

Smokers all want smoking to be considered a vice. They must feel it as something they are doing against themselves. Self-punishment is the basis of most "vice" – doing evil things against oneself. Flagellation, drugs – the deep evil about it is that there is no persuading of someone who is determined to destroy himself. Everyone does it in a way. Writing is a kind of suicide. So is marriage and bringing up a family. Everything is. I don't know that there's any difference really between that and taking drugs. The drug-takers maybe want the full bitterness of knowing what they are doing and being after a time unable not to do it, and then the pleasure of drowning as they <u>get</u> the drug and are carried off once more, beyond knowledge of what they are doing.

(But this might apply to any pattern of life.)
Hypnotism,
Addiction,
Self-punishment,
There's some connection.

It's better for the marriage to be destroyed than for the people to be destroyed. But that is not the view of society, which wishes to preserve the marriage at almost any cost. "Can this marriage be saved?" – as if the people didn't matter, but just the marriage. Preservation of the form and the appearance make rule possible. So long as there's the appearance of a thing working, it can be treated as a unit and governed as that thing, without concern for the details of it or the elements of it.

People are always telling me what my opinions are. I don't know how it is they know them so much better than I do myself.

A story written and a story told aloud are quite different things. I don't like a story which begins by introducing a character and then making the character say, "I mind the time – or words to that effect and then going on and making the story the character's story. Depends. Story within a story within a story. A device. If used to examine story, well, for importance of the story, not so good. You're not quite sure enough of the story just to tell it, so you put it in the mouth of some character and stand back from story and teller and all, uninvolved. This isn't a genuine objectivity.

What does a drawing of a house mean?

The idea of "somewhere else" is always heartbreaking, just the idea that there can be anywhere else.

I wonder if it would be possible to learn anything from the witch doctors by going to the Congo. To meet any in the first place would be the first difficulty. White women would need to be protected, in authority's opinion, so there'd be every difficulty made about going anywhere near any genuine village centre. That part of Africa has always seemed to me about the most <u>real</u> place in the world. Long ago I used to visualize myself going <u>there</u>, to Central Africa, not as a missionary in any sense but just to be there. Going for what is there and not so much for anything I could take there. Even if I was "allowed" by governmental authority there would still be great difficulty in making contact. The language. And the barrier. Distrust of "white". It would take years, I suppose. Would I be able to bring anything back? I have of course found the same thing here, – the essence, the cause, but not the cure. I think really that <u>here</u> is always the place to look. This is the view I have had to some extent for the last seven years and strongly for the last three. It's all HERE. It's really no use my going away there, to their thing. <u>They'll</u> have to use that, develop that. (I only fear they'll deliberately lose it.) I have to seek here, delve here. It's not all lore, it's partly another kind of knowledge. There is lore too, though. Maybe there is healing lore to be found in Scotland. People (folk-lorists!) collect it, but not to use, just as quaint old customs. As they collect "quaint old folk-songs" and in doing so kill something alive and continuing. They can't really kill it though. But where do I find? How do I look? It's no use just looking in the manner of folk-lorists, collecting things cold. It has to be more alive. What I take in through myself, have done in these years, will still do … that's it, really. Hills and hearths. The necessity is to STAY, and not, I think, go. Not go to any Congo or elsewhere, for it wouldn't be valid for here. The John Knox hydra tried to kill all that, in Scotland. Value of song, of poetry. It's in the poetry, – in what I absorb and then in what I form, re-form, put down as writing. All that. That's what I mean. The song. It's in the very words, if they are taken right. <u>Taken</u>, that is, not judged. Not a part of literary life, but of whole life.

Whole life is what people dismiss. They atomise their lives.

YOU MUST HAVE BEEN A BEAUTIFUL BABY
(because, honey, look at you now!)

They brought a great many pots of hydrangeas for the days of the Commissioner's and the Moderator's visits, each year. The black-coated week was a week of holiday for the school. Since then, <u>out</u> in Edinburgh, I see assembly week differently, but never really differently, only differently enough to see how funny it is that it was our week of gala. From here it seems the town suddenly full of black ministers whitened only by their collars. From in there it was open gates, for all that the ministers were <u>was</u> visiting parents. Girls' parents in town. So. The school allowed some going out. And, as I was in no way connected with any minister, for me and other "laymen's daughters" it was simply, Oh God, an open gate for once. Once a year. There was even some unintentional relaxation of the being called for. <u>Evenings out</u>! I think the evening out lasted from 5pm to 7.20pm. Or was it a little later, perhaps 7.40, those evenings only? I remember the gate open – and what happened? I just WENT. Amazing. I walked out of the gate, a big girl, twelve years old at least, and I walked down Kilgraston Road and went to visit my aunt and my cousins. (WITHOUT BEING CALLED FOR.) They weren't particularly thrilled. So next time I went to the pictures (which we weren't allowed to do). Or did something or other. Just wandered about by myself. I went out, and I came in. I traversed some streets of Edinburgh, perhaps had tea in a café. I don't remember. I remember the gate open, and walking out. (I think I was a good deal more than twelve before ever I dared to go to the cinema, forbidden because of 'danger of infection'.) All the week was for the ministers' daughters and their reunions with their collared parents and they didn't care too much about us, about me. I just walked out and no one saw. I was old enough to feel how fantastic, that to be able to walk simply out of the gate and up the street, decorously, responsibly was forbidden. Was wicked.

It taught me a certain scepticism about laws. No talking on the back stairs. No talking in the bathroom. No talking <u>anywhere</u> after 9pm. Those were punishable offences. "I <u>had</u> to talk" was sometimes put forward as a defence. Some emergency where it became necessary for a girl to say something. Maybe she had abdominal pain, felt ill, needed succour. If proved, she might be excused, and <u>not</u> punished by "detention" or "returned lesson". Those were the sentences dealt out. There was one crime I couldn't commit. Whistling was forbidden, for being "unladylike", but I've never been able to whistle. I just can't do it. Shame! So I talked in the backstairs instead.

They are putting in azaleas in Princes Street Gardens. All the pots are standing there on a green cloth spread on the grass. The gardeners are busy inserting them in the plot. Who supplied the hydrangeas for the school, I wonder. They were taken away afterwards. A catering of flowers.

It's pain and oppression at the heart. False laws. I know all about it since. No need to commit more crime, having known the awful shame of being caught talking on the back stairs. Nothing seems like crime after that. Sin is absolved. But the pain of the oppressive laws. Thou shalt not laugh. Thou shalt not speak. Thou shalt not walk out of the gate uncalled for, still battens battens battens.

Blackened feet in black stockings and heavy black shoes hit the pavement. Poor little girl. Poor wee gilly.

They are putting azaleas in the park today. Delicate eastern flowers, I think, related to the rhododendron, inhabitants of mountains, occurring in Japanese art I dare say, delicately odoured, but strong too, tough in an eastern tropical way. Tropical growth is coarser really. The poignant little flowers in the short turf of islands in The North are different. And I am of The North, although I have met The East. And hydrangeas seem to me now like elephants. Like pachyderms. I think somebody else pointed out the similarity to me. In those days long ago I stood astonished, reverent before them as they arrived for their yearly visit. Always exactly so. Blooms unassailable, quite unlike a tender child hidden in ugly clothes and stockings and shoes. Whose eyes were blue or grey and whose hair sometimes gold when sunlight showed it so.

But squashed. "Squash to you!" Schoolgirl repartee. I don't like snubbing people. I feel ashamed to say I've been to Esdaile.

Why do I feel flattered if an Italian says to me, "You're quite Italian" or an Asian, "You're quite Oriental" – when I know that I am about as Scottish as I could possibly be? I think – I suppose – that it means I have universal qualities. I am content for the Oriental to feel me as surprisingly Oriental or for the Italian to say, you know you really could be Italian, because I <u>know</u> that I am the rest, the Presbyterian product, the Picts' distant offspring, even the Vikings' child, and it is reassuring to have ascribed to me also qualities that are described as Oriental or Mediterranean. Realism – excitable, volatile, on top of a deep peace – how Oriental is it, or how Italian? The realistic view. The mystic realistic view. Something went wrong in the Gothic interpretation of things with its romantically fake mystery.

It's all so long. And it's all so far away.

Whatever you say, they explain it by some event in your childhood. Not explaining the event, of course – or, heavens! Sometimes explaining it. That's what they all think they can do.

But I <u>like</u> the insects which crawl into the sun and bask their carapaces and step many-leggedly over the irregularities of stone.

Sometimes I believe I can remember the bees at their work of entering or leaving the hive at Orquil where I was found very very young sitting on the little step of the skep, fascinatedly attentive. Well, I remember the bees of course, but sometimes I think I can remember that very occasion.

A hot sunny day and people in ones and twos and groups all over the grass among the daisies, small children chasing the pigeons, deck chairs. Sound from a concert in the bandstand and inside on the chairs just a few people here and there among the rows and rows. At one time this would have made me unbearably sad. The element of people having chosen used to make me very sad.

A man going into a pub for a drink. This pub, he decides, I'll try this one. Not the same thing as a man going into his usual pub for his habitual drink. That too, though. The choosing. It's too much. "Now I'll go." They are all seeking something. But the thing is, perhaps they find it. Perhaps it is enough. They choose, and it's good. Look! Good! Perhaps what used to make me feel so sad was that all those people seemed to me to have found something and I hadn't. And why it doesn't make me sad now is because I now feel I have as much as anybody. Or I possibly used to feel that they were <u>all</u> just seeking with no possibility of finding. Now I know it is possible to arrive to find, and so I know that they are not all just seeking hopelessly. Some of the seekers still make me hopelessly sad, all the same.

"It is Margaret you mourn for" is no doubt the basis of all sadness.

Some people who seem quite early to have <u>found</u>, unquestioningly, sometimes later to get a terrible drop. And then they seem more lost than those who were seekers all the time.

How I hate that instructive voice on the B.B.C. The commentator, telling how the soil-scraper works, into the microphone of his tape recorder perched up on the actual implement on the actual site. But is that just what I was doing with my "authentic document"; is it why you can't be bothered with "The Lilywhite Boys?" Does it just sound like me perched up there trying to <u>tell</u> you things? I don't really think that anybody can be told anything. Or at least not anything that they are not investigating themselves in other ways too. The interest (the curiosity) has to be there first. People <u>do</u> think that some kind of medical service should be provided. People do think that wars should either be or not be. All I can do is transcribe the results of <u>my</u> observation, or my experiment (my experiences).

Watch out! They are sure to want to belittle you. "Snubs to you!" the schoolgirls say to each other, and "That's you squashed." It is all part of their expensive education.

I suffered from the removal from reality involved in being at a girls' boarding school. For young girls, to be at a boarding school is a completely phoney existence and the view of life and the morals taught there are quite phoney.

Mores Dirigat Caritas.

May love direct (our) ways. May charity direct our customs. As I write this down, "May love direct our ways", I see there isn't any "our" there really in the Latin. Perhaps it is implied. It was always translated like that at school. "Let love direct our ways", and we schoolgirls laughed among ourselves and said it was rather at variance with what the school tried to inculcate in us.

Caritas might be a very nice kind of love. Different from amor.

Mores dirigat amor.

It was really amor the schoolgirls were dreaming of more than caritas. Caritas is either in your character or it isn't. Amor might come to some and not to others. It is the blinding love, powerful and beyond all understanding. Amor cannot be disguised. When I love with amor it is enormous, tremendous, isolated and isolating. I feel caritas for more people than I feel amor. When I respond to someone with caritas it takes me aback if they try to pretend that what I am offering them is amor, as if <u>that</u> was the character of my amor. Caritas hasn't the feeling of hugeness towards one particular person that amor has.

It may be that Mr. David Esdaile or whoever it was who first chose that motto for the school was thinking rather, "May love (caritas) direct the ways of others towards these girls." May the world be charitable to them. May the ways of the world be kind to them. Maybe that's what he thought when he wrote it down hopefully, matching the initial letters with Ministers' Daughters' College. "The M.D.C." they used to call it. M.D.C. Mores Dirigat Caritas, there on the badge. Before I went there the name had been changed to Esdaile, after the founder. But M.D.C. was still on the badge, heading Mores Dirigat Caritas, along with a St. Andrew's Cross and perhaps some other odds and ends. And then ESDAILE written across it.

It is a very curious thing, but my heart still sinks as I write about it, think about it. I have to stop and pause, turn to something else, remember that there are other things, that I am alive.

✻   ✻   ✻   ✻

I need a sort of peace of knowing that I am, believing that I am. I have to savour a sort of assurance that I may walk upon the surface of the world, upon earth, upon ground – <u>may</u> actually go, walk. Am not forbidden.

What is it they try to do, wanting to disgrace your sex? They try to make you feel ashamed. You must not have it, must not give in. It's strange what people do to children – teach them what they call "a proper shame". I see it happening out in the street. And of course I remember it. It is the technique of society – isn't it? – to make all the others do the <u>expected</u> thing. Everyone does what's expected of him and the society "works". That is the ideal of all politicians.

I am not trying to be anything in particular. What I am is AM. I'm not saying this has always been the case. (I'm not really sure about that.)

There is a terrible seduction about <u>wanting to be</u> something or other. It has to be fought for the sake of the AM.

It's not fair to confess. To put my burden upon somebody else and feel absolved. "Oh God, I have greatly sinned." What mean trickery that is! "I'm telling you this because I love you and because you love me." But it is not possible to <u>tell</u> anything, except as a story. A story has enormous value. You know what I think about the value of a story; but it is not confession.

My poetry is all fiction – is folk-song – so that I had to leave some out for an interim edition, in case it was taken for confession, and not only for that but for interdiction. "Basil and two other men from King's Avenance." It's all song, nothing to do with me once it's out and yet everything to do with me. But nothing to do with gossip.

They'd like to pick on lurid details and make a scandal. Doctor Margaret Tait sleeps in her car in George Street. Ooh-ooh. Wait till I tell you. As if there was anything special about that. What I mean about it, it's <u>not</u> special, it is simply IT. It is what it is. It is what is. Ordinary, and yet not ordinary. Perhaps what I mean is that it <u>should</u> be ordinary; but that is impertinence.

I like to walk and walk through Edinburgh. Dun-Eidyn. Odin's Broch. I like to be out in the city. I like to be early in Princes Street Gardens, smelling the roses. While it is still fresh and early morning, I like to walk there, seeing how each rose has come out since yesterday, how some are falling, smelling how the scent varies from day to day, from rose to rose. And walk on the new paths of the heath gardens, new planted with plants still separate. In the summer of 1960 it is sometimes hot before nine o'clock in the morning. There have been people off trains, in the garden, slumbering away the weariness of their journey. They have an aura about them, of having just travelled up from London or from much further, and they are beatifically breathing the foreign air of here, the breath of arrival, as they rest. They are really resting – they have arrived. Here we rest like birds in a wilderness. A little aura or scent of sleep and happiness hangs quite still about them. The sun is so tingling here. It is Scotland. They have come, at last. They are here.

Being an Orcadian, sometimes I identify myself with "the Scots", sometimes I don't. As a Scot, sometimes I identify myself with "the British" and sometimes I don't. Either as Scot or as British, sometimes I identify myself with "Europeans" and sometimes, I don't. I have an idea that I think myself more as Orcadian and European than as either British or Scotch.

When it's just a wet but not pouring Scottish day, India seems further away. I can remember it better on a really drenching day, or when the weather is hot and dry, even although hot and dry here means nothing near the hotness and dryness of the baked and baking plains. It is extremely difficult to remember any conditions other than the condition one is in. It is difficult to remember the heat when it is cold or the cold when it is hot. It is difficult to remember the rain on a sunny day or to remember war in peace time or peace when there is a war on. In a state of imprisonment it is difficult to remember how it is not to be imprisoned. But I am seldom so free that I can't remember the feeling of prison quite clearly. More and more I see that people <u>want</u> to be imprisoned. The state of freedom is a very terrible state – if there is such a thing as freedom. My own greatest fear is of prison or of "invisible prison walls" – I suppose.

It's not prison when the giving and the collusion are for love. That is the "surrender" I innermostly always need. Love and surrender in relation to a man, to "art". It's a miracle that I found both, in the end. It had always seemed it could only be one or the other, and sometimes it seemed it would be neither. It's an emotion of love and surrender but <u>not</u> prison I feel in staying put and getting on with a piece of work. That is the completest freedom I know of in regard to working, living.

In love it's the same. The greatest freedom is being <u>with</u>. Then it is separation that seems like prison.

Prison of separation. Mutilation.

Modern war is prison. It is a condition of no-freedom for all the people in the country. It is subordination to the great greedy lump of war for the sake of war you are separated from whom you love and from work which is your freedom if you are that kind of worker. If you are young and have not yet reached your own love and your own work, it keeps you from them. It keeps you in a prison where they are not allowed.

I have been in prison twice – in school, and in the army.

It is a very very difficult thing to admit that anything that happens to myself is anyone's fault but my own. It was a profound change in myself that had to take place before I could recognise that sometimes I could (or must) blame somebody else. (For actions to me or to others).

Pashardi was ashamed because it wasn't the thing at all for a lady-sahib to do her own scrubbing. He came up to the Hills from the Plains with me, and was out of his element. It was not very easy for him to keep his end up among the strangers, foreigners practically to him, the unfamiliar hill people. He was in danger of losing the place of importance he had in the Plains, just by being unknown to them. They were not to know that he was the important Pashardi with his hand in all sorts of deals we took to be shady, in Jhansi city, a small landowner as well as a bearer of some standing in the B.M.H. Mess. And then I shamed him because the small stone chamber allotted to me for a bathroom was still so greasy and dirty after the servants had cleaned it that I set to with hot water, soda, soap and scrubbing brush and removed the filth myself. I seem to remember that it took several days. Pashardi's chagrin was pathetic. He could have lost caste to do such a thing as to scrub the place himself. He could only order a sweeper to do it. The sweeper pronounced it "clean". But there had been a family living there before, an Anglo-Indian doctor with wife and children, and the stone room had been their kitchen; the slabs of stone which was the sink and ledge beside it was all slimy with grease, and there was greasy blackness spattered all about the place. I went at it with hot water, northern, clearly, white, hard-working, furious. Pashardi could only stand and look, disdainfully unhappy. He never forgave me.

I only stayed there in Jutogh for three weeks and then was posted to S.E.A.C. HQ in Calcutta. Pashardi was deliriously happy at leaving, and had a real booze-up to celebrate. He poked his drunken face in at the window of my carriage where I was travelling along with a florist's consignment to Delhi and enquired, "Having a good time, Miss Sahib?" That is the question I used to ask him when he came tottering drunkenly through my room in Jhansi.

When we got to Calcutta I paid him off and let him go home to Jhansi. I didn't need a bearer after that. I was in S.E.A.C., quite a different thing from India Command.

[Note from the editor: Tait's draft of *Personae* ends here. The following pages are taken from notes for an earlier draft and give an indication of Tait's ideas for how the manuscript could end.]

It is a very very difficult thing to admit that anything that happens to myself is anyone's fault but my own. It was a profound change in myself that had to take place before I could recognise that sometimes I could (or must) blame somebody <u>else</u>. For actions to me or to others.

It is a very very difficult thing to admit that anything that happens to myself is anyone's fault but my own. It was a profound change in myself that had to take place before I could recognise that sometimes I could (or must) blame somebody _else_. For actions to me or to others.

If I ever try to say <u>why</u> I dislike a person, all I'm doing is enumerating all my own faults. As if to put my own errors and defects on to the other. But saying or seeing that doesn't alter it that I <u>do</u> dislike the person. The dislike has nothing to do with why or reasons or anything like that. Any more than love has to do with virtues. They

If I ever try to say why I dislike a person, all I'm doing is enumerating all my own faults. As if to put my own errors and defects on to the other. But saying or seeing that doesn't alter it that I do dislike the person. The dislike has nothing to do with why or reasons or anything like that. Any more than love has to do with virtues. They are seen afterwards in the person loved. The love is more simple, more profound. And hate too is simple and is not <u>because</u> of anything. The same with dislike. You don't stop disliking the person if you see they haven't really got those faults you mention, or not more than anyone else.

are seen afterwards in the
person loved. The love
is more simple, more
profound. And hate too
is simple and is not
because of anything — the same with dislike
You don't stop disliking the person
if you see they haven't really
got those faults you mention,
or not more than anyone else.

Edinburgh's fairy lore is all submerged. The May holiday seems the most Edinburgh of all Edinburgh holidays.

There's a feeling of guilt hanging over the place because of all the witch-burnings. And they're not quite sure whether they are guilty for the witches or guilty for burning the witches. The real guilt is for the false accusation and the burning. It must be at the back of the memory of Edinburgh as a peopled place, along with the fear of being taken for a witch, falsely accused and burned. The "rather you than me" attitude. So there's cowardice and treachery deep in the Edinburgh nature. But on the May holiday there's licence to light the old fires which go back to <u>before</u> the days when "witches" were burnt. There is some lack of fear and a sunniness about that bonfire time.

2) The May holiday seems the most Edinburgh of all Edinburgh holidays

1) Edinburgh's fairy lore is all submerged

(Edinbro would be a better spelling. Or even Edinberg — Dun-Eidyn. Eidynbro)

There's a feeling of guilt hanging over the place because of all the witch-burnings. And they're not quite sure whether they are guilty for the witches or guilty for burning the witches. The real guilt is for the false accusation and the burning. It must be at the back of the memory of Edinburgh as a peopled place, along with the fear of being taken for a witch, falsely accused, and burned. The "rather you than me" attitude. So there's cowardice and treachery deep in the Edinburgh nature. But on the May holiday there's licence to light the old fires, which go back to before the days when "witches" were burnt. There is some lack of fear and a sunniness about that bonfire time

It was just a pagan fire, celebrating the spring of the year, a tribute to some old gods they believed in. So you light it, a braw fire, not for burning anybody, not a <u>stake</u>, and yet by lighting it you show too that <u>this</u> is what you mean by a fire. It's <u>like</u> a stake, but <u>this</u> is our real fire ie. <u>we</u> didn't want a stake! They made us. Which is partly true and partly the dishonest "you <u>see</u>" —

It was just a pagan fire, celebrating the spring of the year, a tribute to some old gods they believed in. So you light it, a braw fire, not for burning anybody, not a _stake_, and yet by lighting it you show too that _this_ is what you mean by a fire. It's _like_ a stake, but _this_ is our real fire. ie _we_ didn't want a stake: they made us. Which is partly true and partly the dishonest "you _see_"---

Maybe – sometime in the future – if you keep quiet and say nothing. That's the kind of promise people give. I'm so tired of half-heartedness.

What exactly is a <u>promise</u>? A statement that you will do something? That you will do it if you can? That you think at the time of saying it that you will do it? That so far as you know when you are promising you will do it? That you would like to do it if you could and if possible you will?

D97/33/1/2

Maybe — some time in the future — if you keep quiet and say nothing. That's the kind of promise people give. I'm so tired of ~~people's~~ half-heartedness.

What exactly is a promise? A statement that you will do something? That you will do it if you can? That you think at the time of saying it that you will do it? That so far as you know when you are promising you will do it? That you would like to do it if you could and if possible you will?

I was twenty years old when the war began in 1939. I was born on the eleventh of November 1918, "Armistice Day", and I have often thought, especially when I was quite young, that there was some significance in my having that birthday. And yet I "came of age" to the start of the war. My 21st birthday was two months after the declaration of war.

Now I know that it is evil to love your enemies.

"The enemy",

meaning a whole nation, is not really an enemy, though! All that removed thing, that distant thing, is no good.

I was twenty years old when the war began in 1939. Two months before my twenty-first birthday. I was born on the eleventh of November 1918, "Armistice Day", and I have often thought, especially when I was quite young, that there was some significance in my having that birthday. And yet I "came of age" to the start of war. ~~I months after the war began~~

Now I know that it is evil to love your enemies. "The enemy", meaning a whole nation, is not really an enemy, though. All that removed thing, that distant thing, is no good.

FEAR

There was a shadow like the shadow
    of a wing dipping down over the window.
It was like the wing of a giant bat
    or vampire —
I thought of witches.
I really saw it,
But what I thought it was came
    out of the imagination of fear.

I was terrified and I thought of
    the enemy's strangling clutch.
I lay exhausted.
Something had seemed to fell me
    and I didn't know what.

I kept seeing the brown jelly
    boggy eyes.
I kept hearing the sort of sucking
    clutch of a bog.
I knew who was against me and
    could do nothing about it.
I was afraid.

I still can see that sludgy bog.
But I have more strength now.
Yes, I'm stronger now.

FEAR

There was a shadow like the shadow
 of a wing dipping down over the
 window.
It was like the wing of a giant bat
 or vampire —
I thought of witches.
I really saw it,
But what I thought it was came
 out of the imagination of fear.

I was terrified and I thought of
 the enemy's strangling clutch.
I lay exhausted.
Something had seemed to fell me
 and I didn't know what.

I kept seeing the brown jelly
 boggy eyes.
I kept hearing the sort of sucking
 clutch of a bog.
I knew who was against me and
 could do nothing about it.
I was afraid.

I still can see that sludgy bog,
But I have more strength now.
Yes, I'm stronger now.

The things I remember
are always the details.
The colour you were one time
And then the colour another time
Mouth-sensations
Quiver – I mean particular quivers.
I don't think this kind of direct
    enunciation is any good.
Anyway I sometimes remember a
    general tone as well as the details.
I remember <u>you</u>: that's what I
    remember about you.
Eyes and multitudes and the
    smell of your skin and all
    the legends and the enormous
    sweetness of your character and
    your ethereal flight-like tremble
And the weight of you upon me.
I remember your fingers.

9 Oct 1960
D97/33/1/12

The things I remember
Are always the details.
The colour you were one time
And then the colour another time
Month-sensations
Quiver   — I mean particular quivers.
I don't think this kind of direct
   enunciation is any good
Anyway I sometimes remember a
   general tone as well as the details
I remember you : that's what I
~~Most's~~ remember about you.
Eyes and multitudes and the
   smell of your skin and all
   the legends and the enormous
   sweetness of your character and
   your ethereal flight-like tremble
And the weight of you upon me.
I remember your fingers.

Do you feel my love?
    From far far away
do you feel my love?
    Do you feel it? Do you?
Do you feel my love, do you feel my love, do
you feel my love, do you hear what
I'm saying, do you feel my love?
    Do you know it's it? Do you feel
my love?
    Are you angry?
      You are too long
away. Far too long away.
      It's time now. Come
now. Come and feel my love. I feel your
love. I dream about you constantly,
    At three
o'clock in the morning do you know I'm there?
Do you?
    Do you feel this love which is always
there between us, which we can't destroy? Do
you feel it? Do you know it's there?
    It's only
an old broken illusion, that love can be
destroyed.
    Feel, feel, feel, feel, feel, feel,
feel, feel, feel, do you feel it?

Do you feel my love? do you feel my love? From far far away Do you feel it? Do you? Do you feel my love, do you feel my love, do you feel my love, do you hear what I'm saying, do you feel my love? Do you know it's it? Do you feel my love? Are you angry? You are too long away. Far too long away. It's time now. Come now. Come and feel my love. I feel your love. I dream about you constantly. At three o'clock in the morning do you know I'm there? Do you? Do you feel this love which is always there between us, which we can't destroy? Do you feel it? Do you know it's there? It's only an old broken illusion, that love can be destroyed. Feel, feel, feel, feel, feel, feel, feel, feel, feel, do you feel it?

Fancy taking Madame Virtue to the theatre! They go and they laugh at the bloodys and damns and then someone tells them and they know not to, so they don't – But the cretins are needed to fill up the theatre, to buy up enough tickets to keep the company performing.

Fancy taking Madame Virtue to the theatre! They go and they laugh at the bloodys and damns and then someone tells them and they know not to, so they don't — But the cretins are needed to fill up the theatre, to buy up enough tickets to keep the company performing.

I seem to need a different pattern to write out of in the autumn from the summer.

Men with guns are the silliest things in the world.

I seem to need a different
pattern to write out of in the
autumn ~~winter~~ from in the summer.

Men with guns are the
silliest things in the world.

Mechanistic defeat!

Mechanistic defeat!

The Bravest Boat, selected pages from Margaret Tait's photograph albums